The Interscholastic Coach

Irvin A. Keller

PRENTICE-HALL, INC., ENGLEWOOD CLIFFS, NEW JERSEY 07632

Library of Congress Cataloging in Publication Data

KELLER, IRVIN A.
    The interscholastic coach.

    Includes bibliographies and index.
    1. Coaching (Athletics) 2. School sports.
I. Title.
GV711.K44   796'.07'7   81-13866
ISBN 0-13-475707-6   AACR2

Manufacturing buyer: Harry P. Baisley

Printed in the United States of America

10   9   8   7   6   5   4   3   2   1

ISBN 0-13-475707-6

PRENTICE-HALL INTERNATIONAL, INC., *London*
PRENTICE-HALL OF AUSTRALIA PTY. LIMITED, *Sydney*
PRENTICE-HALL OF CANADA, LTD., *Toronto*
PRENTICE-HALL OF INDIA PRIVATE LIMITED, *New Delhi*
PRENTICE-HALL OF JAPAN, INC., *Tokyo*
PRENTICE-HALL OF SOUTHEAST ASIA PTE. LTD., *Singapore*
WHITEHALL BOOKS LIMITED, *Wellington, New Zealand*

Contents

CHAPTER 14
In Perspective

Preface

Developments in amateur athletics have exerted influences on the interscholastic athletic programs of the secondary schools and added to the complexities and responsibilities of high school coaching. More and more non-school athletics are being promoted for high school and pre-high school students, culminating in district and national meets and tournaments. The fact that the Soviet Union and other European nations view international amateur athletic competition as a means of gaining political prestige and fostering their ideologies is influencing amateur athletics in the United States. Olympic development programs have been initiated in this country in an attempt to offset any advantages of the athletic boarding schools subsidized by European governments in developing Olympic competitors. The interscholastic and intercollegiate athletic programs are recognized as an important part of the U.S. Olympic effort, and there is an increasing demand for better interscholastic and intercollegiate coaching.

Simultaneously, interscholastic competition is expanding more rapidly than the supply of fully trained interscholastic coaches, stemming from the advent of more interschool competition for girls and the steady growth in the boys' sports programs. School administrators and boards of education have become increasingly concerned to promote the educational values of interscholastic sports so the public will receive its educational dollar's worth from the monies spent on the athletic program. It is essential that the interscholastic coach be well qualified both to coach his or her sport and to teach boys and girls through athletic experiences.

This book has been written specifically to help interscholastic coaches better assume their responsibilities under existing conditions and attain success and satisfaction in their jobs. It presents the general interscholastic knowledge today's high school coach must possess and the professional qualities and competencies he or she must develop to become the kind of coach who can meet the blend of expectations of boards of education, school administrators, athletes, parents, and the public.

All important aspects of coaching are discussed. Practical suggestions are offered for cultivating personal and professional qualities, and effective basic coaching procedures and techniques are recommended. Careful attention is given to the kind of coaching that will make interscholastic athletic experiences more worthwhile. Topics related to outside influences that present potential problems for coaches are examined, and ways of coping with them are considered.

A significant feature of the book is that the help it offers will be valuable to both beginning and experienced coaches. Emphasis is placed on the improvement of coaching, and helpful aids for self-evaluation and self-improvement are provided. It is the type of book that high school principals will want their coaches to read, and chapter bibliographies contain excellent sources for additional readings.

I wish to express my sincere appreciation to those who so graciously gave permission to quote from their materials, and particularly to Brice Durbin for the use of excerpts from some of his excellent works based on his many years of successful experience as a coach and school administrator.

It has been my pleasure to prepare the manuscript for this book, and it is my hope and belief that it will help many coaches to achieve that degree of professional competence that will lead to success and satisfaction in interscholastic coaching.

Irvin A. Keller

CHAPTER 1

The Strategic Position
of the Coach

Introduction

Much has been written about coaching and the interscholastic coach, but there are no historical data which establish when or by whom the teaching of a sport to others was first initiated. There was interscholastic competition before there were high school coaches. The first high school teams, sponsored by the students themselves, had a student manager, but there was no high school coach to teach them the skills and team play essential to the game. The school-appointed coach emerged after problems arose from outsiders offering to coach high school players.

From this humble background the position of the high school coach has evolved into a strategic one in the field of secondary education. We shall note in this chapter how it developed and the factors that have contributed to its significance.

Evolution

The first athletic games involving groups of high school students were initiated by high school boys. Student athletic associations were formed which emulated the athletic clubs of college students. The primary purpose was recreation. The athletes selected a manager from among their own group, but there is no record of any provisions for a coach. The players learned to play by playing and by observing others play. Most of them had never seen a rules book and had little knowledge of the game's rules. Pickup officials, who often knew no more about the rules than the players, were common. Disputes arose and fights among players sometimes resulted. Although they were not sponsored by high schools, the teams often carried high school names, which became a source of embarrassment to the schools when misconduct occurred.

CHAPERONES

High school administrators concluded that something had to be done to prevent disputes and brawls at the student interschool games and the resulting bad publicity for their schools. The first step was the appointment of a faculty representative to accompany the team and to supervise the players' conduct. They acted principally in the capacity of a chaperone, and few had any substantial knowledge of the sport concerned. Coaching the team was not considered one of their responsibilities.

The significance of this action was

1. School officials were no longer ignoring these athletic activities.
2. Some school responsibility was being assumed.
3. Faculty representatives were becoming involved in interschool athletic contests.

VOLUNTEER COACHES

As interest in contests among groups of students from different high schools increased, they began to attract the attention of persons outside the schools. Some of them had been members of amateur and professional teams and a few had played on intercollegiate teams. They began to offer their services to the student athletic associations as coaches of their teams. This was the first coaching high school teams received to any extent, although a few faculty representatives who had been given supervisory responsibilities and who had sufficient knowledge of the sport concerned also had begun voluntarily to give some instruction. The success of teams with volunteer coaches caused the practice to spread.

It was noted that players were learning better skills and team play from such coaching, but problems for school administrators soon developed. Improper language and undesirable attitudes were believed to have been learned from some of the coaches over whom the schools had little or no control. These and other problems caused high school principals and superintendents to conclude that the time had come when high schools must assume full responsibility for interschool games.

TEACHER-COACHES

One phase of the assumption of full control over interscholastic contests was the employment of teachers who had sufficient knowledge of a sport to coach a high school team. They were primarily academic teachers with intercollegiate or amateur athletic experience. Physical education had not been established in the high school curriculum, and few of these coaches had had any formal training in the teaching of athletic or physical skills.

This development increased the school's control over interscholastic athletic games, but some schools persisted in allowing outside volunteers to coach their teams in the absence of any enforceable regulations prohibiting them. Volunteer coaches were not eliminated until state high school associations were formed, which took place during the first quarter of the twentieth century. One of the initial regulations of virtually all state high school athletic associations was that all coaches must be certified teachers employed by their schools. Also, most associations required that some time must be devoted to classroom teaching to meet this requirement.

It was during this period that physical education became established in the high school curriculum as a required subject, and teacher-training institutions formulated programs for the professional training of physical education teachers. A trend soon developed of assigning coaching duties to high school teachers with majors in physical education. The preparation they had received by taking courses in health and safety, care and prevention of injuries, theory and techniques of teaching sports, and other required subjects improved their qualifications for coaching; but the fact that many schools offered more sports in their interscholastic athletic programs than they had physical education teachers meant that many teams were being coached by persons without any special professional preparation. Unfortunately, this situation has continued.

CERTIFICATION

It has been reported that only approximately one-fourth of the head coaches of junior and senior high school teams have had professional preparation for coaching,[1] although there have been attempts to ensure more adequate preparation in the future. A task force was appointed by the American Association for Health, Physical Education, and Recreation Division of Men's Athletics to study this problem and to make a recommendation.[2] It was the conclusion of the task force that special standards should be established by each state for teachers who want to coach high school athletics. These standards would ensure preparation in medical aspects of sports, principles and problems of coaching, theories and techniques of coaching, kinesiology, and physiological

[1] Arthur A. Esslinger, "Certification for High School Coaches," *Journal of Health, Physical Education, and Recreation*, 39 (October 1968), 42.

[2] *Ibid.*, pp. 42–45.

foundations of coaching. Physical education majors would automatically meet the requirements, which would not be applied to classroom teachers who were already serving as coaches. Because of the work of the task force,

1. A wider recognition has been shown for the need of more-professionally trained high school coaches.
2. Programs have been developed by colleges and universities for special coaching certification.
3. Voluntary coaching certification is being practiced. Public colleges and universities have teacher certification authority in virtually all states. Although a coaching certificate may not be required by the state department of education, several colleges and universities are offering special coaching certificates to those who desire them and complete the prescribed requirements.
4. Other qualifications being comparable, secondary school administrators and boards of education select physical education majors or persons holding a special coaching certificate to fill coaching vacancies.

We shall take a further look at the future of coaching certification in Chapter 13.

What Is Coaching?

There are as many concepts of coaching as there are different types of athletics, but the teaching of athletic skills is a constant in all of them. The most common concept, and a rather narrow one, limits its meaning to instruction in athletic skills and play. However, when school officials began to recognize the educational values accruing from athletic experiences under the direction of high school coaches, interscholastic coaching began to acquire a broader meaning, that is, that high school students were being taught to become better persons through athletics. Thus interscholastic athletics came to be considered supplementary to the curriculum, and if so, coaching by certificated persons must be viewed as teaching.

If we accept John Ruskin's theory, which has never been disputed, that education does not mean just teaching an individual what he or she does not now know, but that it does mean teaching the individual to behave as he or she does not now behave, the interscholastic coach is in a significant position to teach.

It is necessary that we clearly understand the three general areas of learning to realize fully what coaching includes. These are knowledge, fixed associations (automatic physical and mental skills), and emotional patterns. Their interaction becomes the controls of conduct that cause each of us to behave as we do.

The attainment of knowledge involves acquiring and organizing information essential in arriving at an understanding that can be applied. Coaching affords numerous opportunities to impart knowledge. An understanding of the rules applied in athletic games is one example. Knowing the standards of eligibility and the school's policies and the reasons for them is another. Becoming aware of how others will react in different types of situations, even in athletic contests, provides some rudimentary knowledge of psychology important to both players and coaches. These are only three illustrations of knowledge that can be taught by coaching, but more will be mentioned in Chapter 6, in which we shall give our attention to the methods and techniques of coaching.

Fixed associations comprise a well-recognized portion of the responsibilities of coaching. These are the automatic responses we acquire when we learn to execute mental and physical skills. To become fixed they must be practiced and repeated until we perform them automatically. Learning the multiplication tables is one of the best examples of mental fixed associations, which generally involve memory in some form. Coaching does not involve any large number of fixed mental associations but is greatly concerned with the development of a large number of automatic physical skills.

No other field of teaching offers more occasions to develop emotional learning than does coaching. Emotional learnings are those to which a feeling is attached, such as ideals, attitudes, tastes, appreciation, respect, loyalty, sportsmanship, and desires. Coaches can and must teach an understanding of them and their importance in everyday life. Ensuring that athletes practice them in interscholastic competition will help to instill them as important controls of conduct. Many advances have been made in the teaching of knowledge and skills, but the teaching of emotional learning lags considerably in the school program. This is regrettable because it is our emotions that frequently determine the purposes for which we use our knowledge and skills.

Successful coaches are those who understand what they are trying to teach and who make adequate plans to teach it. Every teacher, including coaches, should establish specific objectives to be attained in each of the three learning areas. Chapter 6 will offer suggestions for coaches in the teaching procedures to be employed.

Strategic Position

It is easier for us to teach students when they are interested in what we are trying to teach. High school boys and girls have a natural interest in play, and those who participate in interscholastic sports are motivated by the special appeal games have for them. Parental interest and attendance at games further stimulate players, as do community interest and the attention of the news media. The coach is in position to capitalize on these interests in motivating students to learn the skills, knowledge, and emotional patterns he or she is attempting to teach.

It should be made clear at this point that the attention being given to *teaching* is not to be interpreted as any distraction from the coaching of a sport. Neither is there any issue with the desire to win. Winning becomes overemphasized only when other worthwhile learning is neglected. However, this learning is often much easier to teach when a team is winning. Another important purpose of this book is to help us learn to *teach youth through sports*, which will increase the educational values of interscholastic athletics.

CLOSE RELATIONSHIP WITH STUDENTS

The successful coach is idolized by his or her athletes and respected by other students. He or she is one of the more popular members of the school faculty with the student body and is often envied by other teachers. The numerous informal and intimate relationships the coach has with athletes result in an excellent atmosphere for counseling. We must show a personal interest in each player if we want that individual's respect. Coaching provides daily opportunities to observe the attitudes, habits, and other types of emotional behavior of our athletes, which is essential in counseling. As coaches we are in a strategic position for both individual and group counseling. Many coaches utilize incidental methods to counsel athletes whose attitudes, self-control, and so forth are in need of improvement; these can be effective without the player realizing he or she is being counseled. A more direct procedure can be used in the more serious cases. Experienced coaches realize that it is better to counsel athletes than to allow them to practice undesirable habits which will have to be corrected later.

Some coaches do an outstanding job in group counseling by seizing opportunities derived from the experiences of the team in games or on trips to games. College players with whom I was acquainted used to refer with pleasure and admiration to the daily talk sessions by their coach. Each day, after the warm-ups for practice and before the instruction in skills, the entire squad listened to him for some three to five minutes. The players did not know in advance what he would talk about, but they came to realize that each talk had a purpose and would relate to something within their realm of experience. Sometimes a short stanza from a poem or a verse from the bible would be read to introduce or to illustrate what he had to say. He had a profound influence on the lives of his athletes through his teaching and counseling procedures.

Because of his position and the opportunities afforded by it, the coach is often one of the best counselors on the school staff.

GENERAL PATTERNS OF CONDUCT

It is extremely difficult to plan any type of course to teach attitudes and ideals, which have been acquired through our associations with others. They seem to rub off on us. Parents have the most effect in shaping the attitudes and ideals of their children, and the *peer group* has a significant influence. Some have been developed as concomitant outcomes of educational activities but have been learned from teachers much more than from subject matter. The need for better controls of conduct is one of our most serious problems in society. Moral education is an area educators have been inclined to neglect but are now being forced to consider.[3] It is apparent that more attention will be given to the teaching of moral values in the future.

Coaches are in a significant position to influence the attitudes and ideals of youth, and this influence will be positive if we understand the importance of our position and take advantage of it for this purpose. The character traits we display, stemming from our own attitudes and ideals, will be factors in molding those of athletes. One example will illustrate how some of the best lessons in maintaining poise and self-control can be taught incidentally by a coach who takes advantage of opportunities that may arise.

A highly successful basketball coach could find daily something that happened in practice or in a game that could be used to teach a lesson about behavior. He was adept at using illustrations and giving demonstrations. Some of his best players had lost their tempers the previous night in a game they had lost to an arch rival. After the squad had taken its short limbering-up exercises, the players were called over to the bench for one of his frequent short lectures. When they had taken their seats, he placed the two kettles, which he had brought to practice, on a table before them. One was a large kettle, and the other was a small one. He asked which would boil faster if each were filled with water and placed over the same amount of heat. There was unanimous agreement that the smaller kettle would. There was a pause. They were then asked if they thought they had been large or small kettles the evening before and whether this might have been a factor in the loss, the only mention he made about losing. He made his point, and his players learned some lessons they never forgot. They realized that getting

---

[3] David Purpel and Kevin Ryan, "Moral Education: Where Sages Fear to Tread," *Phi Delta Kappan*, June 1975, pp. 659–62.

"overheated" in a game doesn't contribute to success and that it could have the same effect in life. More important, they saw themselves as they really were in the game, and it influenced them to try to be bigger persons by learning to hold their tempers.

Who else is in a better position to teach such lessons than a coach? By trying to teach beyond the skills of the game and practicing a little ingenuity as the occasion occurs, we can have a profound influence on the lives of athletes.

Not only does this kind of coaching help boys and girls, but it also gains respect for the coach and his or her profession. The coaches who are forever remembered by their athletes, and for whom a warm feeling endures, are those who have taught them important lasting values which carry over into adult life. Such values help to give them a *sense of direction*. The skills they once were able to perform well may have faded, but the emotional patterns they concurrently acquired live on.

DISCIPLINE

One of the strongest criticisms of public education is the lack of discipline in the schools. Disciplining students has become increasingly difficult for high school teachers and administrators as a result of the permissiveness of parents, the concern for individual rights, the tendency toward legal action, and the insistence of the courts that schools provide due process.

Discipline is defined as training that is expected to produce a specified character or pattern of behavior, including moral improvement, and as coaches we are in a favorable position to provide this training. Participation in interscholastic athletics is considered by the courts as a privilege rather than an inherent right, which makes it more difficult for a plaintiff to prove that disciplinary procedures interfere with his or her individual or civil rights. The desire of students to enjoy this privilege makes it easier to discipline them. The rules of a game include disciplinary principles. Athletes soon learn that a violation of good conduct results in a penalty against the offender, which may be banishment from the game in serious cases. We should frequently remind students that this is typical of everyday life: If they violate the rules of society, consequences will follow. If we ignore such opportunities to teach, we are neglecting our responsibility. Interscholastic athletics are viewed by some as the last bastion of discipline in our schools.

Our goal in disciplining students should be to help them achieve self-discipline. The establishment and enforcement of reasonable training standards are significant aids in helping us attain this objective. Athletes who understand this purpose and the personal values offered them will not look upon training rules as mere restrictions on their individual liberties. We must teach them that the game will present situations in which self-control must be exercised and that players who discipline themselves sufficiently to maintain their composure and emotional control under trying circumstances become better athletes and better citizens.

TEACHING ON DISPLAY

Each week during a season the product of the coach's teaching is displayed in the games played. How athletes play will demonstrate the teaching of playing skills whether the game is won or lost. The teamwork, alertness, and understanding exhibited by players will reveal the knowledge they are acquiring through interscholastic competition. The elements of sportsmanship shown will be testimony to the attitudes and ideals being shaped. This display puts coaches on the spot, but it has its advantages.

Despite the pressures games cause us and our players, they motivate us to do our best teaching. The public has an opportunity to view the effects of our coaching and gain an understanding of what we are accomplishing. What effect would it have on all teachers if the results of their teaching were to be demonstrated each week before the school and the community? It might help them to become better teachers.

PUBLIC RELATIONS

A good high school coach is an asset in a school's public relations. Schools are often judged by what is observed on the athletic field or gym. There are relatively few occasions to view directly other phases of the educational program. The conduct of the players, coach, and student spectators will reflect on the school. Coaches are in a strategic position to serve as public relations ambassadors for their schools. They have many contacts and opportunities both within and without the community to represent the high school, and the respect they have earned adds to their influence on others.

One of the nation's outstanding athletic coaches—who had a clear understanding of the philosophy and objectives of athletics at all levels—the late Clark Shaughnessy, former coach of the Chicago Bears, stated on two occasions in presentations made at meetings of the National Federation of State High School Associations that the main purpose of interscholastic athletics was to *make men and women out of boys and girls* and that providing entertainment must be secondary. His philosophy, accepted by high school administrators and directors of athetics, places the coach in a key role in the educational process. We must realize that maturity is the primary goal of education and that interscholastic athletics will contribute to it. If they should cease to be educational, they could no longer be justified as part of the total school program.

Summary

The evolution of requirements for high school coaching reflects the significance attached to the position of the coach and has resulted in more-professionally prepared high school coaches.

Coaching involves the teaching of physical skills, knowledge, and emotional controls, and interscholastic athletics offer wide opportunities for teaching these basic controls of conduct.

The coach occupies a strategic position because of his or her close relationship with students, occasions to teach emotional learning, and conditions that make it easier to discipline students. The results of the coach's teaching are publically displayed each week in the games played, which stimulates coaches to improve their coaching and teaching methods.

The place of the coach is important in public relations both within and without the school community.

It must be realized that *making men and women out of boys and girls* is a primary function of interscholastics and that coaches can make interscholastic athletics a still more significant phase of the educational program.

QUESTIONS AND TOPICS FOR STUDY AND DISCUSSION

1. Trace the development of qualifications established for high school coaching. Give reasons for each stage in this development.
2. What is the latest development in the standards for interscholastic coaching? Say why you think this requirement is important. Can it be made mandatory for all coaches and assistant coaches? Why or why not?
3. Write a definition of coaching.
4. Why is it important that coaches understand the three areas of learning inherent in coaching and teaching?
5. Explain how the coach is in a favorable position to teach emotional controls. Give examples to substantiate your explanation.
6. Why is the close relationship of the coach with students conducive for counseling? Has any coach provided counseling to you? Explain.
7. Prepare a brief outline of a plan to teach better attitudes and ideals through coaching.
8. Why is it frequently easier for coaches to exercise discipline than it is for other teachers?
9. Enumerate and explain ways in which you think coaches can become good public relations representatives.

10. Do you agree with the late Clark Shaughnessy's philosophy of interscholastic athletics. Explain why or why not.

BIBLIOGRAPHY

Esslinger, Arthur A. "Certification for High School Coaches." *Journal of Health, Physical Education, and Recreation,* 39 (October 1968), 42–45.

Fretwell, Albert K. *Extra-Curricular Activities,* p. 407. Cambridge, Mass. The Riverside Press, 1931.

Gallon, Arthur J. *Coaching Ideas and Ideals,* Chap. 1, Boston, Houghton Mifflin, 1974.

Hartman, Paul E. "Selecting the Right Person to be Coach." *The Bulletin of the National Association of Secondary School Principals,* 62, No. 418 (May 1978), 23–27.

Lawther, John D. "Role of the Coach in American Education." *Journal of Health, Physical Education, and Recreation,* 36 (May 1965), 65–66.

Lindholm, Karl. "Coaching As Teaching: Seeking a Balance." *Phi Delta Kappan,* 60, No. 10 (June 1979), 734–36.

Purpel, David, and Kevin, Ryan. "Moral Education: Where Sages Fear to Tread." *Phi Delta Kappan,* June 1975, pp. 659–62.

"A Survey of Special Coaching Requirements of Athletic Coaches of High School Interscholastic Teams." *Journal of Health, Physical Education, and Recreation,* September 1970, pp. 14–16.

CHAPTER 2

The Kind of Coach We Want to Be

Introduction

There is a tendency to classify coaches into two types, successful coaches and unsuccessful coaches. But success in coaching means different things to different people. Some categorize success by whether coaches are winners or losers, whereas others consider their attitudes and approaches to coaching. There are frequent discussions among school patrons about good coaches and poor coaches, but little is said to indicate that any significant number are just *average* coaches.

Coaches are remembered for different reasons. Some are remembered for the lasting impact they have on the lives of athletes, others primarily because of their winning records, and a number for just having been at one time a high school coach.

We shall take a comprehensive look in this chapter at what kind of coach students, parents, administrators, boards of education, and communities want. The type of coach each of us will become will be determined largely by our individual abilities and attitudes and by how we want others to remember us.

Why We Want to Coach

We all have different reasons, generally multiple in nature, for deciding to coach, and these reasons will be influential in the kinds of coaches we become.

LIKING FOR ATHLETICS

We all have liked athletics or we would not have been high school players, and this experience was instrumental in stimulating our desire to coach. Coaching affords an outlet for us to continue an active, participating interest in athletics. Some of us who may have aspired to become professional athletes, or who were professional athletes, turned to high school coaching as one way to continue to participate in what we really like.

EXCITEMENT OF COMPETITION

Participation in athletic competition is both satisfying and exciting. After our playing days are over, becoming a coach affords an opportunity to pursue the excitement we felt as players. We will identify ourselves with the team's successes and thrills, and it will be a challenge to outcoach our rival colleagues.

ATTENTION AND RECOGNITION

It is a normal human trait to seek attention and recognition, which may be attracted in various ways. The publication of our team's successes by the media stimulates a feeling of satisfaction within us. The popularity of high school sports places us in the limelight when things go well, and we are inclined to forget critical statements published when our team loses with the anticipation and hope of future success.

INFLUENCE OF A COACH WE ADMIRE

Many of us were fortunate in having had coaches whom we respected and admired because of both their coaching abilities and the type of persons they were. They impressed us by the attitudes and ideals they demonstrated and the personal interest they showed in us. The enjoyment and satisfaction they exhibited from working with boys and girls motivated us to emulate them.

SUPPLEMENT TO OUR LIVELIHOOD

If we are honest about it, one of the reasons a number of us considered coaching was as a means of supplementing our livelihood; but if a livelihood was our only reason, we would not have become coaches. We understand that the primary source of income will be from teaching, but we will gladly accept and expect some extra increment for the time we devote to our coaching duties. Some teachers did coach in the early days for no more pay, but those days are gone. Boards of education and high school administrators now consider interscholastics a part of the total educational program, and paying coaches for their extra duties is only fair.

Each of these, when viewed in proper perspective, is a legitimate reason for deciding to be a high school coach, but no one of them is sufficient to make a successful coach. If we want to become an outstanding athletic coach who contributes to the welfare of high school students, we must have other worthwhile reasons. Some of them and their significance may be realized while we are gaining experience. It may be that a few of us were drafted to coach as the result of an expanding interscholastic program for which there was an inadequate supply of qualified coaches, and we are now attempting to improve our qualifications. Unless we have good reasons for continuing to coach, most of us will drop it.

AFFECTION FOR STUDENTS

Great high school coaches genuinely like boys and girls and get a feeling of satisfaction from helping them to develop both as players and as individuals.   Trying to help each student become a better person through athletic experiences is looked on as a challenge and a responsibility.

The close personal relationship with athletes develops a lasting sense of empathy, and a feeling of satisfaction results from observing them mature physically, mentally, and emotionally. Coaches who are remembered most sincerely are those with an abiding interest in each athlete, whether a substitute or a star, which continues long after he or she is gone. This type of relationship not only helps the students but also helps the coach continue to be an important person in the lives of others.

OPPORTUNITY TO TEACH

If we are to be dedicated to making interscholastic athletics an important phase of the total educational program, we must view athletic competition as providing significant opportunities to teach. As a certified teacher-coach this must be one of our reasons for accepting a coaching assignment. Otherwise, we should stick strictly to the classroom.

The excitement of games and the exultation of winning must not cause us to neglect the educational objectives of interscholastics, whether the games are won or lost. As a means for self-improvement, players should be taught to diagnose mistakes to determine their causes and to avoid rationalization. They must be helped to understand that such has an important value in later life. Both victories and defeats will provide many opportunities for learning such lessons.

There will be many occasions to try to instill better attitudes and ideals. It must be realized that our own attitudes and conduct will be important in influencing proper ideals of sportsmanship, honesty, fair play, respect, and courtesy. Many who have taught and coached sincerely believe that the field or gym offers an excellent laboratory for this emotional learning.

The Kind of Coach Others Want

In attempting to be the coach of our own ideals, we dare not be unconscious of the type of coach others want, nor should we be blinded by our self-image. The degree of success to which we aspire can be increased if we are aware of the expectations of those persons who have a vital interest in interscholastic athletics. They include the athletes, their parents, the school administrators, board of education, and the school patrons.

In considering the prospectives of these various groups, we need to exercise considerable care and judgment. Each group may differ in its priorities. Fans will be primarily concerned that the coach is a winner and may not give much significance to anything else. All other groups will be interested in winning, but they will want to see additional traits in the coach. Their requisites need to be evaluated to determine whether they will contribute toward our development as a coach or whether they represent vested interests. It can be very helpful to us to understand what they want and their reasons for it.

ATHLETES

The Minnesota State High School League[1] and the Indiana High School Athletic Association[2] have conducted studies relating to what athletes like and dislike about coaches. Also, each of us can recall what qualities we respected most in our coaches and who made a good impression upon us. It will be helpful in building a good relationship with members of our athletic squads if we are aware of what they appreciate in a coach, but their desires and reasons for them will need to be evaluated carefully.

The following, from the Minnesota and Indiana studies and inciden-

[1] Minnesota State High School League, *Listening to Athletes* (Anoka, Minn., 1975).

[2] Indiana High School Athletic Association, *Are We Listening?* (Indianapolis, 1977).

tal comments from former high school athletes, are the qualities student athletes want to see in a coach:

1. A coach should know the fundamentals of the sport and teach the necessary skills to excel in it.

2. A coach should really care about students personally and be one to whom they can turn for personal help and counseling.

3. A coach should show no favoritism regardless of the players' abilities. The substitutes who sit on the bench during the game want to feel that their coach has an interest in them and that they are being treated fairly.

4. A coach should want to win but should not act as if it is a castastrophe if the team loses.

5. A coach should want students to enjoy athletic competition and should realize that this is an important reason for their participation in athletics. Ninety-six percent of the athletes replying in the Indiana study indicated that they would participate in interscholastic athletics even though no awards were given, which is evidence that one of their primary purposes of competing in athletic games is to have fun and recreation. [3]

6. A coach should realize that boys and girls have interests in addition to sports, and unnecessary conflicts with other interests they consider important cause frustrations.

7. A coach should give constructive criticism after defeats and not lose his or her temper. Players and teams want to be criticized privately. Public criticism before spectators or through the news media is resented and does not achieve any worthwhile purpose.

8. A coach should be reasonable in the amount of time demanded of athletes. Practice sessions that are consistently too long exceed the athletes' optimum span of concentration and become boring to them, resulting in staleness. The students also object to year-round practice in any one particular sport. [4]

9. A coach should command respect and be a worthwhile example.

10. A coach should have firm but reasonable standards. The great majority of athletes appreciate training rules and policies when they understand the reasons for them. They do want them to be consistently applied.

[3] *Ibid.*, p. 2.

[4] *Listening to Athletes*, p. 5.

11. A coach should be someone to whom the students will feel devoted after their athletic experiences have been completed.

These are resonable expectations, and we will be wise to give them serious consideration.

PARENTS

What parents want can be confusing if we fail to consider their individual desires and expectations in the total perspective of parental concerns. A few parents will be extremists with vested interests. All will be primarily interested in their own children, but for different reasons. They will want to see their progeny in the team lineup, and some of them will claim that favoritism is being shown if their sons or daughters do not play as much as they think they should. The ultimate goal of some will be a collegiate athletic scholarship for their son or daughter. The materialistic value of the scholarship may take precedence over personal values, and they will want the coach to be a tool in helping to achieve this objective. In fact, there may be some parents who will rate us as coaches by the number of college athletic scholarships our players receive.

We must not allow the preferences of a minority, who may be the most vocal, to obscure those commonly accepted qualities that the majority of parents want the coaches of their children to have. These parents will desire the same characteristics in a coach as do the majority of athletes. In addition, they will want the following:

1. An individual who has a good understanding of the most worthwhile values of interscholastic athletics.
2. A coach who will have a positive influence on the lives of youth.
3. A coach who will make them feel certain that their daughter or son is in good hands with proper supervision, particularly on out-of-town trips.
4. A coach who can and will communicate with parents about personal problems of athletes, the standards and policies applied and the reasons for them, and other matters of mutual concern.

SCHOOL ADMINISTRATORS

The high school administrator, the athletic director, and the board of education are in the best position to know what kind of coach the community wants and the kind of coach the school needs. If they do their job properly, they will balance community desires with the needs of the students, the latter taking precedence in instances of conflict. These persons will be responsible for selecting the coach and giving the supervision necessary to help him or her develop into the kind of coach they are convinced will contribute toward the overall educational objectives of the school. It is important to have a clear comprehension of the kind of coach they want.

School boards and administrators may differ from school district to school district, but there are some common traits they will look for:

1. A coach should provide leadership for the youth and citizens of the community by his or her character, ability to instruct, and example.

2. A coach should be loyal to the school and the teaching profession.

3. A coach should be cooperative with other faculty members and the school administrators.

4. A coach should have a philosophy of interscholastics compatible with the educational philosophy and objectives of the school.

5. A coach should communicate directly with the athletic and school administrators regarding athletic matters. Differences of opinion and complaints made to others and through the news media do not serve any worthwhile purpose or benefit the coach.

6. A coach should be an ambassador for the school. Administrators recognize that the coach is in a strategic position to create either a good or a bad impression for the school and can be an asset or a liability in public relations, which causes them to be concerned about the kind of image the coach will help to create.

7. A coach should win his or her share of games but should not have an obsession for winning. Unfortunately, some individual members of boards of education, and occasionally a school administrator, may be obsessed with winning. When the majority of a school board and the school administrator are so obsessed, the best advice is to seek a coaching position elsewhere.

8. A coach should adhere to established school district policies. As we gain experience and establish ourselves on the school faculty, we will be able to influence policies, but we must make certain that the policies are approved by the administration before they are applied. Just as we will expect our athletes to abide by already adopted training rules and regulations, school boards and administrators will expect us to

comply with established school policies and regulations until such time as they may be officially changed.

It will enhance our position if we know what is expected of us by the board of education and administration and to give support to their policies. It is good administrative procedure for them to consult coaches in regard to policy considerations, and we will become instrumental in framing school policies after we prove ourselves an asset to the school and community.

Summary

The kind of coach we become will be determined primarily by each of us. We must be ourselves, and one should not attempt to be somebody else. It will help us to understand the type of coach others want us to be, which can enhance our development, but there are also some inherent dangers. Their reasons must be examined for validity. Those which are excessively vested are seldom sound. The common qualities which the students, parents, and school administration wish to see in a coach can be of great help to us in creating an image of the kind of coach we would like to have others see in us and that we would like to see in ourselves.

Methods and techniques for self-improvement will be discussed in Chapter 12.

QUESTIONS AND TOPICS FOR STUDY AND DISCUSSION

1. Why have you chosen to be a coach? List reasons in order of their influence upon your decision.
2. How does coaching provide opportunities to teach students through interscholastic athletics? List the types of learning in which there will be opportunities to teach.
3. If you were, or are, the parent of a high school athlete, list the qualities you would like to see in the coach of your daughter or son.
4. List the reasons why you should have a clear understanding of what the school administration expects of its coaches.
5. Give a description of the kind of coach you would like to be.

BIBLIOGRAPHY

Gallon, Arthur J. *Coaching Ideas and Ideals*, pp. 18-21, Boston: Houghton Mifflin Co., 1974.

Indiana High School Athletic Association. *Are We Listening?* Indianapolis, 1977. A report on a study of the views of high school athletes toward interscholastic athletics.

Minnesota State High School League. *Listening to Athletes.* Anoka, Minn., 1975. A report on student forums.

Sabock, Ralph. *The Coach*, pp. 39-69. Philadelphia: W. B. Saunders Co., 1973.

Snyder, Eldon E. "A Study of Selected Aspects of the Coach's Influence on High School Athletes." *The Physical Educator*, 29 (May 1972), 96-98.

CHAPTER 3

History, Philosophy, and Objectives of Interscholastic Athletics

If we are to understand the place of interscholastic athletics in secondary education, it is essential that we understand its history. An insight into its development will help us comprehend the philosophy that emerged to give it direction. A perception of both the history and the philosophy of interscholastic athletics is essential in evaluating present practices, trends, and prevailing regulations.

Our fundamental beliefs about why we provide interscholastic competition furnish the basis for our objectives as coaches. Objectives incompatible with the accepted philosophy of secondary education will not be our most significant goals.

In this chapter we shall trace the general history of interscholastic athletics, note the evolution of its philosophy, and examine its most worthwhile objectives.

History of Interscholastic Athletics

The development of interscholastic athletics can be seen as periods or stages, which will provide a better understanding of how they became a part of the secondary school program. Authors sometimes differ in the number of stages and in the titles designating them, but there is general agreement regarding the developments that took place. Those that follow are descriptive of the periods through which interschool competition emerged to become a vital part of high school education.

STUDENT SPONSORSHIP AND CONTROL

As previously stated, interscholastic athletics were initiated by high school students who formed student athletic clubs or associations. The manager, chosen from among their own group, selected the players for the team and scheduled the games, some of which were against town teams, which included adults. As competition became keener, outsiders were allowed, and sometimes recruited, to play on their teams. One of the first student-sponsored teams on record was formed by some high school boys in Worcester, Massachusetts. The name chosen for the team was the Worcester High School Baseball Club, although not all the players were students of the school.[1] All of these student-sponsored games were for one purpose—to have fun.

High school administrators at first ignored these student-directed activities; they did not consider them to be any business or responsibility of the schools. However, because the schools' names were adopted for many of the teams, people in the communities thought that they were school-related functions. Disputes among players, occasional fights, and misconduct at contests ultimately became a source of embarrassment for high school principals. Although the games were not school sponsored, which was not clearly understood by school patrons, the administration was criticized for the misconduct of players and fans. Some serious injuries and a few deaths which occurred in football caused great concern among high school principals.[2] Conditions surrounding student-sponsored athletic contests eventually reached a point which made it clear that they could no longer be ignored.

PERIOD OF OPPOSITION

As problems multiplied, opposition began to develop, part of which came from professional physical education organizations which were being formed in the late 1800s. Physical educators during that time were strong proponents of *physical culture*, which primarily consisted of such activities as calisthenics and gymnastics. Their negative attitude toward athletic games as a part of physical culture caused them to voice their objections to interscholastic sports.

Also, many classroom teachers thought that the time devoted to athletic contests interfered with the academic work of students and that they should not be allowed.

The abuses noted caused a number of school administrators to consider taking steps to abolish student-sponsored athletic teams and contests. Others, although opposed to what they observed, took the position that it would be impossible to outlaw them because of the interest in them that had developed in some communities. It was their belief that if the schools were to attempt to stop games between teams made

[1] Albert K. Fretwell, *Extra-Curricular Activities* (Cambridge, Mass.: The Riverside Press, 1931), p. 407.

[2] Lewis L. Forsythe, *Athletics in Michigan Schools: The First Hundred Years* (Englewood Cliffs, N.J.: Prentice-Hall, 1950), pp. 70-72.

up largely of high school boys, community groups would take over and support them. It was obvious to them that the students were interested in and wanted to compete in athletic games and that there was no effective procedure to eliminate them.

PERIOD OF TOLERATION

The result was that school officials resolved to tolerate these student activities and to exercise some supervision over them. This was the period when faculty members were appointed as chaperones to accompany teams to help prevent misconduct at games. Volunteer coaches began to offer their services, and eventually some faculty members who had played games in the sport concerned and had some knowledge of it started to do some coaching. A few eligibility rules were established, and improvement began to be noticed after the schools officially assumed more responsibility over interschool games during the first two decades of the 1900s.

RECOGNITION OF EDUCATIONAL VALUES

High school administrators gave little attention to any educational values of interscholastic athletics during the stage of toleration. Toward the latter part of the period, schools began to employ teachers for coaching duties to eliminate the volunteer coaches over whom they had little, if any, control. Some of them provided good leadership to teams and players, and it began to be observed that some worthwhile educational results were being developed. By 1925, several professionally trained coaches were employed, and it was becoming more evident that interscholastic athletics were contributing to the educational objectives of the high schools. Sports by this time had also become an important part of the physical education program, and there was less conflict between physical education and interschool competition. Many coaches were physical education teachers, and athletes who excelled in physical education were competing on school teams. Additional eligibility standards in the form of academic requirements and good conduct were having wholesome effects, and principals recognized that interscholastic competition, when properly planned and administered, was supplementing the academic program.

FULL SUPPORT OF SCHOOL ADMINISTRATORS

School administrators and boards of education began to accept interscholastic athletics as an integral phase of the total educational program. They started allocating funds to support the games, and by the 1930s it was evident that sports had become a permanent fixture in the high schools.

The extent of the support sports receive can be noted by the increasing amount of funds they are provided. Some sports that do not obtain any financial aid from admission fees are financed from school district funds. Two schools in Missouri, Clayton High School and Horton Watkins High School of Ladue, finance their athletic activities entirely from board of education funds and do not charge any admission for athletic games. Financial crises infrequently cause a temporary reduction or elimination of district financial support, but public pressures result in its restoration as soon as feasible. School laws in many states contain specific provisions providing boards authority to use school funds to support interscholastic athletics.

The attitude of school officials and school boards has been influenced further by the recognition of the importance of interscholastic activities given by such national and regional educational organizations as the National Association of Secondary School Principals and the North Central Association of Colleges and Secondary Schools. School administrators, in general, do not consider a high school program complete without interscholastic athletics.

PERIOD OF EXPLOITATION

It is typical that after a high school activity becomes popular with students and attracts public attention, there are attempts by outside groups and organizations to exploit the students and the school program. Soon after the schools assumed responsibility for interscholastic athletics, individuals and groups began to solicit talented high school athletes to play on independent teams, which caused conflicts with interscholastic play and the academic program. This problem eventually was alleviated by the adoption of limited team standards by state high school associations, which provided that athletes would be ineligible for interscholastic competition if they competed on an outside team during the season they were representing their school in the same sport.

Others sponsored special events, such as meets and tournaments, to which they invited high school teams to participate. These efforts also were thwarted by statewide regulations established by schools through their state high school associations.

Beginning in the 1940s and continuing to the present, there have been an increasing number of nonschool-sponsored promotions, which in numerous instances involve exploitation of interscholastic sports. The primary purposes of the majority of these projects are to benefit the sponsor more than the students or their schools by using them to raise funds, gain recognition for the sponsor, or advertise products. Additional attention to them will be given in Chapter 13.

That interscholastic athletics had educational values was recognized by the 1920s, but for several years they were generally developed incidentally from athletic participation. Attention to interscholastics as a better tool for learning began to be emphasized in the 1940s and was given impetus by the adoption of the Cardinal Athletic Principles by the National Federation of State High School Athletic Associations and the American Association for Health, Physical Education, and Recreation in 1948 and 1949, respectively.

To be of maximum effectiveness, the athletic program will:

1. Be closely coordinated with the general instructional program and properly articulated with other departments of the school.

2. Be sure that the number of students accommodated and the educational aims achieved justify the use of tax funds for its support and also justify use of other sources of income, provided the time and attention which are given to the collection of such funds are not such as to interfere with the efficiency of the athletic program or of any other department of the school.

3. Be based on the spirit of non-professionalism so that participation is regarded as a privilege to be won by training and proficiency and to be valued highly enough to eliminate any need for excessive use of adulatory demonstrations or of expensive prizes or awards.

4. Confine the school athletic activity to events which are sponsored and supervised by the proper school authorities so that exploitation or improper use of prestige built up by school teams or members of such teams may be avoided.

5. Be planned so as to result in opportunity for many individuals to explore a wide variety of sports, and in reasonable season limits for each sport.

6. Be controlled so as to avoid the elements of professionalism and commercialism which tend to grow up in connection with widely publicized "bowl" contests, barnstorming trips and interstate or intersectional contests which require excessive travel expense or loss of school time or which are bracketed with educational travel claims in an attempt to justify privileges for a few at the expense of decreased opportunity for many.

7. Be kept free from the type of contest which involves a gather-

ing of so-called "all-stars" from different schools to participate in contests which may be used as a gathering place for
representatives of certain colleges or professional organizations who are interested in soliciting athletic talent.

8. Include training in conduct and game ethics to reach all non-
participating students and community followers of the
school teams in order to insure a proper understanding and
appreciation of the sports skills and of the need for adherence
to principles of fair play and right prejudices.

9. Encourage a balanced program of intramural activity in grades
below the ninth to make it unnecessary to sponsor contests of
a championship nature in these grades.

10. Engender respect for the local, state and national rules and
policies under which the school program is conducted.[3]

State high school associations and individual schools have since that
time devoted much more effort to establishing more specific educational objectives for interscholastic athletics and plans and procedures
for attaining them, but the potentials of athletics as a medium for learning have not been reached and will be discussed further in Chapters
6 and 7.

Evolution of Coaching

Coaches have had a great influence upon the history of interscholastic
athletics. It was the engaging of qualified high school coaches and the
result of their teaching that were largely instrumental for athletics
being recognized and supported by administrators and boards of
education. The leadership of those early outstanding coaches helped to
shape a program of great interest and value to high school students.
Just as many of the improvements in the academic program have en-
sued from the efforts of individual classroom teachers, so the eleva-
tion of interschool athletics has come from the initiative, foresight,
attitudes, and efforts of dedicated coaches.

Development of Philosophy

The term *philosophy* has several connotations. Some think that it involves the abstract and does not have practical application, but in our
discussion we shall limit its meaning to understanding answers to ques-

---

[3] National Federation of State High School Associations, *Official Handbook*,
1974-75, pp. 9-10.

tions of *why*. Our beliefs as to why we have interscholastic athletics in our schools constitute our philosophy, which will influence our efforts as coaches. It is important to realize that the philosophies of sports will differ among coaches, administrators, players, and parents. There may be some misunderstandings about why sports are included in the school program. This makes it wise for a school to have an official statement of the philosophy that gives direction to its athletic program, and to educate all concerned to it.

A philosophy was present when students initiated athletic contests with students of other schools. Athletic games were looked on as a way to have fun, and the fact that it was more fun to win than to lose may have accounted for many of the practices which crept into their activities and to which school officials objected.

It is evident that during the early days of interscholastic competition there was no prevailing school philosophy to give it direction. Ideally, all educational programs should start with fundamental beliefs from which objectives are developed to guide them. It was not this way with athletic contests. Schools found them in their hands after concluding that it was better to exercise some control and tolerate them than to have students manage them. It was not until after educational values were recognized that coaches and school administrators began to give serious consideration to formulating statements of philosophy to guide their programs. The basic prevailing belief that began to emerge in the 1920s was that interscholastic athletics provided opportunities for students to acquire physical, social, and moral values.[4] Prior to that time, winning was considered most important and any benefits to students were secondary.

State high school associations and the National Federation of State High School Athletic Associations began to emphasize the importance of sound philosophy to guide school athletics in the 1940s. Interscholastic activities by this time were seen as a supplement to the academic program, a premise still held. State associations began to suggest statements of philosophy for consideration by their member schools, which were encouraged to use them in formulating an official athletic philosophy of their own. Some state high school associations have included the accepted philosophy of their schools in their constitution and by-laws. The following is the statement contained in the Constitution of the Missouri State High School Activities Association:

Interscholastic activities shall supplement the secondary curricular program and shall provide most worthwhile experiences to students that shall

[4] Samuel M. North, *Athletics in High School*, Proceedings of the Sixty-Second Meeting of the National Education Association of the United States, CXII, Washington, D.C., June 29-July 4, 1924, p. 647.

result in those learning outcomes that will contribute toward the development of the attributes of good citizenship. Emphasis shall be upon *teaching through* school activities. To this end only can interscholastic activities be justified.

The philosophy of the National Federation of State High School Associations is well stated in its Official Handbook:

NATIONAL FEDERATION
STATEMENT OF PHILOSOPHY

The purpose of the National Federation of State High School Associations is to coordinate the efforts of its member state associations toward the ultimate objectives of interscholastic activities. It shall provide a means for state high school associations to cooperate in order to enhance and protect their interscholastic programs. In order to accomplish this, the National Federation is guided by a philosophy consistent with the accepted purposes of secondary education. Member state associations' programs must be administered in accordance with the following basic beliefs:

Interscholastic athletics shall be an integral part of the total secondary school educational program that has as its purpose to provide educational experiences not otherwise provided in the curriculum, which will develop learning outcomes in the areas of knowledge, skills and emotional patterns and will contribute to the development of better citizens. Emphasis shall be upon teaching "through" athletics in addition to teaching the "skills" of athletics.

Interschool athletics shall be primarily for the benefit of the high school students who participate directly and vicariously in them. The interscholastic athletic program shall exist mainly for the value which it has for students and not for the benefit of the sponsoring institutions. The activities and contests involved shall be psychologically sound by being tailored to the physical, mental, and emotional maturity levels of the youth participating in them.

Any district and/or state athletic meet competition to determine a so-called champion shall provide opportunities for schools to demonstrate and to evaluate the best taught in their programs with the best taught in other schools and in other areas of the state.

Participation in interscholastic activities is a privilege to be granted to those students who meet the minimum standards of eligibility adopted cooperatively by the schools through their state associations and those additional standards established by each school for its own students.

The state high school associations and the National Federation shall be concerned with the development of those standards, policies, and regulations essential to assist their member schools in the implementation of their philosophy of interscholastic athletics. Interschool activities shall be kept in proper perspective and must supplement the academic program of the schools.

Nonschool activities sponsored primarily for the benefit of the participants in accordance with a philosophy compatible with the school philosophy
of interscholastics may have values for youth. When they do not interfere
with the academic and interscholastic programs and do not result in exploitation of youth, they shall be considered as a worthwhile supplement to interschool activities.

The welfare of the schools demands a united front in sports direction
policies and the high school associations provide opportunity for this unity.
They must be kept strong.[5]

It is evident from these statements of philosophy that interscholastic
athletics are thought of as an important part of the total secondary
school program. That they are considered as supplementing the curriculum does not diminish their importance. They differ from curricular
offerings primarily by the fact of voluntary participation, and in almost
all high schools no units of credit are offered for them. The curriculum
consists of both required and elective subjects, and a sufficient number
of credits must be accumulated to meet graduation requirements. State
departments of education prescribe certain subjects which must be
taken to obtain a high school diploma, and the balance of the total
units required are chosen from elective subjects.

Physical education is generally a required subject which offers credit
toward graduation. A few individual schools have permitted interscholastic competition to be substituted for physical education, but this is
prohibited in most states. Neither is interscholastic athletics listed as
an elective course.

There are some who feel that credit should be given for interscholastic sports, which would make them a part of the curriculum and
give them greater educational status, but this could result in some
difficult problems. If they were to become a curricular subject, participation would then become an individual right rather than a privilege, as the courts have considered it in the past. The question would
arise as to whether the schools could afford to offer interscholastic
opportunities to all the students who might insist on being provided
this right. What effect would it have on the enforcement of eligibility
requirements? Could the same standards be applied if it were a right
rather than a privilege? Would coaches be free to select the best players
for interscholastic teams? Would more court suits result if students
were denied what would then be considered a right? These are some
of the questions which must be given serious study before there is any
concerted attempt to include interscholastic sports in the curriculum.

Privileges are often cherished more than rights and serious thought
should be given to the possible effects that changing the basis of inter-

[5] *Official Handbook*, 1977-78, p. 8.

school athletics from that of a privilege to that of an inherent right might have on the total interscholastic program. The recognition now given them as a significant part of the total educational program in supplementing the curricular offerings indicates that it is not necessary, and the potential problems and uncertainties involved indicate that it might not be wise.

Athletic Philosophies Differ

Different philosophies of athletics exist, even within the school program. Interscholastic athletics preceded physical education in most high schools, but physical educators were committed to a philosophy earlier than coaches. There were differences in their philosophies of physical education before it was established in the curriculum as a requirement for virtually all students. Those who were proponents of physical culture promoted gymnastics, calisthenics, and dance to develop strength and grace. They were opposed to athletic contests, and there was controversy when other physical educators began to advocate games as a part of physical education. Eventually, the philosophies merged, and they are all included in modern physical education programs.

Opposition by physical education teachers to interscholastic contests occurred in the late 1800s and early 1900s. After colleges developed programs to train physical education teachers and coaches, such negativism began to subside—largely because many who majored in physical education became coaches, and courses in the coaching of sports were initiated into the physical education curriculum. That high schools tended to employ coaches with physical education majors both to teach physical education and to coach athletics had considerable influence on the conciliation of the two philosophies. Although there are still some differences, there is general agreement that the primary purpose of both physical education and interscholastic sports is to teach youth through the experiences both afford. Physical education is a part of the curriculum, and interscholastic athletics supplement curricular experiences. Each is guided by educational philosophy.

PROFESSIONAL

The converse of interscholastic athletic philosophy is that of professional athletics, which operate under a business philosophy. The owners of professional athletic clubs expect to make a profit by selling entertainment to the public, and players consider it a means of livelihood. Championships and all-star games are sponsored to increase attendance and gate receipts. A winning team is essential to sell the entertainment, and the services of players are bought to help ensure success. There have been attempts to emulate professional athletic practices in interscholastic athletics without a clear understanding of the professional athletic philosophy and how it differs from and conflicts with the educational philosophy on which school athletics are based.

INTERCOLLEGIATE

We may have difficulty trying to define the philosophy which guides intercollegiate athletics. It is considered as having educational values, but it has objectives that differ from other types of school athletics. This need not be considered a criticism, but it results in the situation in which we find collegiate athletics today. Many college and university athletes look upon sports as an opportunity to receive training for professional athletics. It is affected a great deal by professional athletic philosophy. The costs of the intercollegiate programs are financed largely by gate receipts, which makes it important to produce winning teams. The most talented high school senior athletes are recruited and awarded athletic scholarships to enhance the teams' successes. Intercollegiate athletics offer values to the players and provide wholesome entertainment to the public.

AMATEUR

Following a period of chaotic conditions in the last quarter of the 1800s, during which promoters offered cash and merchandise to entice athletes to participate in events they sponsored and considerable corruption existed, a movement toward a philosophy of amateur athletics developed. It was based on the view that competition in athletic activities should be for pleasure and social benefits, with any awards to be only symbolic. The formation of the Amateur Athletic Union in 1888 gave great impetus to this belief, and its philosophy became the accepted one for many amateur athletic organizations.

Because school athletics are amateur, they have been considered by many to be in the same category as all other types of amateur athletics. The actual fact is that school athletics are amateur, but not all amateur athletics are school athletics, nor do they have the same philosophy or objectives. Although the philosophy pertaining to awards is essentially the same, interscholastic sports are guided by an educational philosophy and objectives which are broader than those of other types of amateur athletics.

Statement of Philosophy

Just as each of us will be guided in our coaching by our philosophy of interscholastic athletics, a school's interscholastic program will be guided by the philosophy that prevails in it. We must not become confused by the various philosophies guiding other athletic programs, and we must remember that school athletics are for the educational and personal benefits of high school youth.

Schools have formulated statements of philosophy which were influenced by the coaches who helped to implement them. It is important that such statements be approved by the boards of education, which make them official for the school district. Publicity will help provide better public understanding and give proper direction to the interscholastic programs. The following is a statement of philosophy and objectives adopted by the Parkway School District of St. Louis County, Missouri, which has proved helpful in planning and administering its fine program:

STUDENT ACTIVITIES
Philosophy

We believe that the opportunity for participation in a wide variety of student-selected activities is a vital part of the student's educational experiences. Such participation is a privilege that carries with it responsibilities to the school, to the activity, to the student body, to the community, and to the individual student. These experiences contribute to the development of learning skills and emotional patterns that enable the student to make maximum use of his or her education.

Parkway student activities are considered co-curricular to the school's program of education which provides experiences that will help to develop boys and girls physically, mentally, socially, and emotionally.

DISTRICT GOALS

1. Provide a superior program of student activities that includes appropriate activities for every boy and girl.
2. Provide opportunity for a student to experience success in an activity he or she selects.
3. Provide enough activities to have an outlet for a wide variety of student interests and abilities.
4. Provide those student activities which offer the greatest benefits for the greatest number of students.
5. To create a desire to succeed and excel.
6. To provide for the students' worthy use of leisure time now and in the future.
7. To develop high ideals of fairness in all human relationships.
8. To practice self-discipline and emotional maturity in learning to make decisions under pressure.
9. To be socially competent and operate within a set of rules, thus gaining respect for the rights of others.

10. To develop an understanding of the value of activities in a balanced educational process.[6]

Objectives of Interscholastic Athletics

The objectives of interscholastic athletics must stem from and be compatible with the school's philosophy. When definite objectives are established and plans developed to achieve them, they will help implement the educational philosophy of the school.

Goals can be divided into three categories: the school's objectives, the students' objectives, and the coach's objectives. It is only natural that we shall be concerned with achieving our own personal objectives, but we must also understand and attempt to help our students and school attain their goals.

THE SCHOOL'S OBJECTIVES

The school's objectives will be general and will be a part of its overall aims of education. They will include:

1. Mental, physical, and emotional development of individual students.
2. Enhancement of the educational objectives of the school by providing experiences not otherwise afforded.
3. Provision of wholesome recreation and entertainment to students and spectators.
4. Fostering school spirit.
5. Gaining community support for the school.

The first three of these objectives relate to the aims of the schools to develop better and more competent citizens. They are consistent with the ultimate goals of education and the needs of our society.

The last two pertain to the schools themselves. Fostering school spirit promotes a "we" feeling and cohesiveness within the student body and pride and loyalty to the school. Support to the school is important in furthering the cause of education. Demonstrating to the public the results of good coaching on the play of athletes and the attitudes and behavior of all students creates a favorable impression for the school and gains support of the community, not only for interscholastic athletics but also for other phases of the school program.

---

[6]Parkway School District, *Handbook for Interscholastics*, 1979, p. 3.

THE ATHLETES' OBJECTIVES

If it were entirely left to athletes, their primary objectives would be to have fun and win games. These were their goals when athletic games were first initiated by them. Little thought was given to anything but the pleasure of playing the game, and winning made it more fun.

It is one of our responsibilities as coaches to acquaint students with other important and worthwhile objectives and the values they will receive by striving to achieve them. They must be stimulated to adopt these goals as their own. Among the aims athletes should be motivated to adopt and to try to achieve are the following:[7]

1. *They should understand why the school offers a program of interscholastic athletics.* If they gain this objective, they will have a rudimentary knowledge of the school's philosophy of athletics, which will increase their appreciation of school sports and of their school. Understanding why schools give students opportunities to participate in athletic activities will help them as adults to realize the differences between school athletics and other types. One of the problems facing the schools, and us as coaches, is that too few adults realize the difference in the purposes of interscholastic athletics compared to other amateur athletic programs and to those of professional athletics. For example, adults plan youth athletic programs that are not fully appropriate for their age levels and frequently involve practices more appropriate for the adults, who project themselves through the children who participate. This problem can be alleviated by attaining a better understanding of the philosophy and objectives of junior and senior high school athletics, which are planned for youth.

2. *They should know the values that athletics have for the individual and for society.* The objectives listed in this section reveal most of the values interscholastic sports offer athletes. Collectively, they can be seen as helping the individual to become a better person, which is an ultimate value. Athletes should understand that each objective has an inherent value. The lasting values have the most significance for the athlete and should be emphasized. The attitudes and ideals acquired will help to provide a sense of direction and influence the students' adult lives. Our society will be a better one if we develop better citizens, and interscholastic sports have great potential in this regard.

3. *They should understand the standards of eligibility and their significance.* Athletes sometimes look on eligibility requirements as

---

[7]Charles E. Forsythe and Irvin A. Keller, *Administration of High School Athletics* (Englewood Cliffs, N.J.: Prentice-Hall, 1977), pp. 10-11.

restrictive rules, which often creates a negative attitude toward all standards. This attitude will be avoided if we teach them the reasons eligibility regulations were formulated and their purposes in the interscholastic program. One of the significant reasons for their understanding the standards of eligibility is to protect their privilege to participate in interscholastic competition. Athletes and their parents are apt to blame coaches for negligence if players commit an inadvertent violation because they were not fully informed of the standards. It is imperative that we make every effort to help them attain this objective.

4. *They should understand the rules to play the game and to be intelligent fans.* Without rules there could be no games worthy of playing. Athletes should realize that their purposes include fairness and equity in competition and the physical welfare of the players. Specific instruction in and interpretation of the rules should be provided, and the personal and team benefits of knowing them should be emphasized. Student spectators also will be better fans if they are acquainted with the rules, through school assemblies or other means, and parents and adult fans can be given information at PTA meetings and special occasions.

5. *They should be able to think as individuals and as members of a group.* Athletics regularly provide opportunities for decision making and thus enhance the ability to think. The player must also think with the team, which instills in the individual the basic element of cooperation needed in our democratic society. One of the pleasures of coaching is to observe players thinking and working together as a team toward a common objective, to do their best in competition.

6. *They must have faith in democratic processes.* One of the virtues of our society is that the competition among its members is instrumental in stimulating each to become more competent. Some of those who excel are selected for public office to represent others, and qualifications are established to ensure that they have the background and are the type of person worthy of such privilege. Interscholastic athletics afford excellent opportunities to teach the meaningfulness of democratic processes and to practice them. Those who excel in physical skills are selected to play on the team, and the standards of eligibility make certain that the players possess the qualities and character to represent the school, student body, faculty, community, and team. Student athletes are too immature to develop these concepts without our help, but it will not be difficult for them to understand if we make this type of analogy. Interscholastic athletics are popular in our society and should be used to build greater faith in our democratic processes.

7. *They should understand the values of group ideals and goals.* An ideal is an idea to which a strong emotional feeling is attached. It often

originates in one individual who may influence others until it is instilled in them and becomes a group ideal. When it does, it influences behavior and enhances human relationships. There is no better place to build high ideals of honesty, fairness, respect, cooperation, dedication, and loyalty than the athletic field or gym. The importance of group ideals can be made clear to athletes by helping them to understand that all members of the team must have them if it wishes to receive respect and support, and that the team and each individual may be misjudged and affected if any one player fails to uphold the team's ideals.

The value of group goals can be established by illustrating how winning must be a team (group) goal if the team is to be successful. A player whose goal is to score the most points in a basketball game may not contribute as much as one who is more interested in the team winning, regardless of who scores the most points.

An organization of persons with common group ideals and goals will accomplish more than one person acting individually without concern for the ideals and goals of others. Understanding this value will yield meaningful benefits in later life.

8. *They should improve their motor skills.* Athletes understand and have this objective, but they must be reminded not to become self-satisfied. When they fail to improve their skills, they will have reached their maximum performance and other players may pass them by.

9. *They should improve their health and physical fitness.* We may suppose that all athletes have this objective, but we may find that they do not. Both good health and physical fitness can be temporary. Some students may not give attention to diet, proper exercise, and rest during off-seasons or after their playing days are over. We must emphasize the importance and value of continuing efforts toward this goal.

10. *They should appreciate wholesome recreation and entertainment.* Students engage in sports for fun and diversion and should be taught to appreciate the opportunities the school provides. If an appreciation is instilled in them, they will continue these activities as a worthy use of their leisure time, which should be emphasized.

The interscholastic athletic program offers one of the most wholesome forms of entertainment for student and adult spectators. It continues to afford enjoyable vicarious experiences long after active participation.

11. *They should have a desire to succeed and to excel.* All of us have a desire to succeed, but not everyone has the desire to do his or her best and to excel. Cultivation of the drive to reach one's potential can have significant value in later years. Interscholastic competition tends to create within us the will to excel over others, which helps us

to succeed in a competitive society. The desire to win can be translated into a healthy desire to excel.

12. *They should have higher ethical and moral standards.* Some of the critical problems facing our society include the breakdown of family life, rising crime, political corruption, lack of respect for the property of others, decline of personal honesty, and changes in sex mores, which are causing much concern among educators.[8] These involve ethical and moral issues which schools have been reluctant to treat directly through the curriculum; instead schools have relied largely on informal means of teaching these values. School activities, including athletics, are considered important features of the informal programs.[9] There is a trend among educators toward the position that more attention must be given to teaching moral and ethical values, and some are suggesting a formalized method. Basic to this issue is the development of better attitudes and ideals that influence behavior.

Interscholastic athletics is one of the best ways to teach these standards effectively. The very nature of the interscholastic program makes this possible. Rules of eligibility are instrumental in helping students to understand the importance of meeting ethical and moral standards for good citizenship, which we should emphasize as the most significant requirement of eligibility. Provisions in the rules related to conduct and sportsmanship influence better citizenship, and penalties assessed for violation of these and other rules stimulate better behavior.

Athletes, and student spectators, should be taught the need for higher ethical and moral standards in our society, which can only be met by inculcating them in individuals. The importance of this objective of interscholastic sports should be stressed and emphasized.

13. *They should learn self-discipline and emotional maturity.* Self-discipline is one of the paramount goals of education. Students should be helped to realize its personal value and the consequences of not achieving it. Those who grossly fail to acquire it are found in our correctional institutions. The training received in athletics helps to build self-discipline and should be emphasized to athletes as being for this purpose.

Emotional control correlates closely with self-discipline and is essential to it. Athletic contests present numerous occasions for practicing it. The loss of emotional control results in mistakes and penalties, a fact students will learn through athletic competition. These experiences will help them mature emotionally, and we should frequently remind

[8]Kevin Ryan and Michael G. Thompson, "Moral Education's Muddled Mandate," *Phi Delta Kappan*, LVI, No. 10 (June 1975), 663-66.

[9]David Purpel and Kevin Ryan, "Moral Education: Where Sages Fear to Tread," *Phi Delta Kappan*, LVI, No. 10 (June 1975), 659-62.

athletes of the value of proper emotional control now and in adult-
hood.

14. *They should acquire social competence.* The widening of ac-
quaintances inherent in interscholastic athletics offers opportunities to
develop social competency. Students should be taught how to be good
hosts and good guests. The pep club can play an important part in helping to achieve this objective if the coach and pep club sponsor cooperate: It is essential that both the team and pep club look upon students
from other schools as *friendly opponents* and not as *enemies.*

15. *They should realize the values and benefits of conforming to
rules.* Rules for any activity or undertaking are established for the benefit of the majority of persons involved. Without them a state of anarchy
would exist. We must teach students the basic reasons for rules and
emphasize how the importance of conforming to rules in athletics is
analogous to the value of adhering to laws, which have been adopted
for the betterment of society.

All of the preceding are among the significant and worthwhile objectives for students participating in interscholastic athletics. They
must be helped to understand them and the inherent values achievement offers to each individual and the team, which is comparable to
the conditions they will find in later life. Attention will be given in
Chapter 6 to methods and techniques for teaching students how to
achieve these objectives.

THE COACH'S OBJECTIVES

What shall our own personal objectives be as coaches? This is a
question we should frequently ask ourselves if we wish to continue to
improve in our profession. Our goals must include helping our schools
and students to achieve their own objectives. In addition, we should
have personal objectives compatible with those.

1. *We should develop a personal philosophy consistent with the
accepted philosophy of interscholastic sports and of secondary education.* Our basic beliefs must guide us toward the ultimate goals of
education.

2. *We should improve our personal qualities.* Our character is what
we are, and our personality is what others see in us. We should be concerned about the development of both if we are to improve our effectiveness as coaches. (Ways to accomplish this will be discussed in
Chapter 8.)

3. *We should be recognized as a teacher and a coach.* If we are realistic, we will acknowledge that we must succeed both as a teacher and
as a coach. A coach is a teacher through athletics, but we must also

become a competent teacher of school subjects in our field. More time will be devoted to teaching courses included in the curriculum than in coaching. It must be our goal to be recognized as both a good coach and a good teacher.

4. *We want to win athletic games.* This is a worthy objective and there is nothing wrong with it unless it becomes our only aim, and thus other worthy objectives are neglected. If the desire to win stimulates us to make every effort to help boys and girls reach their potential as players and as better individuals, which will help them become better athletes, it will contribute to the goals of education .

5. *We should develop a lasting personal relationship with our athletes.* Some of the best lifetime friendships have developed between coaches and their players. Personal attention given to players, counseling offered, working together toward common goals, and athletes responding to the efforts of the coach—all build a mutual feeling of respect and friendliness that becomes permanent. These are the conditions that cause many adults to credit their coaches for much of their success and result in a relationship that endures.

6. *We should attain professional advancement.* There are two general types of advancement within any profession. One is to move to a higher position within the profession; the other is to become a more proficient technician in some particular phase of the profession. Coaching is one phase of the profession of education. We must decide whether we wish to continue as a coach or whether we want to become an athletic director or school administrator or specialize in some other area. Unfortunately, too many of our coaches have considered it necessary to advance to another field in education and have discontinued coaching. Those who have resolved to devote their lifetime to coaching have contributed most to the advancement of the position.

7. *We should contribute to the general objectives of education.* Many coaches feel that they can contribute more to the education of students through coaching than they can through any other phase of teaching. Although the winning of athletic contests may appear to be their immediate goal, they are dedicated to helping boys and girls develop personal traits and abilities that will assist them in becoming more capable and better citizens.

8. *We want to supplement our livelihood.* Most of the high school coach's salary is for teaching, but the additional pay for coaching does provide some extra income in a profession in which members are not paid as well as in some other professions.

9. *We want to achieve a feeling of satisfaction.* When we were younger, we enjoyed the excitement of active competition in sports. As we grow older and are not as physically capable of playing, coaching pro-

vides an avenue of satisfying participation and enjoyment. Many coaches continue to coach *simply because they like it.*

Summary

Athletic activities involving high school students were started before any interscholastic athletic philosophy and objectives were established to guide them. They were initiated by students for the purpose of fun and recreation. As competition became keener, abuses and undesirable practices resulted.

Interscholastic athletics have gone through several stages in their development. In the initial stage they were under the control of students and were generally ignored by school administrators. After abuses started causing embarrassment and problems for the schools, a period of opposition began in the late 1800s, during which attempts were made by some schools to abolish student-directed athletics. A general conclusion was reached among high school principals that it would be impossible to eliminate student athletic games and that it would be better for the school to exercise some control over them than to drive them outside the school. Chaperones and sponsors were appointed to accompany teams during the period of toleration which followed in the early 1900s, and a few faculty members began to provide some coaching. Conditions surrounding contests began to show some improvement.

As the control by schools increased, some educational values of school-sponsored athletics began to be noted. The establishment of more regulations and standards during this period led to further improvements and caused school administrators to realize that interscholastic athletics were affording experiences which were contributing to the aims of education. During this stage attention began to be given to the formulation of a philosophy of interscholastic athletics and the establishment of objectives, and by the late 1920s they were accepted as a part of the secondary education program.

By 1930, interscholastic athletics had received the full support of school administrators and boards of education. Although limited at first, money was budgeted for them by some boards of education; this has become a common practice and is evidence of their educational importance.

After interscholastic sports were recognized as a significant part of the educational program and were becoming increasingly popular, there were attempts by nonschool organizations and individuals to exploit them. This period is still with us and it has been necessary for the high schools and their state associations to adopt regulations to prevent such exploitation.

The educational values of interscholastic athletics had been proclaimed for quite some time, but there is little evidence that much direct attention was given to implementing them until the late 1940s and 1950s. State high school associations and their member schools began to emphasize the need for more attention and were formulating plans to increase the educational values by the 1960s. Programs to improve sportsmanship, the training of cheerleaders in their responsibilities, and manuals for pep club sponsors and coaches have all contributed to making athletic games more educationally significant.

Although it followed rather than preceded the initiation of interscholastic athletics, the philosophy which emerged now gives direction to the program, and the objectives established make clear what interscholastic sports are to help achieve.

QUESTIONS AND TOPICS FOR STUDY AND DISCUSSION

1. Explain the conditions surrounding athletic contests while they were under the control of students. What type of student organizations were formed to administer them?
2. Discuss the abuses and undesirable practices which caused school officials to oppose athletic games sponsored by student-athletic associations.
3. What was the general attitude of school administrators toward interscholastic contests during the period of toleration? Discuss steps taken by the schools during this period which led to improvement and the ultimate recognition of the educational values of interscholastic sports.
4. When do attempts to exploit high school athletes and the interscholastic program generally occur? List three purposes nonschool organizations usually have for promoting contests and meets for high school athletes and school teams.
5. Explain steps taken by high schools and high school organizations to implement the educational values of interscholastic athletics. Discuss the importance of the Cardinal Athletic Principles.
6. Summarize the history of interscholastic athletics by listing the stages, or periods, in their development from their beginning to the time they received the full support of school administrators and boards of education.
7. How could you support a contention that as the qualification of coaches improved, so did the educational values of interscholastic athletics?

8. Why were interscholastic athletics sponsored by high schools for a number of years without an established philosophy to guide them?

9. Discuss how interscholastic athletic philosophy differs from the philosophy of professional athletics and from other types of amateur athletic philosophy. Explain how you can note the influence of professional athletic philosophy by the practices observed under it.

10. Why were objectives for interscholastic athletics slow in being established?

11. Presume that your athletic director or principal may ask you to prepare a statement of objectives you would like to have the board of education consider for adoption; write a statement of the objectives you would recommend.

12. Why is it important that we teach our athletes the objectives of our athletic program?

13. Enumerate objectives you will want your athletes to have for participating in interscholastics.

14. State and give reasons for the personal objectives you will have as a coach.

BIBLIOGRAPHY

"Cardinal Athletic Principles." *1974-75 Official Handbook*, pp. 9-10. Elgin, Ill.: National Federation of State High School Associations.

Dannehl, Wayne E., and Jack E. Razor. "The Values of Athletics—A Critical Inquiry." *The Bulletin of the National Association of Secondary School Principals*, September 1971, pp. 59-65.

Forsythe, Charles E., and Irvin A. Keller. *Administration of High School Athletics*, pp. 1-13 and 70-72. Englewood Cliffs, N.J.: Prentice-Hall, 1977.

Forsythe, Lewis L. *Athletics in Michigan Schools: The First Hundred Years*, pp. 70-72. Englewood Cliffs, N. J., :Prentice-Hall, 1950.

Fretwell, Albert K. *Extra-Curricular Activities*, p. 407. Cambridge, Mass.: The Riverside Press, 1931.

Gallon, Arthur J. *Coaching Ideas and Ideals*, pp. 25-31. Boston: Houghton Mifflin, 1974.

Montgomery, James A. *The Development of the Interscholastic Movement in the United States 1890-1894*, pp. 31-32. Ann Arbor, Mich.: University Microfilms, 1962.

North, Samuel M. *Athletics in High School*, p. 647. Proceedings of the Sixty-Second Meeting of the National Education Association, Washington, D.C., CXII, June 29-July 4, 1924.

Parkway School District. *Handbook for Interscholastics*, p. 3. Chesterfield, Mo., 1979.

Purpel, David, and Kevin Ryan. "Moral Education: Where Sages Fear to Tread." *Phi Delta Kappan*, LVI, No. 10 (June 1975), 659-62.

Ryan, Allan J. *Philosophy of Athletics at the Junior High School Level. Contemporary Philosophies of Physical Education and Athletics*, pp. 92-110. Columbus, Ohio: Charles E. Merrill, 1973.

Ryan, Kevin, and Michael G. Thompson. "Moral Education's Muddled Mandate." *Phi Delta Kappan*, LVI, No. 10 (June 1975), 663-66.

Seaton, Don Cash, Irene A. Clayton, Howard C. Leibee, and Lloyd L. Messersmith. *Physical Education Handbook*, pp. 7-9 and 12-19. Englewood Cliffs, N.J.: Prentice-Hall, 1974.

Shapiro, Leonard, and Donald Huff. "False Hopes and Broken Dreams." *The Basketball Bulletin*. National Association of Basketball Coaches of the United States, Summer 1977, pp. 86-93.

"Statement of Philosophy." *1977-78 Official Handbook*, p. 8. Kansas City, Mo.: National Federation of State High School Associations.

CHAPTER 4

Working with the Administration and Faculty

Coaching involves more than just working with athletes. There are others who make the interscholastic program possible and who help to administer it: the superintendent of schools, the high school principal, the athletic director, members of the faculty, and the board of education. It is vital for the school administration and faculty to function as a team if the interscholastic program is to provide maximum benefit to the students, and the purpose of this chapter is to help us learn how to gain their cooperation and support.

Responsibilities of the Board of Education

The board of education is elected by the citizens to provide the education desired by the community for its youth, which consists of both the curricular and extracurricular programs, including interscholastic athletics. Because of its responsibilities to the community, it has the final authority over all phases of the district's educational offerings.

AUTHORITY

State law provides the board of education with broad powers. The statutes of virtually all states allow the local board of education to adopt whatever policies and regulations it deems necessary to govern the schools of the district and to implement the educational program as long as they are not contrary to law. Such policies and regulations officially adopted by the board of education have the effect of law, which the courts have recognized.

Members of boards of education do not have the time to attend to the details of administering the educational program, and most of them do not have the certification requirements to do so. The board employs qualified administrators and teachers to implement the district's educational program under the policies and regulations it establishes. It further is empowered to delegate responsibilities to others and to determine to whom those persons are accountable, which will be considered further below.

DEVELOPING PHILOSOPHY AND OBJECTIVES

Every school district should have a general statement of philosophy and objectives which has been officially approved by the board of education and which gives direction to its total educational program. This statement should be complemented by a more specific statement of philosophy and objectives by each school within the district. Departments within the school should have a statement of departmental purposes and goals consistent with the philosophy of the school and school district. The interscholastic athletic department falls into this last category. It is important that all such statements be officially approved by the board of education, which will give them added weight.

It is impractical for each department in the several schools in some districts to meet directly with the board of education, but administrators and teachers should be involved in recommending statements for its consideration. In most cases they will be formulated under the supervision of the school principal and submitted to the superintendent to be presented to the school board. Some lay persons may be invited to participate in this process, which may have some advantages, but care must be exercised in their selection.

It is important to make certain that the board of education understands the philosophy and purposes of interscholastic athletics. Some members may consider the winning of games as the only goal, whereas others may be opposed to interscholastic competition. We must attempt to learn the board's views, and if there is any indication that members fail to comprehend the educational values offered, we should work through the school administrators to educate them.

DELEGATION OF RESPONSIBILITY

It must be recognized that the superintendent is the chief representative of the board of education. He or she is delegated general authority, is charged with the supervision of the district's total school program, and is responsible to the board. Except in the smallest districts, the many details of the superintendent's office will make it necessary for him or her to delegate responsibility and authority to principals and other administrators. The responsibility for the interscholastic program may be assumed by the principal or it may be delegated to an athletic director under his or her supervision. It will be one or the other to whom coaches will be accountable.

The following diagram illustrates the delegation of authority and responsibility in several large high schools. Some of the positions may not be found in smaller high schools.

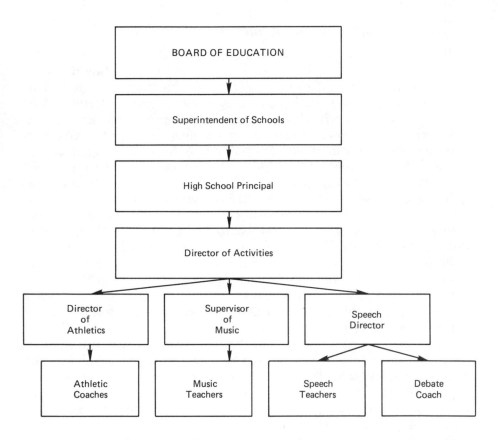

Figure 4-1. Administrative organization for interscholastic activities

If the school does not have an activities director, the director of athletics may report directly to the principal or a vice-principal, or a vice-principal may be the activities director or even the athletic director. In the very smallest schools, coaches may be under the direct supervision of the principal or superintendent. It is important to know who is our immediate supervisor, and we should avoid going around that person to an administrator on a higher level. If it is deemed necessary to consult a higher authority, the immediate superior should always be first consulted and invited to take part in any discussions.

DISTRICT POLICIES

Some school policies are district-wide, whereas others apply to individual schools within the district. The board of education has the final responsibility for and authority over all policies. Coaches will be setting policies for their athletes and must make certain that they are acceptable to the school administration and board.

The successful high school coach understands the responsibilities and authority of the board of education and that the board must have the power and final determination necessary to carry out its functions. Coaches and teachers have a right to expect their views to be heard and considered, but they cannot presume that they should each have the authority to make final decisions, which would lead to a state of administrative anarchy. There must be mutual respect between the board of education and the school faculty of which the coach is a member.

Working with the Faculty

In this discussion we shall consider the faculty comprising both administrators and supervisors, but we must realize that the superintendent is the chief representative of the board of education. It will generally be through him or her that we will work with the school board.

THE INTERVIEW

The interview for a coaching position should be looked on as more than a procedure in the process of being hired as a coach. It is important to us for two significant reasons: (1) to determine whether we want to accept the position if it is offered and (2) to provide the foundation for working with the faculty in the school in which we become employed.

We should learn as much about the school and its interscholastic philosophy and objectives as we can through the interview. If we are not voluntarily given the opportunity to ask questions, we should ask for this privilege. In our preparation for the interview we should think through carefully the information we desire and formulate tentative questions to obtain it. Among the things we will want to learn will be the following:

1. *Does the school have a statement of philosophy and objectives for its interscholatic athletic program?* If it does, we should ask for a copy. If not, we will want someone, preferably the superintendent, to explain them. We must be certain that we will be satisfied to work

under that school's approved philosophy and goals, and we may want to seek a position elsewhere if we feel that we cannot.

2. *What established policies does the school have for interscholastic sports?* As a new coach, we must realize that the best judgment will be to follow established policies. We may find that additional policies may be needed, but recommendation of new policies should wait until we have had time to get oriented to the school program. We will be able to influence policies after we gain experience in the school. It is often a mistake to begin a position with the idea that we are immediately going to make revolutionary changes in school regulations.

3. *What is the attitude of the faculty toward interscholastic athletics?* Do the members cooperate in supporting the program? Do teachers show an interest in the athletic activities by regularly attending games, supervising the conduct of students, and helping in the administration of athletic events?

4. *What is the general attitude of the athletes toward the school's athletic program?* Has discipline been a problem? Do they expect any special privileges? We will want to know whether the team morale has been good or poor and what material we will have to work with, although this should not be one of the most significant factors in our decision.

5. *Does the student body support the team and show a sense of loyalty to the school's interscholastic program?* We will also want to know whether good sportsmanship and conduct are displayed at games.

6. *Does the community support the interscholastic program by interest in and attendance at games?* Are there any pressure groups within the community to influence athletic policy? If there is a booster's club, we will want to know something about its program and activities.

7. *How does the school finance the athletic program?* It is important to learn if the program is expected to finance itself through admission receipts and what support is received from the board of education funds, as well as to understand the general financial condition of the district.

8. *What do the school board and administrators expect from their coaches?* What is their first priority? It is not unheard of for some board members to be most interested in employing a coach who they believe will win conference and state high school series championships. A winning record is not good enough for them if it does not produce champions. We should be wary about accepting a position under these conditions.

The information such questions will provide is fundamental in accepting or rejecting a coaching position. We need not be afraid to ask them if the information is not provided voluntarily. They will be recognized as intelligent queries by any knowledgeable school administrator and board of education and will generally increase our opportunity of being hired. If we are offered the job and accept, this information is equally important in providing a foundation from which to work.

Also, we should anticipate and be prepared to answer questions, some of which might be the following:

1. *Why are you interested in a coaching position in this particular school?* It is advisable to learn as much as we can about the school and its interscholastic program before the interview. We must convince the board of education and school administrators that it is the type of school in which we would like to work and that we are confident that we can make contributions to its objectives.

2. *What is your philosophy of interscholastic athletics?* Does your philosophy of junior differ from that of senior high school athletics? Your reply must be compatible with the general accepted philosophy of interscholastic sports (see page 27). Most school administrators, including athletic directors, will appreciate the point of view that extending sports in junior high school to as many students as practical should be emphasized, with less emphasis on winning records. We should also be prepared to state our philosophy of education.

3. *What do you consider the most important objectives of interscholastic athletics?* This question must be answered with care. We should explain without hesitation that our *immediate* objective is to win contests but that a more important goal is to produce men and women of high character and good citizenship, whether the games are won or lost. Our response should be clearly stated so that our purposes are well understood.

4. *Of what professional organizations are you a member or plan to be a member?* If we expect to be a respected teacher and coach, we should join the community and state teachers' associations. We should also join the state association for health, physical education, and recreation if our field is physical education. Membership in the state coaches' association adds to our credentials if we explain that our reason for joining is to become better prepared professionally. I am not in favor of coaches' associations trying to control the interscholastic program. It must be realized that administrative organizations must and will supersede the authority of coaches. Fortunately, all the associations in almost all states have learned to work together in building a better athletic program.

5. *Can you work well with others?* Other coaches? Classroom teachers? School administrators? We must show respect for coaches of other sports and be willing to cooperate with them. There will be some classroom teachers who do not look favorably upon the athletic program. We should explain that we will respect their opinions but will try to influence them in the other direction. The board of education, superintendent, principal, and athletic director will be particularly concerned about your attitude toward school administrators and whether you respect their positions and responsibilities.

6. *What is your attitude toward boosters' clubs?* These clubs sometimes try to become pressure groups and influence school policy. You should answer that you can work with a boosters' club provided it is a supportive organization without any vested interests of its own. You might suggest that you think such an organization can be an asset if its projects include improving sportsmanship, stimulating attendance, and helping to host events.

7. *Do you think you will be satisfied working under the policies and regulations of this school?* Unless you think you cannot work under current policies and do not plan to accept the position, your response should be that you certainly expect to accept them, and that you will not have any suggestions until you have had time to evaluate them in practice.

8. *What do you expect of players?* The first part of your response should be that you will want your athletes to try to do their best. You should explain that you will insist they put academics first and receive satisfactory grades. Emphasize that good sportsmanship during games and good conduct in and out of school will be of concern. Respect for others is important to you, and you will expect the athletes to follow the regulations and policies of the school.

Other questions will, of course, be addressed to you. Think through them carefully before answering. Be sure you understand them and their purposes. It is a good technique to ask occasionally that a question be repeated if you do not have a ready answer and if you need time to think. If you do not have a reply, do not hesitate to state that you do not have sufficient knowledge about the matter to respond to the question.

POLICIES AND STANDARDS

No program is any better than the standards established for it and the policies formulated to uphold the standards. Standards and policies relating to the students' eligibility, good conduct, discipline, and out-of-town trips must be adopted. Others regarding the sportsmanship of fans and the cooperation of nonschool organizations will contribute to a better program. Clear administrative policies on budgeting and the purchase and care of equipment, the duties and responsibilities of coaches, and the delegation of authority help coaches avoid making embarrassing mistakes. The need for policies should be anticipated, and it is much better to develop them before difficulties arise than to adopt them as corrective measures.

There are a few basic procedural principles for developing any standards or policies, including those we shall formulate for players, such as training rules.

1. *The reasons for the standard or policy should be established first.* This step will help in its acceptance and support.

2. *Those to be affected should be involved in the development.* This does not mean that the persons included have the authority to accept or reject the policy or standard. Their sole responsibility is to make recommendations.

3. *Standards and policies established must be clear.* Those that are not lead to confusion and controversy.

4. *They should be publicized before they are made effective.* Adequate effort must be made to see that they are well understood.

5. *Simple procedures for due process should be established and publicized to handle violations without fear of court action.*

6. *Policies and standards must be consistently enforced.* Enforcement procedures should be planned in advance to avoid any charges of inconsistency and discrimination.

The athletic director or high school principal will be responsible for developing the school's standards and policies. Coaches should have the opportunity to make recommendations, but they must remember that this is the limit of their authority. There are some tactful ways of exercising influence. It is much more effective to inform a superior of conditions that warrant consideration, and ask if he or she thinks a policy is needed, than to tell him or her that a particular policy *should be* established.

It is wise to have all necessary standards and policies approved by the board of education through the superintendent. Official approval makes it much more difficult for anyone to challenge the policies before the board or in court.

If we have not been instructed about school policies, it is wise to inquire whether there are any. Occasionally there is negligence in preparing statements, and unwritten ones may exist. We should put our own policies in writing, give each athlete a copy, and post other copies in conspicuous places.

Our concern here is with those who share responsibilities for the athletic program. If the school has an athletic director, he or she will be the person to whom we will be immediately accountable and with whom we will work most directly. It is unwise in any organization to bypass the immediate superior, except in extreme cases when that individual proves to be incompetent or is guilty of general negligence or malpractice. Most schools will have an athletic director, but if they do not, coaches will report to either the principal or a vice-principal.

Any suggestions or recommendations should be made to our immediate superior, and any questions should first be asked of that person. It is best to put recommendations in writing and to ask for a conference to present them. After carefully explaining the reasons for them, we should ask the administrator to study them and to schedule a second conference after doing so. If the recommendations are approved, we should urge that they be presented to higher officials for their endorsement and that we would be glad to attend any conference for this purpose. Those of sufficient significance should be presented through the principal and superintendent to the board of education for official adoption.

The direct contact we have with the principal and superintendent will depend on the size of the school. It is a good practice to recognize the athletic director, principal, and superintendent at all public functions. A personal expression of appreciation to them for their support and assistance helps to make communication easier.

FINANCIAL MATTERS

Financing interscholastic athletics, like any other part of the educational program, can be a sensitive area and a source of friction unless there is mutual cooperation between the faculty members concerned and the school administration. It is reasonable for coaches to expect and to request sufficient financial support from the school budget to provide the type of program that will meet the interests of the students, but it is important that they cooperate by being as economical as feasible.

Submitting justifiable budget requests, soliciting volunteer help to save expenses, avoiding unnecessary expenses, and seeking ways to increase interest in and attendance at games are among the ways coaches can help. Coaches cannot take the attitude that providing the funds we want for our sports is the responsibility of the administration. We must be willing to lend our cooperation in helping to find ways of securing the necessary funds.

It is important to remind ourselves from time to time that we are first a classroom teacher (including physical education), and second, a coach. We shall be communicating with other teachers from both positions, but for now we shall be concerned mostly with our relationships as a coach.

Coaches are expected to be cooperating members of the faculty, and I have already mentioned the professional organizations we should consider joining. Regular attendance at faculty meetings is important, although other teachers and administrators will recognize that it may be necessary to miss some meetings during a sports season. You should demonstrate an interest in other teachers' work and offer assistance when you can. Ask about their responsibilities, methods of teaching, and goals. One of the best ways to get their cooperation in your program is to help them in the extracurricular activities they sponsor.

You should request that teachers report to you when any player is failing to perform satisfactorily in the classroom. Let them know that you will support their academic standards and that you will counsel your athletes, but that you will not intercede for the students regarding their grades. Athletes should be taught that classwork comes first, as demonstrated by that eligibility requirement. Coaches can be some of the best motivators of better academic performance. They can also be unofficially one of the best school counselors. Your athletes should feel that you are sympathetic toward any academic difficulties they may be having, and that you will arrange a conference for them with the teacher for individual attention.

Conflicts in dates of athletic contests and those of activities sponsored by other members of the faculty can cause friction. This can be avoided by a school policy regarding the scheduling of events and use of the gymnasium or playing field. If difficulties do arise, it is wise to suggest that any future problems be resolved by long-range planning, and coaches should show a willingness to cooperate in accommodating as many students as possible. Teachers need to realize that athletic facilities must be reserved for contests during the various seasons, but coaches recognize that they must also be used for some nonathletic events. We should support the reservation of some time between sports seasons for special programs.

A close working relationship should be established with the school counselors. They should understand the standards of eligibility, but they should be advised to refer any questions regarding eligibility to the athletic director or high school principal. It is generally best for one knowledgeable individual to be delegated the responsibility for answering questions about eligibility to provide for accuracy and consistency in interpretations. Athletes with serious personal problems should be referred to their counselor, to whom the coach should relay any information he or she may have.

RELATIONSHIP WITH CUSTODIANS

The custodian of the gymnasium and dressing rooms is generally interested in the interscholastic program. Because his or her work often brings that individual into frequent contact with the players, he or she will know much about their attitudes, their behavior, and the type of individuals they are. Occasionally this information may be of assistance to the coach, but it should be kept in confidence if it is obtained from the custodian. *It should be used only to help the players.*

The custodian performs many services and favors for coaches and we should express our appreciation. Players should be taught respect for custodians and cooperation in helping to keep a neat, sanitary dressing room and an attractive gymnasium or playing field. Providing the custodian with passes to both home and away games when possible will contribute to his or her cooperation.

Summary

If we wish to be a respected coach who works successfully with the school administrators and other faculty members we must

1. Recognize the authority and responsibility of the board of education.
2. Respect the positions of the superintendent, principal, and athletic director.
3. Adhere to the established philosophy and objectives of the school's interscholastic program and its total educational program.
4. Understand and conform to school policies.
5. Communicate and work through proper channels.
6. Establish a good relationship with other teachers.
7. Take an active part in professional organizations.
8. Become a contributor to the interscholastic and curricular programs by suggesting and recommending worthwhile changes for improvement.

Coaches are popular when the team is winning, but we must be careful not to exploit this popularity or to overestimate its value. A good relationship with the administration and faculty will gain support when our winning record is not outstanding; this support is essential to our continuing success.

QUESTIONS AND TOPICS FOR STUDY AND DISCUSSION

1. Explain the basis for the authority and responsibility of the board of education.
2. Write a statement of philosophy of interscholastic sports that you would recommend and explain the procedure you would follow in seeking its adoption by the board of education.
3. Why is it sometimes important to educate members of the board of education to the philosophy and objectives of interscholastic athletics?
4. List what you consider the most worthwhile objectives of interscholastic athletics.
5. Why are district and school policies significant?
6. Discuss how the interview can be mutually beneficial to the school administration and the coach it employs. What information would you want to obtain from the interview?
7. Explain the steps you plan to follow in developing policies for your athletes.
8. Discuss ways of building good relationships with classroom teachers.
9. A teacher says to you that interscholastic athletics have no educational value and cause too much conflict with academic work. Discuss how you would respond.

BIBLIOGRAPHY

Forsythe, Charles E., and Irvin A. Keller. *Administration of High School Athletics*, pp. 191–204. Englewood Cliffs, N. J.: Prentice-Hall, 1977.

Gallon, Arthur J. *Coaching Ideas and Ideals*, pp. 237–38. Boston: Houghton Mifflin, 1974.

Interscholastic Manual for Boards of Education. Columbia: Missouri State High School Activities Association, 1977.

Massengale, John D. "Coach-Faculty Strain: Some Occupational Causes and Considerations." *The Principles and Problems of Coaching*, pp. 99–105. Ed. John D. Massengale. Springfield, Ill.: Charles C. Thomas, 1975.

Resick, Mathew C., and Carl I. Erickson. *Intercollegiate and Interscholastic Athletics for Men and Women*, pp. 24–29. Reading, Mass.: Addison-Wesley, 1975.

CHAPTER 5

Public Relations

As coaches we must also learn to work with parents, school patrons, athletic fans, community organizations, and the sports media. If we desire their cooperation, we must help build sound public relations for both ourselves and our school.

Basic Elements

Good public relations will not happen by accident, nor can they be the result of showmanship or propaganda, which generally lack a sound basis. We are concerned with public relations built on a solid foundation, which will make it difficult to refute our claims and justification of interscholastic athletics.

A SOUND PHILOSOPHY

The total athletic program of a school involves more than interscholastic sports. It also includes physical education and intramural activities.[1] An important part of the inherent philosophy is that athletic experiences should be provided to all students, but the interscholastic part is designed to meet the needs of the more physically talented. It must be kept in proper perspective within the total program and should not cause any neglect of the needs of the great majority of high school students.

---

[1] Don Cash Seaton *et al., Physical Education Handbook,* 6th ed. (Englewood Cliffs, N. J.: Prentice-Hall, 1974), pp. 6–7.

It is strongly recommended that the objectives of interscholastic athletics be put in writing and be well publicized. There will never be an issue about winning as an objective unless it is overemphasized to the point that it causes neglect of the educational and recreational objectives.

The principal and athletic director will understand and explain the school's philosophy and objectives, but frequently the coach has many opportunities to present and discuss them also. Individuals and groups in the community are sometimes more inclined to listen to coaches than to administrators, and their comments can be effective. Thus each of us must be prepared to spell out clearly the philosophy and objectives of our school's interscholastic program. Coaches are sought after as speakers in many communities; often they are expected to discuss the team's chances of winning or to review games already played. These occasions afford opportunities to relate the objectives in an effective manner. In addition a discussion of interscholastic philosophy and objectives can be an interesting PTA program.

GOOD COACHING AND ADMINISTRATION

A well-coached team which displays fine sportsmanship makes a favorable impression for the school, which is important in public relations. (Principles and techniques of coaching will be discussed in Chapters 6 and 7.) Well-planned and well-administered athletic contests involving the cooperation of coaches, faculty, and students, including the extension of courtesies to followers and guests, helps to create a favorable image for the school. The appearance and sportsmanship of the coach adds dignity and has great influence on the attitudes of school patrons. Unless these basic elements provide the foundation, it will be difficult to maintain the interest and support desired.

Relationships with Parents

Vital to good public relations and to success in coaching is the establishment of good and proper relationships with parents. It is essential to assume leadership in this matter, and plans to gain parental interest and support should be made well in advance of the sport season.

UNDERSTANDING PROGRAM'S
PHILOSOPHY AND OBJECTIVES

We cannot assume that parents know what and why we are attempting to accomplish through interscholastic sports. A number of coaches have held preseason parent-athlete meetings to provide them important information. This is an appropriate time to discuss the philosophy and objectives of interscholastic athletics by simply explaining the program and providing a written statement of it. It is wise to include the standards of eligibility, values of athletic participation, and training standards. Parents and athletes often blame coaches for inadvertent violations of eligibility standards. Written copies will help to avoid this problem. Some schools require that both the athlete and his or her parents study and understand the requirements for eligibility before he or she is certified eligible by the administrator. Parents and athletes should understand that eligibility is a privilege to be attained by meeting the standards established for it, and that this definition is recognized and upheld by the courts.

It is important that training standards are discussed and their benefits to players reviewed. Giving athletes and parents a copy of the training rules will increase understanding and make them easier to enforce. The cooperation of parents in upholding all established standards and policies should be solicited. If they clearly understand the reasons behind them, it is generally easy to get their support.

It is wise to suggest to parents that they support all parts of the school program, of which interscholastics is only one. This advice will demonstrate that as coaches we are interested in the total educational program.

INTEREST IN PLAYERS AS INDIVIDUALS

Parents should understand that we are interested in each member of our squads, whether they are regular players or substitutes, and that we want them to enjoy their participation and to develop their potential. It is generally unwise at parent-athlete meetings to indicate who will be the starting players or the ones expected to be outstanding. This act contributes little, or nothing, to the purpose of the meeting and may cause ill feelings on the part of some parents and athletes or adversely affect the attitudes of others. It is also unwise to make any predictions for the team's record or the performance of any individual players, except to say that you plan to help the team and each of its players to do their best.

Parents should know that attending games and exhibiting good sportsmanship are appreciated by their children. Failure to attend may be interpreted as a lack of interest in their daughters and sons, and unsportsmanlike conduct is a source of embarrassment to them. Parents should be requested not to boo officials and to avoid public criticism of them. The method of selecting officials, requiring approval of both schools, should be discussed, and they should be informed that if an official proves to be incompetent, he or she will not be approved for future games. It should be explained that officials are only human and may make an occasional error, but that they will not make as many mistakes during the entire game as the team will make during the first few minutes of play. They should understand that team mistakes, or lack of them, will determine the outcome of the game.

PERSONAL CONTACTS WITH PARENTS

There will be many occasions for person-to-person contacts with parents. We should welcome and take advantage of them and learn as much as we can about individual parents beforehand. Being the first to smile and say hello makes it easier to start informal conversation. Asking questions about their work, interests, and activities exhibits a personal interest, as does inquiring about their son or daughter. These informal contacts are important in beginning your relationships with parents.

We should always be friendly but *businesslike* when discussing interscholastic matters. Any praise of their daughter or son must be sincere and not excessive. If questions are asked about her or his athletic potential or personal problems, a careful but honest reply should be given. If the matter is serious, it is often wise to ask some questions before responding; sometimes it is best to suggest that mutual thought and study be given to the problem and that another meeting be arranged.

There will be times when some parents may make complaints or express their concerns. In these situations, the parents should be allowed and encouraged to do most of the talking. You should ask questions that will reveal the reasons for the complaint, and these should be evaluated carefully to determine whether or not they are legitimate and the complaint has any real basis. If it appears advisable, time should be requested to study the matter and assurance given that it will be given immediate attention. It is always prudent to avoid taking the defensive in these situations and to ask the parents first what recommendations they would make. Reasons for your response to the complaint should be fully explained. If a personal error is discovered, it should be readily admitted with thanks for it being brought to your attention. Complaints should not be invited, but parents should feel that they will be heard. In all cases, appreciation should be expressed for a complaint being made personally and for the willingness of the parents to take time to discuss it. Even complaints can be used to establish desirable relations with parents when handled properly.

Public Relations with Community Organizations

There are organizations in almost all communities that have an interest in the interscholastic program, and you should obtain information about them before relations are established. Some will want the coach as a speaker, and others will want to assist the school in its athletic program. A few may try to exploit it. You should try to understand each organization's reasons for its interest to determine how to establish proper relationships with it.

GENERAL ADVICE

You should welcome opportunities to speak to community groups. Knowledge of and practice in the fundamentals of good speaking will be an asset, and you should take time to study them. Being an effective speaker is important in building relationships and in daily coaching duties. You should use speaking occasions to educate members of the various organizations about the history, philosophy, and most worthwhile objectives of interscholastic athletics—but they must be presented in an interesting manner. You can add interest by using true stories from the history of school athletics and illustrating why standards had to be adopted.

You should avoid predictions and you should not single out players for excessive praise. Emphasize that the team will be just as good as each player helps to make it, and praise team effort. This does not mean that players cannot be recognized for their team contributions, but it must be done in such a manner as not to be offensive to other players or their parents, some of whom may be in the audience. Avoid public criticism of the team or individual players. Criticism of any one player must be constructive and done in private.

Criticism of the school program or of the administration or board of education has no place in speaking to community groups. It is far more beneficial in establishing good public relations to recognize your administrators, if any are present, and to express appreciation for the opportunity to work with them. Even though a criticism may be justifiable, it should be made directly to the party concerned through established channels.

You should always express appreciation to the organization for the opportunity to speak and solicit its support and cooperation. Encourage members to attend games, and suggest that they support the school's sportsmanship objectives. Some organizations occasionally express a desire to help the school financially or in some other material way. Such proposals should always be referred to the administration. Any such assistance must be without any specific designation of purpose to avoid having a nonschool organization determine policy for the board of education. The school should have guidelines concerning such financial support.

SERVICE ORGANIZATIONS

Most communities will have one or more service clubs, which by virtue of their purposes are generally interested in the interscholastic athletic program and in supporting it. They will include some of the most influential persons in the community. Some follow the tradition of having the high school coach speak to them just prior to the opening of the sports season. It is appropriate to talk to them about the values and benefits interscholastic competition has for the students and for the community and to solicit support. The importance of good sportsmanship should be stressed.

BOOSTERS' CLUBS

Booster's clubs are formed by supporters of athletics in many communities for various purposes. They can be an asset or a liability. When the team is winning, they will be generous in their praise of the coach; but when it is losing, they will be among the most vocal critics, sometimes suggesting that the coach be fired.

If a boosters' club is to be an asset, it must be provided leadership. There will usually be an inclination for close communication with the coach. We must be certain that the club gets the school's approval for any projects or activities it wishes to sponsor and that established school policies and the reasons for them are understood and honored. The administration should anticipate those policies needed to guide the boosters' club in its support of the school program. Suggesting that the club help the school in various other phases will keep it from becoming a vested-interest group and make it of greater benefit to the community.

A school administrator or the coach should attend all meetings of the boosters' club. Worthwhile projects can be suggested, such as working to improve sportsmanship at games and acting as hosts to visiting fans. Any financial support should not be accepted for any specified purpose. Allowing the designation of the use of any money is permitting the club to determine policy for the school, which is not a good precedent to set. The board of education and school administration should determine the use of any funds received. The person attending the club meeting can influence it to keep winning in proper perspective within the total educational program.

As coaches, we must make certain that our cooperation with the boosters' club has the approval of the administrators. When proper channels of communication are followed and good leadership is supplied, such an organization can help to improve the interscholastic program. However, it must not be allowed to become a pressure group.

PARENT-TEACHER ASSOCIATIONS

The PTA is an important organization in many communities. The same principles and procedures should be applied in working with it as suggested for boosters' clubs.

SETTING AN EXAMPLE

Attitudes and ideals are taught by example more effectively than by most other means. The attitudes and ideals displayed by parents have a profound influence on those formed by children at an early age. Later, those of the peer group are a potent force, and the examples set by teachers have an effect. The result may be good or bad, depending to a large extent on what students observe in the examples set by individuals with whom they come into contact.

The coach is in a strategic position to influence the attitudes, ideals, and tastes of high school students. The coach is the single most important person in creating an atmosphere conducive to good or bad sportsmanship by his or her example.

Coaches should take an active part in community activities and organizations. They must not be "joiners," which can take too much of their time and result in nonperformance of their responsibilities, but they should assume their fair share in community matters. There will be opportunities during off-seasons and during the summer to help plan and administer activities and programs. The coach's leadership and example are often greatly needed in organizing summer athletic programs for high school and pre-high school students. Some coaches are employed during the summer by community organizations to manage recreational programs.

We must understand that the example we set is significant in the education of the young. Moreover, the respect we are shown in the community will be influenced by the kind of example we set.

Relations with the News Media

The support of the news media is important in educating the public to the school program in any community. Good relations with representatives of the press, radio, and television are essential and must be cultivated. The interscholastic program is one area of education that receives much publicity, and full advantage should be taken of this fact. Techniques for securing the cooperation and support of the media can result in better community understanding of the interscholastic program.

The first meetings with a member of the news media are significant in establishing an atmosphere of understanding which will influence our relationship with a reporter and his or her cooperation. If one is a new coach in the community or there is a new sportswriter or sportscaster, it is typical in either case for both personal and professional questions to be asked of the coach. This is an appropriate time to explain our philosophy of interscholastic athletics and to discuss some of the most important objectives and values. It can be suggested that this is one area in which the public needs more information and has too little opportunity to get it.

We should acknowledge that we understand the competition for space in the newspapers and that sports space is limited. It usually is not the fault of the sportswriter when coverage is not as extensive as we would like it to be, and we should indicate that we understand this problem.

After a sportswriter or sportscaster is sufficiently known, it is appropriate to talk about mutual concerns. You should express your desire that interscholastic athletics be treated as a *school sport.* Help the reporter understand that high school athletes are still emotionally immature and that public criticism or excessive praise may not be in the player's best interest. Reporters should be encouraged to ask questions about interscholastic matters, but they must be answered carefully and accurately.

WORKING WITH THE MEDIA

It is common for reporters to want preseason interviews with the coach, and time should be made for them. If desired, a time should be arranged for taking pictures of the squad and individual players. All interested reporters should be informed and invited to take pictures at that time. This step helps to avoid unnecessary interference with practice sessions. Predictions of the team's success should be avoided or qualified, and information about athletes must be accurate. The preseason interview provides a good opportunity to discuss the schedule, practice plans, importance of training rules and the reasons for them, changes in game rules, desire for public support of the interscholastic program, importance of good sportsmanship, benefits of athletics to players, and significance of interscholastic sports in teaching attitudes and ideals. There is a great need to get such information to the public, and it is easier to get it in preseason articles than in reports of games during the season.

Pre-game information is of interest to the public and is desired by sportswriters and sportscasters. The starting time, admission charge, instructions for fans, and any administrative details they should know should be included. Any special half-time activities may be described. The probable starting lineup will be expected as well as information about individual players: their age, year in school, weight, height, and previous varsity experience. All remarks about the opposing team must be correct and stated in a manner devoid of any criticism. The style of play expected and any outstanding players to watch may be mentioned. It is wise, when possible, to praise the opposing team, players, and coach. This will make your team look better whether it wins or loses. Appreciation should be expressed for the opportunity to compete with the school concerned.

Arrangements should be made to gather statistics for postgame reports. Student assistants are frequently helpful in compiling these records, which can be passed on to reporters. It helps to analyze the play of both teams and to describe any highlights and turning points in the game.

Sportswriters and sportscasters frequently wish to interview players immediately following the game. Statements are sometimes made then to the media which are later regretted. It is wise to prepare players for answering questions directed to them. They should be instructed to avoid making any critical remarks about the opposing team or individual players and the officials. To prevent such inappropriate statements, you should establish a policy that players are to go immediately to the dressing room following the game and before talking to reporters, and that members of the media are not permitted to enter until the coach has had a few minutes to settle his or her team. Athletes are inclined to be stimulated emotionally after games and may be upset after losses. They should be reminded that that particular game is over and helped to regain their composure. Reporters will accept this policy if they understand the reasons for it and there is no unnecessary delay in their admittance.

Common courtesies should be extended to those reporters covering contests. Press passes should be furnished and space at games should be provided. Fairness must prevail in dealing with multiple newspaper and radio reporters. Some schools have found regular press releases a helpful procedure. They are generally made through the office of the athletic director with the help of his or her coaches. Care must be taken not to give anyone a scoop on a story or advance significant information that is not given to others at the same time. In return, we should ask reporters to honor off-the-record statements and not criticize officials or the opposing coach or team. It is proper to ask for cooperation in publicizing the most worthwhile objectives of interscholastic sports.

Radio broadcasting of games is traditional in many communities. An issue sometimes arises as to whether there should be a fee charged for this privilege, which is generally resisted by some radio stations. School officials occasionally feel that broadcasting games, particularly football games during inclement weather, hurts the attendance, but this has never been proved; many think that it helps by stimulating interest. Some schools have found an alternative by requiring the radio station to give statements during intermissions at games publicizing and explaining various phases of the district's educational program. These are prepared by school officials and include objectives of the academic and interscholastic activities, or any information they desire to be presented to the public. Announcing the game before the date it is to be played tends to increase attendance. This type of policy is usually well received by the broadcasting company and is worth a lot to the school. A wide audience listens to game broadcasts, which provides a way to get information about the school program to the public. If the same amount of time on radio were to be purchased, it would cost a considerable amount of money. We should suggest such a policy to our administrators if one is not already in effect. Figure 5-1 is an example of an agreement form used for this purpose.[2]

A different view is generally taken in regard to television. Athletic administrators are inclined to agree that televising local games hurts attendance, and there is only a limited amount of it, except for state high school basketball tournaments. If there is any proposal to televise local games, rates for television should be established which protect the school from any loss of attendance; there should be a written contract which includes details for preparation for televising; and the school should reserve control over the half-time activities that are televised. Sponsors of both television and radio broadcasts should not be permitted to advertise any products contrary to good athletic training standards.

Relationships with the Student Body

It is important to establish good relations with the student body. (Relations with parents were discussed earlier, and relations with athletes will be discussed in a later chapter.) The values of interscholastic athletics to students who are not athletes should be discussed with them, and the recreational and educational benefits explained. The assembly program is used for this purpose in many schools. Demonstrations of plays can be presented by using the gymnasium for the assembly. All students should be made to feel that inter-

---

[2] *Radio Broadcast Agreement Form,* Missouri State High School Activities Association, Columbia, MO.

MSHSAA TOURNAMENT RADIO BROADCAST AGREEMENT

_____, a MSHSAA Tournament Manager, who
is empowered with the authority to act in behalf of the schools of the
MSHSAA and _____, a radio station desiring to
broadcast live or delayed one or more games in the _____
_____, enter into the following agreement as approved
by the MSHSAA Board of Control.

The Radio Station is granted broadcast rights for the games
involving _____ High School, for which
it is agreed:

1. That no charge be made to the radio station for the
   broadcast rights to the above mentioned event(s).
   That the radio station announce at least FOUR times
   during each game statements prepared and provided by
   the MSHSAA Office advertising the purpose of the
   MSHSAA program. The station is also required to give
   advance publicity to the event being carried.

2. That no individual or organization be permitted to
   sponsor a broadcast for the purpose of advertising
   alcholic beverages, tobacco, or any other product
   which is contrary to the principles of good high
   school athletic training. That NO political parties
   or candidates be allowed to sponsor any of the
   broadcast.

3. That the radio station provide a list of sponsors
   before the broadcast, and that such sponsors be
   approved by the tournament manager or committee in
   accord with (2) above.

4. That the MSHSAA Board of Control reserve the right to
   discontinue the broadcasting rights of the station at
   any time in the event previous broadcasting by that
   station is considered to have been in poor taste or
   incompatible with the educational objective of the
   MSHSAA.

Agreed to and accepted: Date_____ 19_____

SIGNED_____, MSHSAA Tournament Manager

SIGNED_____

RADIO STATION_____

ADDRESS_____

CITY_____

ZIP CODE_____

Figure 5-1. Sample Radio Broadcast Agreement Form

scholastic athletics are for their benefit, and their cooperation should be solicited to make it as good a program as possible. Many students who are not athletes like to participate in sports in some way. The pep club is the best example, but many students help their schools as student managers, record keepers, student reporters for the school paper, and ushers at games. All should be helped to understand the need for good sportsmanship and for their assistance in supporting it. Coaches should show an interest in nonathletic activities by attending functions and giving assistance during the off-seasons. The support of the student body is essential in the success of any public relations program.

The players can be of great assistance in fostering good relations with the public and with other schools by the impressions they make. Neatly dressed and well-groomed athletes are respected. Their good manners reflect favorably on the school's athletic program and the teaching of the coach. Their sportsmanship during games influences the conduct of others and helps to create an atmosphere conducive to good public relations. Athletes should be taught the importance of good relationships with others and how to work to achieve them. They can be some of the best press agents for the interscholastic program of our schools.

Summary

The most important factor in building good public relations is a sound interscholastic program based on a solid philosophy of school athletics and most worthwhile educational and recreational objectives. Satisfied students and parents are the best salespersons for interscholastic sports.

We must develop the ability to explain why there is interschool competition and what the school wishes to accomplish through it. Careful attention must be given to developing good relations with parents and community organizations.

Setting a good example at all times is significant in developing proper attitudes and ideals in high school students and helps us to develop better public relations.

Effort must be made to create good relationships with members of the news media and to receive their cooperation. Assistance provided to them will help to get the type of reporting coaches want.

Maintaining good public relations is a continuing process which must have our continual attention.

QUESTIONS AND TOPICS FOR STUDY AND DISCUSSION

1. Enumerate and discuss the importance of the basic elements of a sound interscholastic public relations program.
2. Explain ways you plan to establish good relations with parents. Why would you discuss eligibility regulations with them?
3. If a parent comes to your office to complain that his or her son is not getting to play enough, how will you handle this situation?
4. Explain the kinds of support you would like to have from community organizations.
5. If a local service club or some individual expressed to you the desire to purchase some athletic equipment for your school, explain how you would deal with this offer.
6. Why are some boosters' clubs an asset to some schools and a liability to others? Outline some guidelines you plan to follow in working with the boosters' club for your school.
7. What types of learning are developed in students and others by the example set by the coach?
8. Discuss possible ways of establishing good relations with members of the news media. What types of assistance can you give them?
9. Prepare a one-minute statement about your interscholastic program appropriate for a radio broadcaster to give during an intermission in a game.
10. Do you think a policy which does not allow reporters to enter the dressing room until the coach feels the players are emotionally ready to be interviewed is wise? Why or why not?
11. Outline the program you would prepare if you were put in charge of planning an athletic assembly program.
12. Explain how you would try to get players to help establish good public relations.

BIBLIOGRAPHY

Gallon, Arthur J. *Coaching Ideas and Ideals*, pp. 243–46. Boston: Houghton Mifflin, 1974.

Keller, Irvin A. "The Interscholastic Program: A Sound Plan Spells Good Public Relations." *Interscholastic Athletic Administration*, 2, No. 3 (Summer 1976), 17–18.

National Federation of State High School Associations. "Competing for Public Relations." *Interscholastic Athletic Administration*, 2, No. 3 (Summer 1976), 22–25.

Pernice, Sue. "Coaches—Let Your Players Think." *Journal of Physical Education and Recreation*, September 1976, p. 23.

Resick, Matthew C., and Carl E. Erickson. *Intercollegiate and Interscholastic Athletics for Men and Women*, pp. 201-12. Reading, Mass.: Addison-Wesley, 1975.

Seaton, Don Cash, Irene A. Clayton, Howard C. Leibee, and Lloyd L. Messersmith. *Physical Education Handbook*, pp. 6-7. Englewood Cliffs, N. J.: Prentice-Hall, 1974.

Tamerilli, Al, Jr. "The Coach as a Public Relations Man." *The Coaching Clinic*, 9 (December 1971), 21-22.

CHAPTER 6

Educationally Significant Coaching

Athletic coaches praise interscholastic athletics for their educational values, which have been recognized by school administrators and others. Interscholastic competition is considered today an integral part of the total secondary school program, although it is not in the same category as the academic curriculum. No school is required by statute to offer interscholastic athletics; they are not a requirement for students, offer no academic credit, and are traditionally held after scheduled class hours.

The most significant question is not whether they have educational values, but whether these values are as worthwhile as they ought to be. There has been considerable controversy for many years over the types of interscholastic competition found in junior high schools.[1] The financial crisis has caused boards of education to question whether competitive sports are worth what they cost and whether they are developing character values more easily than those taught through physical education.[2]

However, despite scattered criticism, there does not appear to be any general inclination to discontinue interscholastic athletics. The best way to offset these criticisms is to make these sports more educationally significant—which is the purpose of this chapter.

[1]Charles E. Forsythe and Irvin A. Keller, *Administration of High School Athletics*, 6th ed. (Englewood Cliffs, N.J.: Prentice-Hall, 1977), pp. 341-48.

[2]"All About the Real Cost of School Sports and How Not to Get Your Signals Crossed," *The American School Board Journal*, 162, No. 6 (June 1975), 19-33.

Prerequisites

If athletic experiences are to produce important educational results, there are certain basic prerequisites for the coaches who direct them. Maximum educational values are the result of good coaching, and good coaching occurs only when the coach possesses certain fundamental views, knowledge, and abilities.

BASIC PHILOSOPHY

In addition to developing a personal philosophy of school athletics which is compatible with the recognized interscholastic athletic philosophy (discussed in Chapter 3), we must have a basic understanding of and be committed to the philosophy that gives direction to secondary education. The primary purpose of interscholastic athletics is to *make better men and women out of boys and girls.*

WORTHWHILE OBJECTIVES

Coaches have numerous objectives that can be classified in several ways; daily, weekly, seasonal, and long range. The coach's personal objectives, those of athletes, and the school's interscholastic goals were discussed in Chapter 3. Each of us must formulate what we consider to be the most worthwhile goals for us, our players, and our school through the sport we are coaching. It is advisable to have fewer objectives—which are definite and which we strive to accomplish—than so many that few are really achieved.

We should never apologize for the fact that winning is one of our specific and immediate objectives. Teaching students to excel is a worthy goal when kept in proper perspective among other objectives. Winning is not being overemphasized as long as we do not neglect to stimulate and direct athletes to achieve those goals which will have more permanent and ultimate values for them.

BASIC PRINCIPLES OF TEACHING

All of us will agree that coaching is teaching. It involves the teaching of sports and the teaching of youth through sports. For maximum learning to result, certain fundamental principles of teaching and learning must be applied. Some of the most significant include the following:

1. *The apperceptive background of the learner (player) must be determined.* The apperceptive background is comprised of the student's ability and previous learning. In athletics it is dependent upon his or her previous playing experience and mental and physical innate abilities. Most often it is ascertained through observation. Some formal tests of skill have been used on a very limited basis, but generally it is determined from observing the performance of individuals in tryouts and practices. The apperceptive background of the athletes determines their readiness for learning certain skills, knowledge, and emotional patterns. For example, contrast coaching a junior high school sport with coaching a senior high school sport. We would be more concerned with teaching fundamental skills to junior high athletes, providing more simple drills in developing these skills, and using less complicated plays in teamwork. Coaches sometimes make the mistake, even in senior high school, of trying to teach patterns of plays they used as collegiate players, which are often beyond the apperceptive background of their players. It is best to develop *plays to fit the athletes than to try to fit the athletes to the plays.*

Skillful coaches note what a player can now do and envision what he or she is potentially capable of doing in the future with proper coaching. Some senior high school coaches are inclined to select players for their varsity squads from the students' performances in junior high school. Others, aware that boys and girls at the junior high school level vary greatly in physical maturity, have the ability to envision what some of the more physically immature will be able to do in senior high school. There has been no scientific study to show that there is any high correlation between the performances of athletes at the seventh-grade level and below with performances at the twelfth-grade level. A number of potentially good athletes conceivably are eliminated from senior high school interscholastic athletic competition by coaches who fail to realize both their achievements in junior high athletics and their abilities to continue to develop as they gain maturity. Fortunately, basketball coaches for one, are becoming more aware of this problem; they realize that the taller players in junior high school, who are often still uncoordinated, can develop into fine basketball players by the time they are seniors in high school. There was a period of time when they were considered too awkward to ever make the team.

2. *The learning activities must be appropriate.* Learning activities are appropriate when they are in fullest agreement with the types of learning involved in attaining the desired objectives. Skill drills must contribute to the automatic performance of the skill in games. Repetition is required to cause them to become automatic. A clear demonstration of how the skill is performed is necessary for athletes to gain knowledge through observation.

It is essential for coaches to understand the three types of basic learning and to provide different types of learning activities and techniques of teaching to produce the physical skills, knowledge, and emotional patterns inherent in the objectives. As already stated, skills require understanding and repetition. Knowledge involves the organization of bits of information which enables the player to develop the ability to think. Emotional learning is taught by creating a feeling which influences conduct. For example, an idea becomes an ideal when it is accompanied by a strong feeling which sways behavior. The examples set by the coach are important in developing attitudes and ideals. Personal attributes—such as punctuality, fairness, accuracy, neatness, tolerance, broad-mindedness, respect, and good sportsmanship—can also be developed by citing examples of their importance and by stimulating athletes to practice them.

3. *Psychologically sound motivating techniques must be used.* The desire to win and to excel in athletics provides considerable motivation, but it is not always sufficiently effective, particularly when the team is losing. Further stimulation is necessary if players are to continue to improve their skills through practice drills, which may become monotonous, and to develop desirable personal attributes. The soundest motivational technique is to create a feeling of need for what is to be learned. Illustrations and examples showing the benefits of this learning are effective.

4. *Provisions must be made for individual differences.* The football coach employs this principle exceedingly well. The heavier players are taught how to play in the interior line; the faster, lighter players are coached to play in the backfield; and the tall, more ambulatory athletes are groomed for end positions. There are other individual differences which must be taken into consideration. How to handle players of different personalities and temperaments is important. Some players will need continual encouragement and praise, whereas others would become too self-satisfied from such treatment. Diverse attitudes will be noted among squad members, and different ways of changing attitudes and building better ones will be necessary. Also, drills and practices must be planned to meet the needs of athletes at divergent levels of accomplishment.

5. *Diagnostic and remedial teaching is essential.* The distinguishing factor between the outstanding teacher or coach and the average one is often the ability of diagnostic and remedial teaching. Developing the capability to analyze the little weaknesses or mistakes and supplying remedial measures to correct them adds greatly to the success of the coach.

6. *Learning must be unitary, not fragmentary.* Learning is not complete until it can be applied by the learner. Information does not be-

come knowledge until it can be organized and put to use. Fundamental skills become valuable to the athlete when he or she understands how and when to use them in athletic games. It is important that the teaching of sports skills be done under conditions as similar to game situations as practical. This does not mean that isolated drills should never be used. They are often needed for the necessary repetition required to develop the skill, but players should understand how they are to be used in games before engaging in the drills. Otherwise, the learning may be fragmentary and not of maximum value.

7. *The physical and social environment for learning must be ideal.* Students learn from their environment, and the social and physical environment for learning must be kept as ideal as possible. Neat, sanitary gymnasiums, playing fields, and dressing rooms are important factors in developing attitudes toward and habits of health and sanitation.

Misbehavior on the athletic field or in the gymnasium distracts from learning just as it does in the classroom. Good discipline enhances learning in all situations. Creating an attitude of respect for others and requiring it in daily practice and in athletic contests helps to provide an environment conducive to learning.

All good teachers apply these basic principles. The remaining portion of this chapter and the following chapter will be devoted to what we should teach and how we should teach it.

Content

The major attention of coaches is given to teaching fundamental sports skills and game patterns to win contests. Winning games is an immediate objective, and a coach who cannot stimulate players to win and to excel in sports will not succeed. However, if interscholastic competition is to have significant educational values, it is important that the following matters be taught.

HISTORY

A rudimentary understanding of the history of interscholastic athletics will add to the appreciation of school sports and the opportunity to participate in them. (This history was discussed in Chapter 3.) Asking students what they think interscholastic sports would be like, or whether we would have them, if outsiders and some of the coaches were permitted to play can create desirable attitudes toward the interscholastic program of today. A brief review of the evolution of school control will help students understand that the schools have collectively adopted minimum standards to provide equity and fairness among players; thus they will appreciate the need for regulations.

PHILOSOPHY

In explaining to athletes why the school offers interscholastic competition we can discuss the school's interscholastic philosophy.

VALUES AND OBJECTIVES

Among the objectives discussed in Chapter 3 were those of the school and those of the athletes. Players should understand both, especially the ultimate values. Each athlete should be urged to consider adopting personal goals which will have lasting values. It is advisable to suggest that students formulate a few significant goals which they think they can attain and to give them their continuous attention rather than to recite a long list of objectives which they will make little effort to achieve.

A better public understanding of the philosophy, objectives, and values of interscholastic athletics will result if all athletes are taught them while engaging in the interscholastic program. This is significant when criticisms arise and support is needed. Adults who have been so taught in high school are more inclined to be supportive of the total school program.

EMOTIONAL CONTROLS

The basic controls of conduct are knowledge, physical and mental skills, and emotional patterns. Learning is not complete without the last, which determine how and for what purpose knowledge and skills are used. Outstanding teachers give careful consideration to the development of proper attitudes and ideals; respect for others, honesty, integrity, fairness, and so on.

STANDARDS OF ELIGIBILITY

Coaches must teach athletes that eligibility is recognized by the courts as a privilege rather than an inherent right guaranteed by the United States Constitution. They must also teach what standards students must meet to enjoy this privilege. Failure to do so sometimes results in charges of negligence against the coach and his or her school. Training rules, which will be considered later, are another important way to develop emotional controls and self-discipline.

Many high school athletes have competed in a sport without acquiring any knowledge of its history. Athletes will have a greater appreciation of the sport—although they may not play it better—if they know who invented it, when it was started, and the extent to which it is played.

Good coaches help athletes to understand themselves, to analyze their strengths and weaknesses, including their attitudes and ideals, as a basis for self-improvement. They should also be motivated to understand others better. Knowing opponents sufficiently well to know their habits and how they will react enables many defensive players to become outstanding performers. A knowledge of possible psychological influences and how to counteract them helps avoid a lack of emotional control. Competent coaches are much aware of the importance of applying psychology in coaching and in competition.

All high school athletes should be given information about their state high school association. It is a voluntary organization founded by the high schools of the state through which they work cooperatively in adopting standards and regulations to provide a wholesome and worthwhile program of interscholastic competition for the primary benefit of boys and girls. The standards and regulations of the association have been adopted as those of their school and by all other member schools of the association to ensure fairness and equity in competition among high schools and high school students.

All state high school associations belong to the National Federation of State High School Associations, which provides such services as publishing games rules specifically written for high school players, producing films on interpretations of rules, keeping records of high school performances, and publishing player handbooks in some sports. It works for more uniformity in regulations from state to state by recommending uniform standards of eligibility and other athletic requirements.

Good sportsmanship and conduct do not result automatically from athletic experiences. Players must be taught the importance of good sportsmanship, the standards of conduct contained in the rules, and the penalties and consequences resulting from violations.

Procedures and Techniques

After determining what skills, knowledge, and emotional learning we plan to teach, our attention must then turn to how we are going to teach them. There are many methods and techniques of teaching that we might use, but we must select those which are most appropriate for the type of learning involved and which we understand sufficiently to employ. Both formalized and informal, or incidental, methods should be used. Procedures, methods, and techniques will be discussed by simulating the beginning of a sports season in which we are meeting the squad for the first time. It is important that both daily and long-range planning be done in advance as the first meeting with the squad is a significant one. Athletes will realize whether or not there has been adequate preparation, which can be an important factor affecting the relations between the coach and the team.

INITIAL SQUAD MEETING

Some state high school associations will allow a squad meeting for the purpose of orientation before the first allowable date of practice; others will not. We must adhere to the regulations of our state association.

Most state associations will permit athletes to have their physical examinations before the first practice date. Their physical fitness for practice and competition must be verified by a doctor before they are permitted to participate.

The procedure for the first squad meeting may vary with the tenure of the coach and his or her familiarity with the players. This is the time to start learning to know the players better. Some coaches ask questions of the athletes, whereas others use personal information cards; these may be completed at the meeting but are most often only distributed and returned later. The usual information is requested: birthdate, names of parents, home address, telephone number, and so on. Additional information may include the number of years of participation in the sport, seasons of competition on the varsity team, and positions played. If cards are used, I strongly recommend that this question or a similar one be included on the back: "Why do you want to compete in interscholastic athletics?" The answer will provide an insight into the player's attitude and reasons for participating in athletics and his or her understanding of the philosophy and objectives of interscholastic sports. One important advantage of the card system is that it provides a ready reference file when the coach needs to contact parents or an athlete. Also, this background information will be important if it becomes necessary to counsel the player. The following are samples of the front and back of a personal information card:

PLAYER PERSONAL INFORMATION CARD

Name _____ Birthdate _____

Address _____ Telephone _____

Father's name _____ Occupation _____

Mother's name _____ Occupation _____

Number of years you have been a member of a school squad _____

Did you compete in Little League, Might Mite, Bitty Basketball, etc. (List)
_____

Number of years you competed on a junior high school team in this sport
_____ ; junior varsity team _____ ; varsity team _____

List other sports in which you have participated _____
_____

Do you have a part-time job during the school year? _____

If yes, describe _____

Do you have a summer job? _____ . Describe _____
_____

Have you attended a specialized sports camp? _____. If yes, in what
sports? _____

What is your weight? _____ ; your height? _____

(over)

PLAYER PERSONAL INFORMATION CARD (CONT'D)

Why do you want to compete in interscholastic sports? (Give your reasons)

Date _____ Signed _____

One of the most appropriate times to begin to teach athletes the philosophy and objectives of interscholastic athletics is during the first meeting with the squad. A lecture can be introduced by asking the athletes why the school affords them the opportunity to compete in interschool competition. After some responses, the school's philosophy and objectives can be explained. All the information we will want to present cannot be given in one period, so we must plan what we want to accomplish in the first meeting and what we want to present in future meetings and practices.

The first meeting with the squad is an appropriate time also to discuss training rules and school policies. Reasons for them and their values should be emphasized, including both personal and team benefits. The type of conduct expected in the dressing room and on the practice field or gym should be explained. The responsibilities and authority of student managers and assistants can be outlined and the cooperation of players requested. The importance of maintaining a good academic standing should be made clear. Players should understand from the start that you want them to enjoy being members of the squad, whether as first-team players or substitutes, but that the greatest satisfaction will arise from being athletes who are dedicated to their personal improvement and to the team. They should realize from the beginning that success in athletics requires some sacrifice of other interests during the sports season and involves hard work. The initial meeting can contribute toward a *good tone* for interscholastic sports and for a proper relationship between coach and players.

PRACTICE SESSIONS

A coach will have to plan practice sessions thoroughly to make the best use of the time. Few matters can be properly taught in one session; moreover, it is better to practice a skill ten minutes for several days than sixty minutes on one day.

An outstanding basketball coach used to have a time schedule on a three-by-five-inch card for every practice session. On it was listed what he planned for his players to do and how many minutes were to be used for each activity. His practice periods averaged about one hour and forty-five minutes and never more than two hours. He believed that the attention span of high school players was such that little or no improvement resulted after that amount of practice, and that players were inclined to *just go through motions* after a certain length of time—which could result in practicing careless habits. No time was wasted in his practices, and his teams were noted for their hustle.

The length of practice sessions will vary from coach to coach, and the amount of time that can advantageously be used will differ with the players. It is wise to plan our sessions so that they will be most appropriate for the players involved.

TEACHING THE HISTORY

Athletes will appreciate the privilege of participating in interscholastic athletics more if they understand some of its history. Presenting it in story form is a good method. Use any incidents you have heard that describe the conditions prevalent when athletic competiton was in the hands of the athletes themselves. There are some to be found in every state.

In Missouri, for example, a high school senior coached the football team because no other coach was available; previously the players had recruited an unemployed miner and a young railroad worker to load the team in a game with a neighboring school, but they still lost.[3] A football team in Massachusetts on which its coach also played was badly beaten in a game; they found that a young local dentist, who a few years previously had been a star tackle on a university team, was the player who hurt the team members and their coach in this particular game. This incident led to the formation of a school league, which adopted a rule providing that all players must be bona fide students of their high schools.[4]

Even after schools assumed some control over athletic competition, coaches sometimes played on their teams. A Missouri basketball coach played on his team for two years. One game he remembers quite well. Not only did he coach the team and play the entire game, but he officiated the last half as well. He decided later that it was his officiating that caused the great big fight that followed the game.

TEACHING THE VALUES AND OBJECTIVES

Athletes should be informed that the ultimate goal of the school is to help them to become better persons. The values for players are found within the objectives for athletes discussed in Chapter 3. Some coaches have found it a good procedure to discuss these incidentally throughout the season rather than to devote one session to them. Analogies of their benefits in everyday life should be made at every opportunity.

TEACHING ATTITUDES AND IDEALS

An attitude is a predisposition to act or react in a certain manner; it is influenced by a state of mind and enforced by a feeling. An ideal is an idea supported by a strong feeling, which becomes a pattern or model for perfection. Both, or the lack of them, are strong forces in determining how the knowledge and skills an individual possesses are used. They are sometimes referred to as attributes of conduct. In interscholastic athletics attitudes toward rules and regulations, authority, and discipline are not difficult to observe. The ideals of fairness, courtesy, and sportsmanship are reflected in the actions of individuals and groups.

There is no generally accepted procedure for teaching these emo-

[3] Irvin A. Keller, *A History—How the Missouri State High School Activities Association Came to Be* (Columbia: Missouri State High School Activities Association, 1979), pp. 13-14.

[4] Frederick H. Pierce, *The Genesis of the State High School Association* (Kansas City, Mo.: National Federation of State High School Associations Press, 1956).

tional patterns, but there are some steps that might be followed:

1. *Diagnose the attitudes and ideals of the players.* This is very important if undesirable ones are to be replaced by desirable ones. If proper attitudes and ideals exist, less time need be given, except to maintain them and to develop additional ones.

2. *Stimulate players to feel that the general pattern of conduct involved is worthwhile.* Telling a true story such as the following to illustrate a value is effective.

One of the best freshman prospects a particular coach ever had was a boy who lived near a college gymnasium and had spent many hours of his leisure time playing in choose-up basketball games with college boys. He was physically mature for his age, being about six feet tall and weighing some 195 pounds. He was well built, strong, and well coordinated. He had learned all the tricks of shoving, tripping, and taking advantage of others from his past experiences. During his first high school junior varsity game, in which he was one of the starting players, his coach saw him intentionally trip an opposing player; this act was undetected by the officials, but the coach promptly removed him from the game for the rest of the evening, although he was beyond doubt the best player on the team. Nothing was said to him that evening about his actions.

The next morning he was called into the coach's office and asked whether he understood why he played less than a quarter of the game the night before. He had figured it out and expressed his regret for his action. In a calm but firm manner the coach informed him that no player, even the best on the team, would be allowed to play if he could not be fair. Before the end of the season, the boy was playing on the varsity team and competed for four years under the same coach. Not once did he repeat any unsportsmanlike conduct; but the coach always wondered whether he had really changed his attitude inside, or whether his good conduct resulted from his belief that the coach would remove him from the game.

The final test came during a state tournament game in his senior year. The apparent strategy of the opposing coach was to have his players try to rough him up in an attempt to get him to lose his temper. Two players guarding him fouled out of the game. Each time he went to the free-throw line, he made some comment to the opposing player who had fouled him. His coach became concerned that he might draw a technical foul, but the officials only smiled at him. After the game, they complimented him to his coach for the way he had conducted himself in the game. When the coach asked them what he was saying at the free-throw line, he was told that the boy had stated each time to the player who had committed the foul against him, "Son, if you don't change your humor, you won't be with us long!" After that incident, his coach was convinced that the boy's attitude had really changed.

This true story has much significance for teaching attitudes and ideals. First, it is clear, and had to be apparent to the player, that the coach had a high ideal of fairness; second, he was successful in getting the player to feel a need for the ideal; and third, it was practiced by the athlete for four years in competition—which leads us to consider further teaching steps.

3. *A plan of action must be developed.* The coach in this story developed a plan of action, which was not to let any athlete play who did not play fair. Although it may have been somewhat blunt, it was effective. The point is that we must decide on a course of action which we consider appropriate to the situation and which we have reason to believe will produce results. Plans may differ with different individuals and with various circumstances.

4. *The attitude or ideal must be practiced in real situations as far as possible.* Some appropriate action must be taken when ideals are not practiced so that athletes will understand their importance and that consequences will follow.

5. *Attitudes and ideals should be generalized.* Occasions when good attitudes and high ideals have been exhibited should be recognized and their values emphasized. Analogies of how they will be beneficial in everyday life should be made. Newspaper clippings commenting on good sportsmanship or conduct should be posted on bulletin boards where the entire student body will see them. It became a feeling of school pride when a coach posted a letter he had received from a motel manager complimenting both his team and other students for the fine behavior they showed while staying at his motel following an athletic game. They were described as the most courteous high school group he had had the opportunity to serve. The principal complimented the coach, team, and student body in an assembly for the fine impression they had made for their school.

In a period when misconduct receives more attention from the news media than do good deeds, *goodness needs a better press agent.*

Slogans and mottos can be effective aids in developing desirable attitudes. Mottos can be printed on cards and posted on a bulletin board in the gymnasium or dressing room. They can be weekly, daily, or periodically displayed. The following samples (Figure 6-1) were suggested by a former coach, later a school administrator.[5]

If You Did Your Best— YOU WON	When You Score— DON'T PURR The Opponents Are On Offense
It Takes A Cool Head To Win A HOT GAME	Enter the Game A GENTLEMAN Leave the Same Way
CROWD BEHAVIOR Reflects TEAM BEHAVIOR	THE BEST PLAYER Helps Others Be BEST PLAYERS
Are You Trying To OVERCOME Your Weaknesses	TEAMWORK Makes GREAT PLAYERS GREATER
OBEY TRAINING RULES For Condition Game Rules FOR HONOR AND RESPECT	The Real Measure of an Athlete is not What he can do in Comparison to others but what he can do IN COMPARISON TO HIS OWN BEST SELF

Figure 6-1. Sample Motto Cards.

[5] Brice Durbin, *Portrait Publications,* Columbus, Kansas.

Motto cards are easy to make, can be interchanged frequently, and can be kept continually before the players.

It is in this area of learning that the least progress in teaching has been made. Ways have not been found to include adequately emotional patterns in the curriculum, and student activities may be the means of teaching moral and ethical values.

Standards of Eligibility

An athlete's attitude toward eligibility regulations derives from the way they are taught and learned. If they are appreciated, they have been taught correctly; if they are viewed as restrictive rules, they have not been taught correctly.

The coach must have a thorough knowledge of the state high school association's minimum eligibility standards and any additional eligibility requirements established by the school. This knowledge must include the history of the eligibility regulations and the reasons they evolved. Nearly all of them will be common standards adopted cooperatively by the high schools through their state association. In general, they will be uniform from state to state, but there will be some differences. The following, which are recommended to state high school associations by the National Federation of State High School Associations, will be found in some form in each state association's constitution and by-laws:

RECOMMENDED ATHLETIC ELIGIBILITY STANDARDS

It is recommended (not required) that state associations adopt eligibility standards at least as restrictive as those contained in this section. Due to increased interstate competition and more numerous non-school sponsored athletic programs for high school age students, the need for more uniformity in eligibility standards between states is increasingly apparent. Minimum eligibility requirements should be re-evaluated periodically to insure they serve their purpose of protecting both the high school participants and the interscholastic program.

1. 19-Year Rule: Students become ineligible when reaching their nineteenth birthday.
2. 8-Semester Rule: In a four-year high school, students may participate for eight consecutive semesters, or in a three-year senior high, for six consecutive semesters. Attendance of 15 days of any semester shall count as a semester of participation.
3. Semester Scholarship Rule: Students are required to do passing work in at least fifteen periods (three full credit subjects) per week. Failure to earn passing semester marks in three full credit subjects shall render a student

ineligible for the following full semester. The record at the end of the semester shall be final and scholastic deficiencies may not be removed for the purpose of meeting minimum eligibility requirements.

4. Amateur Rule: Students become ineligible for participation in all sports if they violate the following Amateur Rule in any sport which their state association sponsors by:

(a) Participating under an assumed name.

(b) Competing on a team on which one of the players is paid.

(c) Entering into a playing contract with a professional club or agent.

(d) Using athletic skill for financial gain.

(e) Accepting a fee for officiating or for working as an instructor in other than a recognized recreation program. (Working as a registered official is a violation.)

5. Awards Rule

(a) Accepting cash or any merchandise award. All awards shall be symbolic in nature with no intrinsic value.

(b) Accepting a symbolic award, from any source, in excess of the amount established by the state association.

(c) Accepting a trip to a University contest which is not within the standards contained in the pamphlet, "A Guide for the College-Bound Student Athlete."

(d) Accepting expenses for attending a summer athletic camp from any person (other than parents or legal guardian) or organization.

A state association may adopt provisions for reinstating a student who has violated the Amateur and Award Rules provided there is at least one year of ineligibility from the date of the violation.

6. Non-School Participation Rules: Participation on a non-school team in a sport during the same season athletes are representing their schools in that sport shall cause them to become ineligible. Each state association shall establish seasons of competition during the school year for out-of-season participation.

7. Transfer Rule: An athlete who transfers enrollment corresponding with a change of residence of parents or legal guardian shall be considered eligible as soon as properly certified. Students transferring schools without a corresponding change of residence of the parents or legal guardian from a district where they had been in attendance to the new district, or if there has been no change of residence, shall attend one calendar year from the date of enrollment at the school to which they transferred in order to establish eligibility.

8. Recruiting Rule: Transfer from one school to another for athletic purposes because of undue influence by anyone connected with the school shall cause a student to forfeit remaining high school eligibility.

9. Enrollment Rule: In order to establish eligibility, a student must enroll not later than the beginning of the eleventh school day of any semester.

10. Grade Rule: To be eligible, a student must be in 9th grade or above and not graduated from high school.

11. Physician's Certificate Rule: A student must present, during the year and prior to competition, a physician's certificate of physical fitness for athletic participation.[6]

Another eligibility requirement adopted by most state associations is that of good citizenship. A student whose character or conduct brings discredit to her or himself or to the school is not considered eligible in those states. Many think this standard is the most important. It is reasonable to expect an athlete—who will represent not only him or herself in competition but also the student body, school, faculty, and community—to be of good character.

The first step in teaching the standards of eligibility is to create an understanding of their importance in the interscholastic program. This can be done by describing conditions that existed before any eligibility requirements were established. Ask players to imagine what school athletics would be like today if outsiders, including adults, played on the teams; if there were only volunteer coaches; if there were no limits on the number of seasons one could compete; if recruiting the best players from other schools were allowed; and if players were permitted to transfer schools at will. They should understand that without eligibility standards, fairness and equity in competition among students and schools would not be possible. An illustration is the following story of what has been called the "bona fide student rule," which spawned other rules found necessary to implement it.

In the beginning, when athletics were in the hands of the students, there were no eligibility requirements. Outsiders beyond high school age and coaches played on some of the teams. After an ex-university player was found on a Massachusetts high school football team, the schools formed a league and adopted the rule that only bona fide students were to be permitted to play on school teams.[7] Other leagues and state high school associations soon adopted a similar rule, but none sufficiently defined a *bona fide student*. It was clear only that the individual had to be enrolled in the school. Sometime later, the eligibility of two football players in Illinois was questioned. It was found that they were enrolled in the high school, but for only one subject, which was spelling. No evidence was found that they were required to pass it.[8] Obviously schools were interpreting the rule differently and an additional rule was necessary. The requirement was adopted that a student had to be enrolled in three subjects to be eligible, but this rule

[6] National Federation of State High School Associations, *1977-78 Official Handbook*, Kansas City, Mo., pp. 37-38.

[7] Pierce, *Genesis of State High School Association*.

[8] Charles W. Whitten, *Interscholastics: A Discussion of Interscholastic Contests* (Bloomington: Illinois High School Association, 1950), p. 3.

did not completely solve the problem either. Some individuals whose primary interest was competing in sports would enroll in three subjects just when practice for a particular sport started and would drop out of school after the last game of the season was played, only to re-enroll again at the beginning of the next season. Some played more than four seasons on high school teams.

These kinds of abuses necessitated the adoption of other rules. One was the scholarship rule contained in the national federation recommendations. Another was the eleven-day, or enrollment, rule, also found in the recommendations. All were adopted to implement the bona fide student rule.

This type of brief history is apt to create a favorable attitude in players toward the standards of eligibility. We should learn all we can about the history and reasons for eligibility standards to create appreciation for uniform regulations.

The second step is to help players develop a full understanding of each eligibility requirement through illustrations and examples of how it applies. All athletes and their parents should be given a copy of the standards of eligibility, and the players should sign a form verifying that they understand them. This step helps to relieve the coach of any responsibility when a violation occurs and ignorance of the law is claimed. Some coaches and principals will not allow an athlete to compete until such a form is signed (see Figure 6–2).[9]

Good Sportsmanship

Sportsmanship is that blend of attitudes and ideals which influences the athlete to be courteous, fair, and respectful and to accept victory or defeat graciously. It is essential in providing the proper environment for interscholastic contests.

The coach is the most strategic person at athletic games to influence the sportsmanship of players and spectators. The attitudes and conduct he or she exhibits stimulate similar reactions of others. For example, many spectators will look to the coach when the officials call a foul against their team to note whether he or she shows an attitude of acceptance or objection and will react accordingly. One of the most effective ways of teaching good sportsmanship is by setting a proper example.

Athletes must be taught that it is a privilege to represent their school, the student body, and the community, and that the sportsmanship they exhibit will create an impression affecting those they represent. They must also realize that their sportsmanship will affect that of others. The

[9]Missouri State High School Activities Association.

MSHSAA PARTICIPATION CERTIFICATE–Physician/Parent/Student

THIS CARD IS TO BE COMPLETED PRIOR TO THE FIRST PRACTICE SESSION. IT CONTAINS VITAL INFORMATION IN CASE OF INJURY. THIS CARD SHOULD ACCOMPANY THIS ATHLETE TO ALL PRACTICES AND CONTESTS!!! CENTRAL FILE IN OFF SEASON.

| Section 1 | ATHLETES APPLICATION AND PERSONAL INFORMATION. |

Name _____ Male _____ Female _____

Age _____ Date of birth ___/___/___ Address _____ Town, City _____ Zip _____

Emergency Phone Numbers (in order) [   ]

This application to represent my school in interscholastic athletics is entirely voluntary on my part and is made with the understanding that I have studied and understand the eligibility standards that I must meet to represent my school and that I have not violated any of them. I also understand that if I do not meet the citizenship standards set by the school or if I am ejected from an interscholastic contest because of an unsportsmanlike act, it could result in me not being allowed to participate in the next contest or suspension from the team either temporarily or permanently.

Date _____ Signed by Student _____

| Section 2 | PARENT PERMISSION AND AUTHORIZATION FOR TREATMENT |

I hereby give my consent for the above student to represent his/her school in interscholastic athletics. I also give my consent for him/her to accompany the team on trips and will not hold the school responsible in case of accident or injury whether it be enroute to or from another school or during practice or an interscholastic contest. If I cannot be reached and in the event of an emergency, I also give consent for the school to obtain through a physician or hospital of its choice, such medical care as is reasonably necessary for the welfare of the student, if he/she is injured in the course of school athletic activities. I understand that the school may not provide transportation to all events, and permit/do not permit my child to drive his/her vehicle in such a case.

The MSHSAA By–Laws provide that a student shall not be permitted to practice or compete for a school until it has verification that he/she has basic athletic insurance coverage. My son/daughter is covered by basic accident insurance for the current school year.

Date_____ 19_____ Signature of Parents or Guardians _____

(OVER)

Figure 6–2. Application to Participate Form

standards of conduct contained in the game's rules and the reasons for them should be made clear.

After players understand the standards, they must be required to practice them. The players should be commended when they demonstrate superior attitudes and behavior. The alert coach will take action to avoid instances of poor sportsmanship. If players show signs of losing their temper or composure, they should be removed from the game for a few moments and informed that they may return to play when they can assure the coach that they can exercise sufficient self-control to make certain they will not cause any embarrassment to the team and school or to themselves. This is a very effective technique of teaching good sportsmanship.

The student body should be informed through assemblies and other means of the need for good sportsmanship at athletic games; students should know that it is one of the best ways of supporting the team. Cheerleaders should show leadership in influencing the pep club and other students to show courtesy and respect toward the opposing team and spectators. When the cheerleaders and the coach show their displeasure toward booing and other types of undesirable conduct, the audience will realize that high ideals of sportsmanship are at work.

Officials are too often the objects of abuse at athletic contests. Most of this can be avoided through proper teaching. Athletes and the student body should be made to understand that the officials are among the players' best friends. They are the persons who see to it that the game is played fairly. Students must realize that officials are human and may make an occasional mistake, but that it is the mistakes of the players, and the coach, that most often hurt the team. Teaching respect for officials helps teach respect for that authority in our society that is necessary to avoid chaos and anarchy.

There is a unique method to build greater respect and appreciation for officials, which one coach found very effective. The varsity players were required to tally all the calls made by the officials in a few junior varsity basketball games. They were given three-by-five-inch cards which contained three headings: (1) I agree, (2) I disagree, and (3) I don't know. All calls were tallied under these three headings. The junior varsity players did the same thing at varsity games. The players were impressed by how few times they actually disagreed with the officials, and by officiating vicariously from the sidelines, they developed a better attitude toward officials and a greater appreciation of their efforts.

Training Standards

Training rules are traditional in all levels of athletics. Players are told they must train if they wish to succeed. The emphasis is on physical conditioning, but there are other values we should implement.

The first step in formulating training rules should always be the establishment of sound reasons for them. The athletes might be asked to recommend a set of training rules and to give reasons why they think they are important. Asking that they be presented in written form will ensure that some thought has been given to them.

Athletes must understand that the coach has to have final authority in adopting and enforcing training rules. He or she is the one held responsible for the particular sports program and must attend to any violation of the rules. Individual athletes must realize that failure to abide by the rules will affect not only that person but also the team, the school, and definitely the coach. If the rules are formally approved by the school administration and board of education, it is easier for the coach to handle any challenge that might arise.

A clear understanding of the training rules and the reasons for them should be given to both the athletes and their parents. Among the more important reasons will be the following:

1. *Training rules develop self-discipline.* Disciplining oneself to put first things first is an important lesson for everyday living. Its significance can be easily illustrated by true stories. For example, when I was a boy and had graduated from reading the funny page to also reading the sports page in the local newspaper, I learned the names of two athletes whom I was to know much better some years later. Both were fine young athletes. One participated on the local college football team and the other was a baseball player on an independent baseball team. The sports page had stories almost every week lauding their athletic exploits. They had only two things in common: both were from families of meager means, and both were considered star athletes. One was working his way through college, whereas the other became a factory worker in his younger years. The former became a teacher and coach and later an outstanding school administrator. The latter eventually lost his job, worked at odd jobs for awhile, and finally became the town bum. Athletic experiences had much value for one, but little for the other. Why?

From information gained later, it became apparent that their attitudes were quite different. The football player learned the necessity of training, both for athletic competition and for life; whereas the other, although many people thought he had the talent to become a professional baseball player, could not resist the temptation to carouse, and he abused his body and mind rather than condition them. He developed no purpose in life and died in middle age.

Stories of this type will help athletes understand the significance of self-discipline, which is a primary goal of education.

2. *Rules improve physical fitness and health.* Regular physical exercise is widely recognized as essential to physical and mental well-being. Watching one's diet, which is recommended as a part of good athletic training, is important to health. Many individuals who learn to eat properly and keep physically fit through athletic experiences continue to do so in later life and are happier, healthier persons.

3. *Rules form good health habits.* There are health factors inherent in athletic training because no smoking or drinking of alcoholic beverages is allowed. Whether there is abstention during the athletic season because of a rule or because they become health habits may be the result of the way such regulations are taught. Preaching about the harmful effects of smoking and drinking on athletic performances is not very effective. Some athletes will ask, "What does it hurt?" However, the important question to have them consider is, "What will smoking and/or drinking contribute to my performance and personal well-being?" Instilling in athletes a desire to evaluate personal habits through this test will lead to their self-improvement. They should understand that strengths contribute to success, and that weaknesses do not, which is just as applicable in everyday life as it is in athletics. Athletes should know that the coach can depend on those who discipline themselves to put first things first, and that these are the ones who are most likely to reach their potential.

Requiring players to cooperate in keeping a neat and clean dressing room helps build good health habits pertaining to cleanliness and sanitation, as does insisting that practice clothing and uniforms be regularly laundered and hung or placed properly. Athletes should not be permitted to leave wearing apparel lying on the floor of the dressing room, even during practice sessions. Reasons for this type of regulation should always be explained. Arrangement must be made for adequate custodial service for sanitary maintenance of dressing quarters. Urging athletes to express their appreciation to the custodian through their cooperation and compliments helps to build better attitudes.

4. *Rules contribute to individual and group success.* A team of self-disciplined and well-conditioned players will more nearly reach its potential than a team whose members are not. The achievement of any group depends on how well each member is physically, mentally, and emotionally prepared. Each has a responsibility to the others to do his or her best. An athletic team, like any other organization, will be just as good as each member helps it to be.

PROCEDURES

The coach must have final authority in establishing training rules, subject to approval of the school administration and board of education, but it is wise to involve players in the process at an appropriate level. They can suggest training regulations and reasons for them. This involvement helps to create a better attitude toward training standards and a willingness to abide by them. It also makes it easier to enforce them. A coach is sometimes surprised to learn that players suggest more rigid rules than he or she would.

It is best to establish a limited number of training regulations based on sound reasons, which can be enforced, than to have a long list which includes some that have little significance and which will receive little attention. Additional rules can be established if the need arises.

After we have selected the training standards for our squad, each one should be carefully explained and the reasons for it reviewed. There is sometimes some resistance to such regulations as dress and grooming standards because of the emphasis in our society on individual rights and freedom of expression. A positive approach should be used in presenting such regulations. Athletes should want others to look for their good traits rather than their faults. People in general are apt to notice the strong qualities in a well-dressed, neatly groomed person, but are inclined to look for faults and weaknesses in unkempt individuals. A team whose members arrive for a game well-dressed and neatly groomed creates a good impression for both the team and its school.

PUBLICITY

Copies should be made of the training regulations and posted in the dressing room and gymnasium. Coaches have found it helpful to prepare a copy for parents and to seek their support in enforcing them.

Some schools publish an interscholastic player handbook which contains training rules. The school newspaper also can be used to publicize training standards. Any publication should include the reasons behind them.

ENFORCEMENT

All training regulations must be consistently and fairly enforced. Failure to do so is a source of real problems. Star players must understand that they are just as subject to the rules as are substitutes. The coach who is fair and consistent will win the respect and support of players and their parents.

Summary

The issue is not whether athletics offer educational values, but whether athletic experiences are as educationally worthwhile as they ought to be, which is dependent on the kind of coaching athletes receive. Basic is a sound philosophy of secondary education and interscholastic athletics.

Worthwhile objectives must be established to give direction to the learning gained through athletics. These include both immediate and ultimate objectives of the coach, the players, and the school.

The coach must have a comprehensive understanding of the basic principles of teaching and learning. The apperceptive background of the players must be determined. The learning activities must be appropriate to the objectives. Psychologically sound motivating techniques must be used. Provisions must be made for individual differences among players. Diagnostic and remedial procedures and techniques must be employed. To enable players to apply what has been taught them, learning must be in as near practical situations as feasible. The physical and social environment must be as ideal as possible to instill proper attitudes and ideals.

Methods and techniques, both formal and incidental, must be developed for teaching through interscholastic athletics. Formal procedures are appropriate at the beginning of the season, and incidental teaching should be continued throughout the season in the areas of knowledge and emotional controls as occasions arise. Illustrations and examples are effective aids.

Eligibility standards must be carefully taught. Athletes should understand the reasons for them through their history and purposes.

Coaches have the responsibility for teaching sportsmanship. The example set by the coach will be a strong influence on the sportsmanship of others. Students should be taught the standards of conduct contained in the game's rules and in the eligibility requirements.

It is good procedure to involve players in the development of training rules. They must understand the reasons for them and the values they have for the individual, the team, and the school. Training standards must be well publicized and consistently enforced.

QUESTIONS AND TOPICS FOR STUDY AND DISCUSSION

1. What three types of learning should coaches plan to teach?
2. What is the difference between immediate and ultimate objectives of interscholastic competition? Give examples of each.
3. Explain the basic principles of teaching that are important in coaching.

4. Explain how you will apply the principle in coaching that teaching must be diagnostic and remedial.
5. List the things that coaches must teach in addition to skills to make athletics more educational.
6. We shall assume that you have been employed as a head coach of a school and that you do not know anything about its athletes. In assuming your duties,
   a. Explain what information you will want about the athletes who wish to participate in the sport concerned and how you plan to obtain it.
   b. Outline a plan for the first meeting with your squad.
7. Discuss how you will help athletes understand the values and objectives of interscholastic competition.
8. You have noted that several players on your squad are inclined to be disrespectful toward opposing players and game officials, seem to resent training rules, and occasionally exhibit poor sportsmanship; discuss the procedures and techniques you will use to improve the attitudes of these players.
9. Why is it important that eligibility standards be carefully taught? How will you get your athletes to understand their importance?
10. Explain how you think sportsmanship contributes to the aims of secondary education. Discuss ways you plan to teach and promote good sportsmanship.
11. Outline the procedure you plan to follow in establishing training rules for your squad.
12. Why should training standards be publicized? Discuss how you will publicize those that you adopt for your players.

BIBLIOGRAPHY

"All About the Real Cost of School Sports and How Not to Get Your Signals Crossed." *American School Board Journal*, 162, No. 6 (June 1975), 19-33.

Bosco, James S. "Winning at All Costs." *The Physical Educator*, 34, No. 1 (March 1977), 35-37.

Briggs, Paul W. "The Opportunity to Be Relevant." *Journal of Health, Physical Education and Recreation*, May 1970, pp. 41-45.

Crase, Darrell. "Athletics in Trouble." *Journal of Health, Physical Education and Recreation*, April 1972, pp. 39-41.

Durbin, Brice. *Portrait Publications*, Columbus, Kan.

Forsythe, Charles E., and Irvin A. Keller. *Administration of High School Athletics*, 6th ed., pp. 341-48. Englewood Cliffs, N.J.: Prentice-Hall, 1977.

Fuller, Link. "Counseling Methods for Coaches and Athletic Directors." *National Federation of State High School Associations: Interscholastic Athletic Administration*, 3, No. 2 (Spring 1977), 14-16.

Keller, Irvin A. *A History—How the Missouri State High School Activities Association Came to Be*, pp. 13-14. Columbia: Missouri State High School Activities

Association, 1979.

Mudra, Darrell. "The Coach and the Learning Process." *Journal of Health, Physical Education and Recreation*, May 1970, pp. 26-29.

Pierce, Frederick H. "The Genesis of the State High School Association." Kansas City, Mo.: *National Federation of State High School Associations Press*, 1956.

Resick, Matthew C., and Carl E. Erickson. *Intercollegiate and Interscholastic Athletics for Men and Women*, pp. 222-27. Reading, Mass.: Addison-Wesley, 1975.

Schultz, Frederick D. "Broadening the Athletic Experience." *Journal of Health, Physical Education and Recreation*, April 1972, pp. 45-47.

Small, George D. "The Learning Process as Applied to Coaching." *Athletic Journal*, 36 (February 1956), 28-42.

Veller, Don. "Compendium of Common Sense Principles in Modern Coaching." *Scholastic Coach*, 28 (October 1958), pp. 68-74.

Whitten, Charles W. *Interscholastics: A Discussion of Interscholastic Contests*, Bloomington: Illinois High School Association, 1950.

CHAPTER 7

Teaching Motor Skills

In this chapter we will consider the teaching of motor skills, which are fundamental in sports. However, although we may treat them separately, we will be teaching all three areas (knowledge, skills, and emotional controls) simultaneously in coaching any sport. Thus, it is essential to vary our methods and techniques so that the activities provided are appropriate to the objectives.

There are general methods and principles of teaching motor skills which may be applied in all sports, and there are special methods used in particular sports. (These are offered in courses on specific sports). We will limit our attention to the more important general methods and techniques and to certain fundamental principles.

Basic Principles

Most of our motor skills were learned by trial and error, and the degree to which the skill was mastered depended on practice. Such a simple skill as throwing was repeated until objects could be thrown more proficiently; but often much effort was wasted because we did not learn how to throw properly. Many early baseball pitchers learned to throw curves by trial and error. Some learned to throw them well, but they may have been capable of throwing them better had they had the benefit of good coaching; and certainly they would have learned to throw them much easier and in a shorter period of time. Such a complex motor skill as throwing curves requires directed instruction to save the time involved in trial and error methods, which is one of the purposes of coaching.

MOTIVATION

Athletes who are well motivated will try harder to master a skill than those who are not. The soundest motivating technique is to create a feeling of need for the skill. This can be done by showing how the skill is significant in competition and by pointing to the success of outstanding players who employ it. Being able to dribble a basketball with either hand is an example. Showing players the advantage of using the hand opposite to the defensive player, as practiced by good dribblers, will create an awareness of the importance of this skill. We should always explain why the skill is important and how it is to be used in playing before providing drills for mastering it.

THE CORRECT START

It is often easier to teach a skill if the athlete has had no previous experience in using it—which is frequently not the situation at the junior and senior high school levels. Students begin learning skills as children on the playground or in their backyards, and by observing the performances of others, but they may or may not learn it correctly. If not, they are inclined to practice the incorrect way until it becomes habitual. Although they may not use the best techniques, some may have learned to perform the skill with considerable success. This presents a problem to the high school coach, who must decide whether to try to break the established habits and instill the recognized correct technique or to allow the athlete to continue the form already established. Great care must be exercised in making this decision. We must be sure that we can help the player improve his or her performance before we try to make any change in it. Some experienced coaches do not try to change a style of performance as long as it is used with a high degree of success. One highly recognized basketball coach tells the story of one of his promising young players who used an unorthodox shot very successfully; the coach had allowed the player to continue for fear of hurting his performance more than helping it. The boy decided to go to a specialized summer basketball camp, where the instructors insisted that he change his shooting style. As a result, according to his high school coach, he was never able to shoot as well again. All of us will face this situation in our coaching, and we must exercise good judgment in what we think best for the individual before making our decision.

The ability to analyze the best movements necessary to perform a skill is basic in teaching that skill, and understanding the fundamentals of kineseology can help promote this ability. There are three important steps in teaching players to start learning a motor skill correctly:

1. *They must be given a clear understanding of the inherent movements.* This can be done by illustrations and verbal explanations; for example, graphic illustrations on a chalkboard may be used for some skills.

2. *The correct form must be demonstrated.* It is especially effective if the coach can demonstrate this form, but if he or she cannot, a member of the squad who practices the correct form can be called on to demonstrate it. The latter may have some advantage in that a student is an individual others can observe in the daily learning process. A simple, effective form devoid of unnecessary movements should be emphasized. Excessive movement, or "showboating," may be crowd pleasing when successful, but it does not leave a good impression for the team when it is not, and it is generally nonproductive.

3. *The initial attempts must be carefully observed and criticized.* Understanding a skill and performing it are two different things. It is difficult for a high school athlete to judge whether he or she is executing it properly in the first attempts. The coach must observe the initial efforts of performance and provide constructive criticism to each player. Those who begin correctly should be complimented, and suggestions should be offered to those who do not. If any athletes are permitted to start performing incorrectly, they will continue to practice in such a manner and form poor habits. It should be recognized, however, that some athletes may be able to use a different form more effectively than the one being taught, and provisions should be made for individual differences when necessary. Teaching each player to perform most effectively through whatever form is most appropriate for that player should be our goal.

CONTINUED PRACTICE

Athletes must be encouraged to concentrate on the correct form and movement until the skill can be performed sufficiently well to no longer need this attention. Eventually, it will become habitual and will be executed automatically, but drills must be continued to maintain this level of performance.

Directing Practice Sessions

Planning and directing practice sessions will occupy the major portion of our coaching time. There are ways of using effectively the time available, both daily and during the entire season.

More time will be available to the coach if athletes report at the beginning of the practice season in good physical condition. All athletes will be required to have a physician's certificate before being allowed to start practice to protect the athlete against physical hazards and to protect the coach from any charges of negligence. A coach who interpreted his state association's requirement for a physical examination to mean that it was necessary only before the player competed against another school had a basketball player die of a heart attack on the playing floor thirty minutes into the first practice session. He was saved from a court suit only after it became known that the parents knew the boy's heart condition from childhood and were informed that it would be shown in court that they were more negligent than the coach, who knew nothing about the case history.

Most state high school associations' regulations will not permit the coach to meet with players before the first official practice date, but they do allow athletes to condition themselves on their own. Many coaches give instructions for individual conditioning for the next season near the close of the previous season, which is permissible and in the best interest of safety for the athletes. Running, weightlifting, and various exercises are recommended. Players should be carefully instructed in the techniques for these exercises to help prevent injury during the off-season. Each coach must check his or her own association's regulations pertaining to preseason conditioning, and any conditioning required before contact drills are begun, to avoid any possible violation.

Athletes must be motivated to condition themselves during the off-season. The coach should emphasize the personal benefits of keeping in top physical condition and the advantages of reporting in excellent condition for the first practice. He or she should encourage participation in summer sports, which will help the athletes stay in shape and provide athletic experiences in different sports.

CAREFUL PLANNING

More can be accomplished in practice sessions when definite objectives are properly planned in series and broken down into specific daily plans. The length of time it will take to develop and maintain certain skills in players must be considered. Each daily plan should include the amount of time to be devoted to each activity, using the following guiding principles:

1. *The practice should be conducted under as near practical situations as appropriate to the objectives.* Situations should be provided so that coordinations may be formed in the way they are to be used in a game. Learning motor skills requires repeti-

tion, but when there is ample opportunity to practice them in a context that resembles games, it is easier for athletes to make the transfer from performing them in practice to using them in competition.

2. *Distributed practice is more effective than massed practice.* Players learn skills better when the amount of time devoted to practice is spread over a period of days. More learning and mastery will generally result from fifteen minutes of practice per day of a particular skill for six days than from one and one-half hours of practice on one day. The amount of time over which the practice should be staggered will depend on the skill being taught and the progress being made. The concentration spans of high school athletes and the nature of motor learning makes this principle important in coaching.

3. *Drills should provide for the active and continuous participation of all squad members.* Maximum learning occurs when each member of the squad is engaged in some way in the drill. Some drills will necessarily involve only a few players at a particular moment, but the others should observe the practice to analyze performance, weaknesses, and possible corrections. The students should understand the importance of observation as an aid in learning motor skills. Competitive drills will add interest and incentives to practices.

4. *Players should be stimulated consciously to improve their skills during practice periods.* Conscious and continuous effort to improve is fundamental in attaining a greater mastery of any skill. When athletes begin to show signs of not trying to improve the skills being practiced, the practice of that particular skill should be stopped. It is better to discontinue than to permit practice of careless habits.

   Also important is providing a type of drill which will in itself stimulate effort to improve. For example, an effective free-throw drill in basketball would be to require each player to shoot twenty-five free throws each day and to keep a chart showing the number of successful attempts; but a more effective one is to require each player to make a certain number each day, regardless of the number of attempts needed. The latter better motivates players to concentrate on improvement, and has the added advantage of requiring additional drill for those most in need of it. The same principle can be applied to various drills in other sports.

5. *Diagnostic and remedial teaching should be used during all practice sessions.* Noticing weaknesses and mistakes during practice and suggesting corrective measures is an important part of

coaching. Attention should be given to the *little things* which are important in preventing the development of improper habits, for example, seeing that players keep their weight balanced on the balls of their feet and fix their eyes before throwing a baseball or shooting a goal in basketball. The efficiency, fluency, and precisiveness of movements should be carefully observed for possible improvement.

Group and individual drills should be devised to correct weaknesses. Players must not be allowed to commit acts in practice that would result in a foul or penalty in a game. Unless corrective measures are taken in such activities as practice scrimmages, the manner or style of play is likely to be repeated in games to the detriment of the team.

6. *Practice sessions must be satisfying to the players.* Although practices may be strenuous at times, they should be enjoyable and satisfying to the athletes. Practice sessions must be conducted in an orderly manner, but this does not mean that players should not be permitted to enjoy a good laugh at occasional funny occurrences. They will also appreciate a sense of humor in the coach. Monotony can be avoided by such techniques as varying the types of drills and balancing criticisms with compliments.

7. *The length of practice sessions must be appropriate.* Coaches differ in their opinions as to how long practice sessions should be. Many base their opinions on what they as coaches want to accomplish, whereas others consider maintaining the enthusiasm and interest of the athletes. Practices for senior high school players can be longer than those for junior high school athletes. When either begin to show signs of diminishing eagerness and enthusiasm, the practice period may be too long. Several experienced coaches have concluded that there is as much danger in having practice sessions that are too long as those that are too short, and that not much is accomplished after approximately the first one hour and forty-five minutes of actual activity. Coaches realize that the interest and concentration spans of interscholastic players are not as long as their own and must be considered in determining the length of the practice period.

The real problem is what some experienced athletes and coaches refer to as *staleness*, either mental or physical or both. It can occur in an individual or in a team. The danger in it is that it may not be recognized by either the athletes or the coach. I had this experience with a good high school basketball team. Although still winning all its games, the team after midseason was having trouble beating teams it was expected to defeat easily. Neither I nor the members of the team could understand why. However, a former university and professional basketball player, who was an official in one of the games, realized that the team had become stale; he recommended that the starting team be excused from practice for a few days and that the practice periods be shortened for these players. Seven of the players did not report for practice for three days and practiced for no longer than an hour each day for the remainder of the season. The reasons were carefully explained to them. The results were impressive: The team regained its sharpness and went on to win fourth place in the Missouri State High School Basketball Tournament. This one case is not sufficient to draw any conclusions, but there seems to be a growing concern about the dangers of staleness by former Olympic athletes and Olympic and university coaches.[1]

Symptoms of staleness can be observed in high school players; for example, they become "draggy" in practice or fail to maintain positions from which movements can most easily be made, such as keeping their weight on the balls of their feet rather than on their heels. If players are stale in practice, it will affect their performances in games. Some experienced coaches believe that this problem is becoming more serious with the trend toward specialization in one sport.

The best solution is to avoid the problem before it occurs, which will obviate the need for corrective measures. Some suggestions, a few of which have already been mentioned under other topics, include the following:

1. Make practice sessions compatible in length with the physical and mental maturity of the athletes.
2. Study the concentration spans of the players and adjust daily practice schedules accordingly.
3. Provide a variety of daily practice activities to prevent any possible boredom.
4. Lighten work in practice just before the games.
5. Advise athletes to get away from the sport periodically by participating in other sports or activities during the off-season.
6. Shorten practice periods after midseason.
7. Give players an occasional day off from practice in the later part of the season.

Some teams are said to have peaked about midseason, meaning they do not improve after that point. We will want our team to continue to improve throughout the season. Being alert to and taking steps to pre-

[1] J. R., Owne, "Athletic Staleness—Fact or Fiction?" *Olympian*, July/August 1975, pp. 6-7, 15.

vent staleness from occurring can be important in accomplishing this goal.

More can be accomplished if we occasionally take time to study our practice sessions. The following checklist can be used to advantage in evaluating and improving practice sessions:

Players and Practice[2]

If answer is yes, circle 3.
If partly true, circle 2.
If answer is no, circle 1.

1. Practice begins on time.	1 2 3
2. Practice ends on time.	1 2 3
3. Practice is kept moving.	1 2 3
4. Rest periods are provided.	1 2 3
5. Practice is varied to avoid monotony.	1 2 3
6. Drills keep all players busy most of the time.	1 2 3
7. There are enough practice balls.	1 2 3
8. Practice sessions are carefully planned.	1 2 3
9. Charts and records are kept so players can be judged objectively.	1 2 3
10. Every member of the squad is recognized at least once during practice.	1 2 3
11. Players must learn to execute fundamentals properly.	1 2 3
12. Competitive drills are used whenever possible.	1 2 3
13. Every player is given an equal opportunity to achieve.	1 2 3
14. Players are required to conform to all school regulations.	1 2 3
15. A personal conference is held with each player at least once during the season.	1 2 3
Scoring: Add numbers circled	
Highest possible score:	45
Lowest possible score:	15

Coaching Team Play

Competition is the culmination for the efforts devoted by players and their coaches in practices. It provides the occasion for applying the fundamental skills, knowledge, and emotional learning developed. Games

[2] Brice Durbin, "When Players Pull Together," *Portrait of a Basketball Player* (Columbus, Kan.: Portrait Publications, 1945) pp. 19–20.

and meets further afford opportunities to demonstrate before the public the best that has been taught in one school compared to the best taught in another. Preparing athletes for competition in team sports differs from individual sports such as golf, tennis, track, swimming, and wrestling. In team sports attention must be given to both individual and coordinated group play.

PREPARING FOR INDIVIDUAL PERFORMANCES

However, there are some common elements in preparing athletes for both individual and team competition. All must know the rules of the sport in which they will be competing, for example, and other common matters are the following:

1. *A proper competitive attitude should be created.* The anticipation of competition will affect athletes differently. Some will lack confidence, and others will be overconfident. The first type will need encouragement and must realize that the primary objective in competition is to do one's best. The fear of losing frequently causes lack of confidence. The individual who is inclined to have this problem should understand that both opponents can succeed in a match when they do their best, although only one will be the winner, and that there will be as many losers as winners in athletic competition. Defeat should not be looked on as failure.

    One of the better ways of offsetting overconfidence is to emphasize the capabilities of the opponent. Examples of contests lost because of overconfidence can be effective. It should be pointed out that an athlete who is sure that he or she is going to win sometimes fails to do his or her best.

    Both types should learn how to accept either defeat or victory. The old adage of being humble in victory and proud in defeat is still an important one, and athletes will understand its significance if they are taught that the attitude they show leaves an impression of the type of persons they are.

2. *An understanding of opposing players should be provided.* An athlete's knowledge of how the opponent will react physically, mentally, and emotionally in competition is important. Coaches must not only know their own players but also be sufficiently familiar with opposing players to provide information about them that will be helpful in competition. Examples would be the holds and techniques applied by a wrestler and how frequently each is attempted; when a long-distance runner is inclined to make his or her move and whether moves are sometimes faked; whether an opposing player is strongest in the

early part of a contest or later, which indicates his or her endurance; the foot habits of an opponent that indicate from which foot moves are generally made and in what direction (important to players on defense in basketball); the emotional composure of opposing players and how they will react under pressure; the susceptibility to fake plays or faking and what type they might employ. Games are frequently scouted, and this kind of data should be included in scouting reports.

3. *Athletes should be movitated for the contest.* Motivation is necessary throughout the practice and playing season, but for different purposes. Emphasis during a practice session is on creating a favorable attitude and need for learning through the various activities involved. The purpose of motivation for a particular contest is to stimulate the players to perform at their best in that particular event.

Coaches have used various methods and techniques for this purpose. Some start as long as a week before the game to get the players emotionally stirred, which in some cases may be too early and result in too much tension and an emotional anticlimax. Other coaches follow a more normal course, teaching their athletes what they need to know about the opposing team and its individual players without any special effort to arouse them until the day before or the day of the game. Both groups apparently feel that their procedures are effective. Coaches should use the procedure most appropriate for their group of players, being careful not to overstimulate them.

Because of the individual differences among players, personal and private comments to some of them are appropriate, the nature of which will depend on the individual. Some athletes must be helped to relax, whereas others will need to be stimulated. Each player should feel that whatever method is used is for the benefit of that person and the team.

Various techniques of motivation have been used with success but more important is the attitude reflected by the coach. Exhibiting confidence helps when players are worried about losing a game, and expressing concern about losing can be appropriate when there are signs of overconfidence. Exuberating enthusiasm rubs off on players, which is why pep talks are given just before the contest. If used wisely at the proper times, special techniques can be effective, such as reading a statement from a pregame sports report about the opposing team. Instilling a belief that the team will perform just as well as each player performs individually, and that failure to do one's best will affect the performance of the team, helps to instill a feeling of individual responsibility.

DEVELOPING PATTERNS OF PLAY

There are many different offensive and defensive formations employed in coaching team sports. Offensive plays may be what are termed set plays, or they may be patterns involving options. Defensive formations are basically person-to-person and zone defenses. All types are presented at the numerous coaching schools and clinics held throughout the nation, and each has been used successfully by some coaches. Because college and university coaches often are the principal speakers at the clinics, a large number of the plays originated in collegiate athletics. However, what works in intercollegiate competition may or may not work in high school athletics. Recruiting the best high school athletes makes it possible for collegiate coaches to *fit players* to their favorite patterns, whereas high school coaches must *fit play patterns to their players*. Each of us must select and devise those that are most appropriate to the members of our squads.

The abilities of interscholastic players, their size and quickness, previous experience, and maturity must be considered in developing the patterns to be used. Another coach's patterns may not be appropriate for our athletes. Whether we have one or two good shooters on a basketball squad or whether we have a team with balanced shooting abilities should make a difference in the type of offenseive patterns we select. The decision to use primarily a running or a passing attack in football should depend on the abilities of our quarterbacks to pass and whether or not we have better runners than receivers. A balanced attack is preferable if we have the players with the abilities to use it.

BUILDING TEAM PLAY

Two players may be of equal ability, yet one may contribute more to the team's success than the other. Often this occurs because one is a *team player*, whose primary concern is the success of the team, whereas the other, more concerned with his or her own personal feats, aspires to be the team's star. Whether or not an athlete is a team player stems from his or her attitude. The team attitude that must be cultivated is uniquely described by Brice Durbin in his booklet, *Portrait of a Basketball Player*:

Did this ever happen to you? (If not, did you ever see it happen to anyone else?) You make a basket, the crowd applauds, the players shout *nice work*, the coach claps his hands, and you dash back on defense with renewed enthusiasm and energy! You have succeeded and you are confident that nothing can stop you!

But do you know what made your success possible? Probably one of your teammates passed the ball to you and another might have screened your opponent—and this assistance on their part was the immediate cause of your success. No doubt the other two helped you indirectly.

Now multiply the enthusiasm you derived from this experience by five and think what a terrific force you have unleashed at your opponents. Team harmony releases this irresistible force. Five boys with energy and enthusiasm are unbeatable, other things being equal.

But this is only half the story. Anyone can be enthusiastic in success but what about failure? Did you ever make a foul or miss a shot in a *hot* contest? How did you feel? Naturally you were depressed but that depression lifts when your teammates all shout, *Don't mind that! Come on! Let's go!* Your coach shouts words of encouragement also! The crowd does likewise! You are back in the game with renewed energy and you are anxious to make amends for your error. Again you have an illustration of what it means to pull together.

If you play with your teammates and you always display real sportsmanship, you will have this player-coach-crowd cooperation.

Did you ever see a selfish player fail? The crowd, coach and teammates laugh inwardly and show indifference outwardly. He receives a salvo of boos and catcalls. The morale of the team sags. A very ordinary team with five boys pulling together can easily defeat them. They will win going away.

The great player plays to win. He knows he will win the greatest possible number of victories when he helps his teammates do their best. He will applaud success to inflame the enthusiasm and energy it kindles. He will shout words of encouragement in failure to lift the depressed spirit it produces.

The team that *pulls together* has five great players. That team will win a majority of its games and many that would be lost if opponents had the wrong spirit. Defeat is the price a team pays for being selfish. Victory rewards the unselfish.

Finally, when the coach is asked why his team won when the chips were down, he will usually say, *My boys were pulling together.* And when he is asked what kind of player you are, he will say, *He's a great player. He plays his heart out for every man on the team.* And every player will say, when asked who won the game, *We won because we were pulling together.*[3]

This excerpt illustrates the type of attitude we will want to instill in our athletes. It further implies some techniques we can use to enhance it, for example, complimenting players on good passes to the player who scored the basket, commending blockers who opened the hole for the ball carrier, and praising the one who blocked the pass or shot. Star players should be reminded that part of the credit for their success goes to their teammates.

Players should understand that teamwork in everyday life is just as important as it is on the athletic field. Individuals pulling together accomplish more than those who pull in different directions.

[3] Brice Durbin, "Players and Practice," *How to Rate Your Coaching Qualities— A Self Analysis* (Columbus, Kan.: Portrait Publications), p. 5.

The importance of preparing players for team leadership is sometimes overlooked by the coaches. Present-day rules for team sports allow coaches to call plays and to make decisions which at one time were the responsibilities of the team captain. But there are still many occasions in today's games when the leadership of players is needed and necessary for maximum success: The quarterback must be capable of making quick decisions on option plays; the playmaker in basketball must quickly observe when the opponents switch their type of defense. Some player must be designated to provide this type of leadership in all team sports. Leadership off the playing field is also important because of the influence it can have on other players.

The team captain has always been looked to for leadership, but the responsibilities of this position have diminished since the rules in several sports were changed, allowing the coach more freedom in calling plays and giving instructions. In some instances it has become only an honorary position, involving such routine matters as calling the toss, selecting the goal, or choosing whether to kick or receive. Regardless of the extent to which the coach dominates, however, there is still a need and plenty of opportunities for leadership by players. A team with player leadership on the field is better than one whose members depend almost entirely on their coach.

There are two general procedures for selecting team captains: elected by the players or appointed by the coach. The former is considered more democratic, but it has some disadvantages unless the position is primarily an honorary one. Players sometimes select captains on the basis of popularity rather than leadership, a quality coaches are inclined to emphasize. Captains should be chosen carefully; they must be players others respect, but not always the most popular, and must possess the mental ability and characteristics for leadership.

The development of leadership has always been proclaimed as one of the values of interscholastic competition, and it can be an important one when it becomes one of our goals in coaching and appropriate methods and techniques are employed to achieve it. Extra time must be spent in conferences with those chosen to captain the team or to serve as quarterbacks. They must understand that the position is more than an honorary one and carries important responsibilities. They must set an example for other players by exhibiting good sportsmanship and good conduct both on and off the field. Play patterns, the reasons for them, and their advantages must be thoroughly reviewed. Such questions as, "What should we do in this situation?" should be asked frequently to help them develop the ability to think. Leadership is developed by practicing it and opportunities for doing so must be given. Practice scrimmages provide occasions for team leaders to make decisions and opportunities for the coach to evaluate their leadership abilities. It is always wise to train two or more individuals to assume the responsibilities of team captain in cases of injury or illness.

TEACHING PLAYERS TO ANTICIPATE

Some players seem to have the knack for being in the right place at the right time and knowing what their opponents are going to do before they try to do it. These are often thought to be innate abilities—and no doubt the athletes were born with the necessary potential—but they were increased through the practice of *anticipatory thinking.*

Athletes can and must learn to anticipate the actions of others in athletic contests, not only their opponents but also their teammates. If there is a vacant space on the basketball court and a dribbler is being pressed, the matter is resolved when both he or she and another teammate anticipate together that a pass can be completed in that area. Conversely, being alert to where an opponent is likely to attempt a pass often enables a defensive player to intercept it. The basic purpose of faking a play is the anticipation that the opponent will react to it in such a way that advantage can be taken of that reaction.

Players should be instructed to practice consciously anticipatory thinking each day just as they do their skills. The more it is practiced, the easier it will become. Coaches can offer helpful suggestions such as these: Always be keenly observant of others; note any particular habits they may have; be alert to the fact that the first movement may be a fake; watch the eyes, facial expression, and stance of the opponent; try to *think with* your teammates; and watch for any *let up* of an opposing player.

GETTING READY FOR A GAME

Getting ready for a game actually begins with the first day of practice and continues until the date of the contest. Mastering the fundamentals and coordinating them into patterns of play are all necessary preparations, but there are certain final plans and strategy that must be attended to for a particular game. It is generally more effective to employ basic offensive and defensive patterns which players have mastered well than to try to teach in a short time new ones for a specific contest for the purpose of surprising the opponents. High school athletes usually cannot master new patterns well enough in a few days to use them effectively, although they may be able to learn some options in a short time. By the time the playing season is well under way, the team should have learned enough offensive and defensive patterns to cope with those of the opponents. But there are final decisions to be made in their selection and minor adjustment.

If possible, the opposing team should be scouted. The scouting record should show strengths and weaknesses, offensive and defensive patterns used, most capable players, any specific habits of individual players, and special matters that warrant consideration. If a film of a previous game between that team and your team is available, the opponents' play should be analyzed from it. It is unwise to use a film from a third party unless the opposing coach approves. Such use tends to cause animosity among coaches unless there is an agreement and both coaches have comparable opportunities. A careful analysis and study of the scouting report will help greatly in the selection of the offensive patterns and defensive adjustments. Some coaches teach both basic types of defense, person-to-person and zone, whereas others use one type and make necessary adjustments in it to meet the competition. Whether to use one or both depends on the capabilities of the players. Some can use both satisfactorily, whereas others lack the maturity and ability to do so. Many high school teams that have tried to employ both types end up not mastering either, and are thus less effective on defense.

From the accumulated information the coach should decide how to defend against the best opposing players (keeping individual records on outstanding players is very helpful), how to take advantage of the other team's weaknesses, and how to counteract any surprise plays or options the opponents may try.

All of this material must be thoroughly discussed with our players and appropriate practices provided to help them meet the competition. The opposing team's offensive and defensive plays must be carefully reviewed. The players guarding the star players on the opposing team should be told of any habits they may have that will help to anticipate their actions. Weaknesses of opposing players can be reviewed to make team and individual offense more effective. Adequate planning and practicing will help to build team confidence.

Several experienced coaches have found that it is wise not to employ any special motivating techniques until just before game time, when an occasional pep talk or unique technique can be used effectively.

The first game is one of the most important of the season. Not only does it provide the first competition for the team, which may be the first for a few players, but also it affords an opportunity to obtain knowledge that will help in preparing for future games.

Some of this will occur during the game. We will be counseling players throughout the contest, particularly during intermissions and time-outs. Substitutions will be made to enable us to give special instructions to individual players. Diagnostic and remedial coaching will be done. Little weaknesses will be noted that will be called to the attention of players. For example it may be noticed that a basketball player who is not hitting his or her usual percentage is starting shots before getting the eyes fixed on the basket. After a quick substitution for a few moments and calling attention to this problem will often help the player regain his or her usual accuracy.

Taking notes during games is extremely helpful in preparing for the next game. Coaches are too busy to both observe play and take notes, but a student secretary can be trained and used for this purpose. Notes can easily be dictated to a secretary seated beside the coach during the game, and the coach need not take his or her eyes off the action. Such procedure will assure the coach that he or she will not forget some details to be reviewed with the players.

A postgame analysis and review with players is significant in helping players to improve and in getting ready for the next game. A game film is one of the best aids, but not all schools can afford to film their games. The postgame analysis provides an excellent basis for the diagnostic and remedial coaching we must do.

Summary

Most of our everyday skills were learned by trial and error, but motor skills necessary in athletics require the application of some basic principles:

1. Players must be motivated to learn and to perform the skill correctly.
2. The learning of motor skills must begin correctly.
3. Athletes must have a clear understanding of the inherent movements.
4. The correct form must be demonstrated.
5. Initial attempts to perform the skill must be carefully observed and criticized.
6. Practice must be continued until the skill becomes automatic.

Procedures and principles for directing practice sessions most effectively include the following:

1. There should be ample individual preseason conditioning.
2. Practice sessions must be carefully planned in accord with definite objectives.
3. Practice sessions should be conducted under conditions as close to real competition as possible.
4. Distributed practice is more effective than massed practice.

5. Drills should provide for the active and continuous participation of all squad members.
6. Players should be stimulated to attempt consciously to improve their skills in practice sessions.
7. Diagnostic and remedial teaching should be applied during all practice sessions.
8. Practice sessions must be satisfying to the players.
9. The length of the practice sessions must be appropriate to the maturity of the athletes.

Care must be taken to prevent staleness in athletes, and preventive measures are better than corrective ones in coping with this problem.

Coaching team play requires preparing individuals for competition and coordinating their efforts into a unit. The preparation of individual players should include the following:

1. Creating a competitive attitude.
2. Providing an understanding of opposing players.
3. Motivating for the contest.
4. Coordinating individuals' responsibilities into a unit.

Offensive and defensive play patterns should be fitted to the abilities and experiences of the players, rather than to attempt to fit players to the coach's favorite formations.

An attitude of team play must be developed which motivates athletes *to pull together.*

Team leaders must be selected and extra time devoted to helping them assume their responsibilities.

Teaching players to anticipate helps to make them better contestants.

Careful game plans must be formulated for each contest. As much knowledge about the opposing team and players should be obtained as possible. The opponent's offensive and defensive patterns and the play of outstanding players must be carefully analyzed as the basis for selecting appropriate offenses and defenses. Alternative options should be considered.

A postgame analysis from notes or film provides significant help in preparing for future games.

QUESTIONS AND TOPICS FOR STUDY AND DISCUSSION

1. Select a skill you will teach your players and explain how you will motivate them to learn and master that skill.

2. Name in order and explain three important steps in helping athletes to begin learning a skill correctly.

3. Prepare a brief outline of instructions you will give athletes as a guide for preseason conditioning.

4. Imagine that you are preparing an early season practice session. Select a sport and prepare a time schedule for a one-hour-and-forty-five-minute session showing the practice activities and the amount of time you will devote to each.

5. Why is distributed practice more effective than massed practice in learning motor skills?

6. Explain some signs you will look for to note whether players are consciously attempting to improve their performances? Why is it wise to sometimes stop practice at this point?

7. Give specific examples of diagnostic and remedial teaching during practice sessions.

8. Discuss ways you will try to make practice sessions satisfying to your players.

9. Explain the basis for determining how long your practice sessions will be.

10. Discuss ways of preventing possible staleness among athletes.

11. Explain some techniques you might use in stimulating a competitive attitude in individual players.

12. Discuss the information you will want your players to have about outstanding opposing athletes.

13. Assuming that you have a tough game coming up a week hence, discuss some of the methods and techniques you will use in motivating your players for the contest.

14. How will you decide what offensive and defensive patterns of play to teach your squad?

15. Explain possible ways of building a team attitude among your players.

16. Why are team leaders necessary? Explain how you will try to develop the leadership qualities they must have.

17. Discuss how you will try to get your players to practice anticipatory thinking in their play.

18. What final steps will you take in getting your team ready for a specific game?

19. Explain how you will use a postgame analysis in your coaching.

BIBLIOGRAPHY

Coppage, Philip R. "Get More from Practice." *The Physical Educator*, 30 (December 1973), 197-200.

Durbin, Brice. "When Players Pull Together." *Portrait of a Basketball player*, pp. 19–20. Columbus, Kan.: Portrait Publications, 1945.

—— "Players and Practice." *How to Rate Your Coaching Qualities—A Self-Analysis*, p. 5. Columbus, Kan.: Portrait Publications).

Gallon, Arthur J. "Coaching Ideas and Ideals." *Motivational Techniques in Coaching*, pp. 46-50. Boston, Mass.: Houghton Mifflin, 1974.

Grieve, Andrew. "Factors Influencing a Coach's Ability to Analyze." *Athletic Journal*, 51 (June 1971), 42-45, 53-54.

Owen, J. R. "Athletic Staleness—Fact or Fiction?" *Olympian*, July/August 1975, pp. 6-7, 15.

Smith, Garry J. "Group Cohesion in Athletics." *Scholastic Coach*, 39 (November 1969), 52-53, 79.

Veller, Don. "Get the Right Boy in the Right Job." *Athletic Journal*, 46 (March 1966), 46-54, 85-87.

CHAPTER 8

Relationships with Other Coaches and Officials

There should be a cooperative and friendly relationship among all those who share responsibilities in making interscholastic athletics a worthwhile program. It is the purpose of this chapter to discuss the type of relationships which should prevail and how they can be established and sustained.

Other Coaches

Except in the very smallest schools, there will be several coaches on the staff: male and female head coaches of various sports and assistant coaches. Each will have his or her individual responsibilities, but all will share the responsibility of providing the best interscholastic program possible for as many boys and girls as the school can afford. Any dissension among them will be sure to affect that program adversely.

OTHER HEAD COACHES

Each head coach has the responsibility for providing the leadership and supervision for his or her particular sport. Commensurate with this responsibility is the authority to make final decisions within the school's administrative policies. However, exercising this authority must not condition the head coach to feel that he or she should make all the decisions. There will be some which will affect several sports and in which other head coaches should have a voice. All coaches must remember that their decisions are subject to the approval of the athletic director or principal and the school administration. They can be made cooperatively and harmoniously when certain conditions prevail.

All coaches must be committed to the school's interscholastic philosophy. They must realize that interscholastic athletics are offered primarily for the educational and recreational benefits of the students. When they share this common basic belief, their viewpoints will be compatible, and even tough decisions will be made on the basis of what are the best interests of the great majority of the students. There is a need for some give and take and there is no place for any selfish interests.

There must be mutual respect of each other's responsibilities. Conditions exist in many schools which cause conflicts in the duties of coaches. For example, inadequate facilities can be a source of friction, and an equitable plan of sharing must be agreed upon. When both boys' and girls' basketball squads use the same gymnasium, practice schedules must be arranged so that there is no favoritism for either sex. Finances can be a problem, as can overlapping seasons—particularly when there are students who wish to compete in both sports. A coach should not try to induce an athlete to start practicing for one sport while he or she is still competing in another. Neither should the coach encourage a player to discontinue participation in other sports to specialize in one, which may not be in the best interests of the athlete.

Professional attitudes and ideals must prevail. The interactions between and among coaches are strongly influenced by the attitudes that each exhibit. Ideals of honesty, integrity, and fairness will foster good relationships. Criticisms of a fellow coach to another must be avoided. Any differences with another coach should be discussed privately with her or him. A sense of loyalty to others and to the school must be shown, and proper channels of communication must be followed. It is wise to discuss previously changes we may want to suggest to the school administration with other coaches who might be affected, and we should never go around these persons to the superintendent or board of education. If a situation should arise which we think should be discussed with the principal, superintendent, or school board, a conference should be requested with all parties who may have an interest in the matter.

ASSISTANT COACHES

There are about as many assistant coaches involved in interscholastics as there are head coaches, particularly in larger high schools. The help they are able to give is largely dependent on their relationship with the head coach. This relationship is better when the head coach is permitted to have some voice in the selection of assistants, and the head coach will have a greater sense of obligation to help assistant coaches improve their coaching abilities. It must be remembered that many assistants aspire to and are capable of becoming head coaches, and they should be given the guidance and supervision that will help them attain this goal. A head coach who demonstrates the ability to develop other head coaches need not fear that he or she may be replaced by an assistant, and there is no place for jealousy in their relationship. The head coach will get most of the credit for what assistants are able to do in securing better performance.

The head coach of one sport may serve as an assistant in another. He or she must be able to adjust to this situation and realize that coaching procedures and techniques are subject to the supervision and approval of a superior. Most coaches can work quite well in such dual capacities.

There must be mutual respect and loyalty. An assistant coach must be loyal to the head coaches and respect their opinions; they will receive most of the credit or criticism for the team's success or failure. Any suggestions or criticisms should be made directly to them, and full support of their coaching must be given in all situations.

Conversely, the head coach must show respect for the assistants. They should be given the freedom and trust to carry out their responsibilities, and their suggestions and criticisms should be solicited and considered. Any criticism of the assistant must be made in private and must be constructive. Recognition and praise, both personally and publicly, should always be given to assistant coaches for any contributions they may make.

The establishment of clear policies helps maintain rapport between head coaches and assistant coaches. It is advisable to formulate policies in consultation with assistants, but they must understand that the head coach must retain the final decision. They should feel free to make recommendations, but this is the limit of their authority.

Some policies which might be considered include the following:

1. *Regular staff conferences should be held.* One of the first conferences should concern policies, that is, outlining individual responsibilities in practices and setting time schedules for daily activities. Pregame and postgame conferences are recommended on the methods and techniques of teaching fundamentals and offensive and defensive play patterns.

   The policy of holding occasional private conferences with individual assistants is mutually beneficial, and should be their primary purpose. Strengths and weaknesses of the assistant can be reviewed, compliments expressed for commendable efforts, and constructive criticism offered. Suggestions and criticisms from the assistant coach should be solicited and discussed. Meetings of this type tend to build better relations and a closer bond.

2. *There should be procedures for assigning responsibilities,* including those applying to practice sessions and contests. Assistant coaches are frequently given the responsibility for coaching and directing the junior varsity teams. If they are given this responsibility, they must be given the necessary authority to assume it. They should be allowed to decide what offensive and defensive plays to use as long as they are compatible with those used by the varsity team. Any deviations should have the approval of the head coach. One of the purposes of the junior varsity program is to help develop players for the varsity team. It would be unwise to have the junior team learn styles of play that would have to be changed later. This type of opportunity provides a means of evaluating the assistant's ability to become a head coach.

3. *There must be policies concerning the supervision of players.* Proper supervision of athletes is important in implementing the educational values of interscholastic athletics. Dressing rooms should be properly supervised, as improper language and conduct often originate in unsupervised dressing rooms. Some coaches assign this responsibility to players. Policies for home and out-of-town games should be established, and standards of conduct should be formulated and enforced. All such policies and the responsibility for upholding them should be understood and shared by all members of the coaching staff.

4. *The school's philosophy and objectives of interscholastic athletics should be set forward.* It is highly important that there be a clear understanding of the philosophy and objectives which give direction to the school's athletic program and that all coaches adhere to and support them.

5. *School policies must be upheld.* All schools will have certain policies concerning the administration of the interscholastic program, which must be upheld by the coaching staff. Nothing will get a coach into difficulty more quickly than a violation of school policy.

6. *Procedure for recommending changes in policy should be established.* It is strongly suggested that a procedure be established for recommending changes in policies of the coaching staff or of the school. Recommendations should first be discussed with the head coach, and if he or she concurs, presented through established channels if they need the approval of higher authorities. A conference with all persons the change may affect should be held before it is made.

Many department heads have found it helpful in building good relations among members of their departments to have them meet at social functions. Some give an occasional party for their staff and spouses and prohibit any shop talk. These strictly social functions provide opportunities for co-workers to learn to know each other better as persons rather than just as fellow teachers.

COACHING STAFFS

The coaching staff should be organized and perform much in the same manner as an athletic team, with the athletic director or principal serving as the captain. A head coach must provide similar leadership by being the captain of the team of coaches for his or her sport.

Opposing Coaches

It is important to maintain a professional attitude toward opposing coaches. Although we oppose them in competition, we must have a fraternal feeling that will enable all coaches to work together harmoniously. If two opposing coaches cannot get along, it will be reflected in the attitudes and conduct of the players. Recognized professional practices will promote good relationships with competing coaches, as will courtesy, honesty, truthfulness, and integrity.

EXTENDING COMMON COURTESIES

If the schools' policies permit, game passes for coaches who wish to observe or scout games promote cooperation and good relationships between schools. Frequently all coaches in a conference are admitted to the athletic contests of schools in that conference. Scouting is a commonly accepted practice, and making sure a coach has a good seat to view the game is a friendly gesture. A coach should never allow another person to use his or her pass. The exchange of schedules before the season opens helps the coach make arrangements for scouting and attending the games of other schools. Some schools provide a hospitality room for visiting coaches and school administrators.

The coach and athletic director of the visiting team should be given advance information about the time the dressing rooms and gymnasium or playing field will be opened, location of the dressing room, game time, spaces reserved for visiting school buses, price of admission, any special halftime activities, seating reserved for the visiting pep club and band (if it is to perform). Also, student managers and ushers should be assigned to look after the needs of the visitors, drinking water should be available on the playing field, a chalkboard provided in the dressing room, and arrangements should be made for students to meet and greet the visiting team and cheerleaders.

DEMONSTRATING MUTUAL RESPECT

The attitudes exhibited by coaches at athletic games are strong influences on the sportsmanship and conduct of players and spectators. If mutual respect is shown by coaches, it helps build mutual respect among players and fans. A heated verbal exchange between coaches, or a similar act, before spectators can have adverse effects. Any discussion in public, or otherwise, should be in a professional and friendly manner. *A forced smile will accomplish more than an uncontrolled show of emotion.* Disparaging remarks about the opposing coach or his or her team should never be made.

AVOIDING CONFLICT AND MISUNDERSTANDINGS

Coaches work more harmoniously when each tries to avoid occasions for conflict and controversy. Problems related to scheduling, game contracts, and numerous other administrative details can often be prevented if the athletic directors or principals assume responsibility for these duties.

The hiring of officials is sometimes a cause of friction between coaches, but it will not be if proper procedures are applied. Most state high school associations have a regulation requiring that the officials for regularly scheduled games must be approved by both schools. A good method is for the home school to send much in advance of the game a list of officials to the visiting school. That school should return the list promptly, indicating those officials who are not acceptable. The officials can then be selected from those who have been approved. They should never be hired until approval has been verified.

A coach should not insist that only those officials be engaged whose officiating may provide an advantage for his or her team. There have been some instances in which basketball coaches, whose teams used a pressing type of defense, would approve only officials who allowed more than the usual amount of contact—which favored their teams. This kind of attitude breeds controversy and is not compatible with the ideal of fairness in interscholastic athletics. Some conferences avoid this type of situation by appointing a person to assign officials to games within the conference. Officials should be selected on the basis of their competencies, including consistency. Consistency in officiating should prevail from official to official, but there are individual differences and some officials call games more closely than others. It is one of the responsibilities of coaching to teach players to adjust their style of play to the officiating.

PROCEDURES WHEN CONFLICTS ARISE

Despite the efforts of coaches and school administrators, occasionally a problem will arise, perhaps a case of ineligibility or an error in the application of a game rule by the officials or the misconduct of a player or fan. Most of these can be resolved satisfactorily if ethical and professional practices are followed.

If one school believes that another has an ineligible player on its squad without knowing it, its first step always is to inform the coach and administrator of that school—who will in most cases investigate and resolve the matter. If the problem cannot be settled satisfactorily between the two schools in this manner, the next step is to suggest that the school administrator request a ruling from the state high school association to avoid any possible violation. The school calling attention to the case should always offer any information it may have about it to the other. If nothing is done and there is ample evidence that the player is ineligible, his or her school should be informed that there will be no alternative but to file charges with the state high school association if he or she is permitted to compete. Coaches and schools hesitate to take such action, but it must be done in fairness to their own players when a school fails to assume its responsibilities for upholding common eligibility standards adopted through the state high school association.

Any protest of an official's error in administering, or failing to administer correctly, a game rule should always be made at the time the error occurs. It must be done in a professional manner, and the opposing coach must be informed that the game is being played under protest when the mistake cannot be corrected under the rules. It is the error that should be protested, not the outcome of the game. It will be the decision of the body hearing the protest to determine whether the official's error affected the outcome of the game and whether any change in it should be made. Decisions of judgment should never be protested. Some state high school associations will not hear any protest of officials' decisions, and others will. All coaches should be familiar with their state association's regulations and procedures regarding protests.

The importance of professional conduct at games cannot be overemphasized. Its value can be illustrated by the attitudes and actions of two coaches in a closely played basketball game. One coach had several years more experience than the other, who was still young. The game was between two rival teams. It was hard played and exciting throughout, the lead changing several times. The fans from both schools were supportive of their teams but well behaved, the players showed excellent sportsmanship on the floor, and the game was well officiated by two brothers. In the closing moments of the game, something happened that frequently causes controversy and unsportsmanlike conduct. With one team leading by one point, a shot was taken by an opposing player just as the horn sounded to signal the end of the game. It was one of those situations in which people's emotions, swayed by whichever team they favored, would determine their opinion about whether the basket should or should not count. Because of the noise from all the excitement, the officials approached the timer to make certain that the signal had not sounded before the official nearest to it heard it. The other official did not know that it had sounded. While they were doing this, the more experienced coach suggested to the younger coach that the best thing for them to do would be to take their seats, wait calmly for the decision, and accept it *cooly*, whichever way it went. Some murmuring and rumbling were starting in the stands. The decision was promptly announced while the coaches were seated on their benches, but they met immediately after the announcement and smilingly congratulated each other before the spectators. Although there was some semblance of groaning from supporters of the losing team, the conduct under the conditions was excellent. The younger coach, who lost the game, contends that he learned one of his most valuable lessons from it. He realized how much the professional conduct of coaches can instill desirable behavior in fans under trying circumstances. He often has wondered what could have happened if objections and animosity had been shown by either coach.

The filming of football and basketball games has become rather common for coaching purposes. Films do afford an excellent medium for analyzing the strengths and weaknesses of players and diagnosing mistakes. But not all schools can afford to film their athletic games. When one school films a game and the other does not, it is good ethical practice to give the latter an opportunity of viewing the film. Films taken of games should not be made available to a third school unless both schools approve or unless a film of a game with the third school is also made available. A coach should not attempt to film a game or any part of a game as a third party for scouting purposes without the expressed approval of both participating schools. The best procedure is a school policy prohibiting filming of games by a third party.

Coaches' Associations

Many coaches are members of local, state, and national coaches' associations. Some of these organizations make significant contributions to interscholastic athletics, but others engage in the promotion of athletic events to which many secondary school principals and athletic directors object, for example, postseason games and national tournaments. A coaches' association should be looked on as a professional organization of which the primary purpose is to help develop the professional competencies of its members.

OBJECTIVES

Among the acceptable goals of coaches' associations are these:

1. *To increase the coaching knowledge and skills of its members.* One method is to sponsor coaching schools and clinics. These clinics afford the opportunity to learn newer methods and techniques from some of the most successful coaches across the nation.

2. *To promote a better understanding of the philosophy and objectives of interscholastic athletics.* Discussions of related topics and encouragement to individual members to make local efforts can be effective.

3. *To keep interscholastic athletics in proper perspective within the total educational program.* Some coaches in the past have viewed attempts to keep athletic contests in proper educational perspective as restrictive, but this belief is unfounded. The stability and strength of interscholastic sports are due in large measure to the efforts of leading coaches and administrators to follow the objectives of education.

4. *To promote the educational and recreational values of athletics.* This purpose has the support of other professional educational organizations and the associations that try to accomplish it are recognized as playing a vital role in interscholastic athletics.

5. *To foster good sportsmanship.* Emphasizing the importance of setting proper examples and formulating a code of sportsmanship can improve the conduct of players and fans and prevent instances of violence.

6. *To prevent and care for injuries.* This is an important topic for consideration at coaches' clinics and should be an objective of coaches' associations.

7. *To promote the professionalism of high school coaches.* High school coaching is recognized as a profession and should be treated as such. Coaches' associations should be concerned that all members adhere to ethical and professional standards, and ways to serve their members better and to improve the interscholastic program should be studied.

Coaches must take an active part in the work of their association and see that it has good leadership. Any organization is just as good as each member helps it to be.

The association must not become a power-seeking organization. Power struggles with administrative groups can be damaging and result in a loss of respect. Efforts should be made to work with such organizations as athletic directors' and secondary school principals' associations rather than against them. A football player who outruns his interference often gets tackled pretty hard. Working with other educational organizations helps provide the type of interference needed to accomplish desirable goals.

College Coaches

College and university coaches have an interest in the interscholastic athletic program. A large number of them were former high school coaches and have a pretty good understanding of the responsibilities of high school coaching. They realize there are differences in philosophy and practices between interscholastic and intercollegiate athletics. The former is seen as a source of talent for college teams, and many high school athletes, some of whom could not afford to attend college without them, are recipients of college athletic scholarships.

High school coaches should try to understand the problems college coaches face and the reasons for the differences in regulations and practices. They are pleased when their athletes receive a college athletic scholarship, but they must be certain that their own program does not become merely a farm system for college athletics. Proper relationships are important to both groups of coaches.

RECRUITMENT

Strict regulations prohibiting the recruitment of players for high school teams are included in the by-laws of all state high school athletic and activities' associations, and severe penalties are assessed for violations. But in college athletics it is a way of life. The entertainment feature at that level and the accompanying pressures to win make recruiting of athletic talent an essential phase of the college coach's responsibilities and necessary to his or her success. Conversely, the college coach must understand that recruiting activities shall not interfere with the responsibilities of the high school coach or with the interscholastic program. Neither must they intrude into the academic and interscholastic activities of the high school player.

The National Collegiate Athletic Association (NCAA) publishes a pamphlet, *A Guide for the College-Bound Student-Athlete*, which is valuable in providing for appropriate relationships between college and high school coaches. It contains a summary of that organization's standards and regulations pertaining to permissible financial aid, eligibility, and recruiting. Two provisions of particular significance for high school coaches are that it is not permissible

> To contact a prospect at his school (high school, preparatory school, or junior college) without permission from the institution's executive officer or his authorized representative.[1]
>
> To contact a prospect at the site of his school's (high school, preparatory school, junior college) athletic competition if he is participating in a contest or competition. No such contact shall be made with the prospect prior to the competition on the day of the competition and then not until the prospect has completed the competition (including all games in a tournament or event extended over several days) and then has been released by his school authority, dresses and departs the dressing room or meeting room facility.[2]

The NCAA makes the pamphlet available to all high schools through their state high school associations. Each school should have one, and all coaches should be familiar with the regulations it contains. High school players look to their coaches for guidance when they are being recruited, and this pamphlet provides much important information for proper counseling. The NCAA further requests that high school representatives cooperate in enforcing its rules by reporting any violations that may occur.

Some of the more serious problems related to recruiting arise when a school has an outstanding senior player whose abilities are widely known. A few such athletes have been contacted by as many as fifty college recruiters. These players often need the help of high school coaches and other school representatives to protect them from such excessive interference. Some schools have found it necessary to arrange policies with parents to alleviate such danger.

PROVIDING INFORMATION

A player's high school coach is the logical person to be contacted for information about him or her for recruiting purposes. Honesty, truthfulness, and accuracy in providing information are important. There will be instances when the recruiter is not sure whether the athlete is of sufficient caliber to warrant an athletic scholarship. Information about this type of player must be valid. If a coach's information is found to be unreliable, it could be damaging to the prospects of another athlete who merits a scholarship in the future.

A high school coach should not expect to be shown any special

---

[1] *A Guide for the College-Bound Student-Athlete* (Shawnee Mission, Kan.: National Collegiate Athletic Association, 1978), p. 11.

[2] *Ibid.*

favors when he or she has a player colleges want to recruit. It is the duty of the coach to help his or her players, not to take advantage of or to exploit their athletic abilities.

Neither should a coach try to help a recruiter by influencing an athlete to attend a particular school. Players frequently consult their high school coaches about choosing a college. They should be told what things they should consider, their intended career and the best preparation for it being a predominant factor. If they plan to be, and have the capabilities to be a professional athlete, that is one thing; but if they contemplate entering another profession after graduation, that is another. In that case, they should consider more seriously the academic program and the school's reputation for producing leaders in their chosen field. Whether to first enter a junior college is a question for some students. The training it offers in preparation for senior college then must be considered. Any institution the student is interested in attending must meet accreditation standards necessary to transfer credits to other colleges. Costs, social and cultural opportunities, quality of the athletic program, and medical care of athletes are among other factors that should be investigated.

Officials

Both coaches and officials must realize that the primary purpose of the interscholastic program is to benefit high school students and that each group has a responsibility toward this end.

PROPER ATTITUDES

The primary function of officials is to enforce the game rules to ensure fairness in competition. Experience has proved the necessity of having some authority to see that players and coaches abide by the rules. This authority is delegated to officials.

Officials' errors are seldom the determining factor in the outcome of a game. "The officials beat us!" is sometimes heard when a close game is lost, usually because one or two controversial calls were made by an official at a crucial point in the contest. In most instances the official was right, but some decisions were based on judgment and could be questioned. But assuming that they were wrong, were they the real cause of the loss? Did the players make any mistakes? How many? Were any coaching mistakes made? Were all the plays called by the coach the best against the defense faced at the time they were called? Were they all successful? Why not? The answers to these questions were in all probability more significant than was the officiating. One experienced football coach in Missouri used to tell his squad before the first game each season that he did not want to hear any complaints about the officiating, because he would see more mistakes by players made in the first play of the game than the officials would make during the entire game. His teams were perpetual contenders, and he was considered an outstanding coach for the more than forty years of his career.

This is the kind of attitude that should be instilled in our players. Blaming the officials for the loss of a game can be a form of rationalization and will not contribute to a team's success, or to the objectives of interscholastic athletics. Players should be taught to analyze their own mistakes and to attempt to avoid them in the future.

Mutual respect must be demonstrated. We would have valid reasons for objecting to an official making derogatory remarks to a player or criticizing our coaching. These are not his or her responsibilities, and any criticisms about players or coaches voiced in public would be unethical. Similarly, coaches should not criticize an official in public or display emotional objections to calls made during the game. A verbal exchange with an official is often followed by boos from the stands and has an adverse effect on the crowd's behavior.

Any criticism of an official should be made directly to him or her in private and after *emotions have cooled.* It should be constructive in nature and made without a show of feeling. In one such situation both the official and the coach criticized each other in a positive way. The official was told that he seemed to be anticipating fouls, which he acknowledged later after evaluating his own officiating and concluded that this fault had to be corrected to avoid any unfairness to any player. The coach was informed that his team seemed tired and that he might be driving his players too hard. He was further told that it did not appear that they were enjoying playing as much as they should. He shortened his practice periods and tried to put some fun into his coaching. The team soon showed considerable improvement, and he acknowledged on several occasions that the advice given by the official helped to improve his coaching. This is the kind of mutual respect that aids both parties. Public criticisms, particularly to the news media, accomplish nothing and cause a lack of respect for the accuser.

Coaches should not fraternize with officials. Coaches and officials should be friends but not *buddies.* Fraternization leads to skepticism on the part of other coaches and officials and can lead to such charges as engaging "homers." Maintaining a friendly but professional attitude is the best policy.

Coaches should try to help the officials. Officials will appreciate any attempts of a coach to help them do a better job. This is not to be interpreted as trying to tell them how a game should be called. One of the best ways to help the officiating look better is to coach players to compete without committing fouls. Ignoring fouling in practice is counterproductive. Players who are allowed to practice fouling daily will be prone to foul in games. Basketball players who are permitted to slap at the ball held or shot by an offensive player in practice foul more than those who are taught to extend the arm with a hook motion of the wrist in guarding an opponent. A game between two well-coached teams whose members have been taught good techniques of offensive and defensive play is much easier to officiate.

Officials make their best efforts when the environment for officiating is good. The coaches are the most strategic persons in this environment. The example they set and the sportsmanship they exhibit influence the atmosphere in which games are played. Keeping the spectators back from the sidelines avoids distraction that could interefere with officiating. Competent timers and scorers prevent sticky situations which must be decided by the officials. Coaches should be alert to and assist in protecting officials from the abuse of fans. Their position at games is not always an envious one. Fans are inclined to be almost 100 percent prejudiced: about 50 percent for the visiting team and at least that much for the home team. Coaches should be prompt to intercede when any of their fans show an inclination to physically abuse officials. In one unfortunate instance of an altercation between a fan and an official, which could have resulted in considerable violence, the football coach had his players surround the two to prevent any other fans from becoming involved. No one attempted to break through the line of padded and helmeted players, and the matter was quickly resolved. The fan was requested to appear before the board of education to show reason why he should not be barred from future games. He did not appear, but neither did he attend any more games that year.

There are usually enough officials, but not always enough competent officials. A number of officials retire each year, several because they are unable to develop the competency for satisfactory work. Some quit because of the discourtesies and abuse shown toward them. To maintain an adequate supply of satisfactory officials it is necessary for young, capable former athletes to be recruited. Officials' associations do some recruiting, but coaches are in the best position to evaluate what young persons have the necessary ability and to influence them to take up officiating. If each coach recruited one prospective official each year, an adequate supply of competent officials would be available.

A mutual understanding of rules is essential. Some controversies have occurred from the failure of the coach or the official to understand thoroughly the rules of the game and official interpretations of them. This is most often the result of the coach not keeping abreast of changes. Coaches and officials should attend the meetings on interpretations of rules sponsored by their state high school associations. Some state associations *require* both officials and coaches to attend these meetings.

The selection of officials can affect relationships. Officials should not be assigned by an officials' association without the approval of both schools. A coach must never attempt to blackball an official from working in conference games or in games in which his or her school is not participating. The coach has a right to approve officials for his or her school, but trying to go beyond that is an unethical practice. Neither should any special favoritism be shown in the selection process.

Courtesies should be extended to officials. Good relationships are fostered when common courtesies are extended to officials, for example, providing an appropriate private dressing room, reserving a convenient parking space, supplying towels, offering a soft drink at halftime, and assigning a student manager to meet and greet them and look after their needs.

Appreciation should be shown. If we take the time to think about what goes into the making of competent officials, we cannot help appreciating their efforts. The great majority of them do not become officials for financial benefits, and they will not last long if that is their reason. The fees received cannot be much of a stimulus. They enjoyed their experiences as athletes and the opportunity to continue to participate in sports is a source of satisfaction.

Much time and effort are required to develop into really competent officials. They must devote hours to the study of rules, take examinations, and attend meetings on rules. A great deal of travel is involved, and there is considerable interference with their family and social life. Yet they become dedicated to the cause of interscholastic athletics and play an important role in them. They deserve our appreciation, which should be expressed to them personally and publicly.

Players should be taught to respect and appreciate officials. The coach should make continual efforts to instill proper attitudes toward officials in his or her players. The best way is through the example he or she sets. The attitudes just discussed are as important for athletes as they are for coaches in establishing relationships which have a meaningful purpose in school athletics.

Summary

It is essential to the welfare of the school's interscholastic program that relationships be established among coaches to enable them to work harmoniously together. There must be mutual understanding and respect among head coaches. They must be committed to the established philosophy and objectives and work cooperatively in a professional manner.

Head coaches must treat assistant coaches as if they were *coaching them to become head coaches.* There must be mutual respect and loyalty. The establishment of clear policies will help maintain rapport.

Opposing coaches must be teated as friendly competitors. Professional practices and the extension of common courtesies will help to create good relationships with them. Occasions for misunderstandings and conflict should be avoided and ethical procedures followed should any occur.

Coaches' associations provide opportunities for broadening relationships when they are led well. They must have interscholastically worthwhile objectives, and coaches should take an active part in their work.

College coaches have an interest in the interscholastic program, which provides a source of talent for their teams. Problems caused by the recruiting of high school players can be avoided by following the standards established by the NCAA, which high school representatives should help to enforce. High school coaches should be prepared to give their athletes information that will help them make wise decisions in selecting the college they will attend.

The values of interscholastic games are enhanced when there is good coaching and good officiating, and the efforts of coaches and officials are more effective when proper relationships are established and maintained.

QUESTIONS AND TOPICS FOR STUDY AND DISCUSSION

1. How will a common commitment to the school's philosophy and objectives of interscholastic athletics provide for better cooperation among head coaches?
2. Assume that you are the head football coach and the basketball coach is urging one of your starting varsity players to come out for basketball practice before the football team plays its last game to avoid getting behind other players. Explain the steps you will take in dealing with this problem.
3. Select a sport you plan to coach and prepare a statement of policies you would want your assistant coaches to follow in working with you.
4. You have delegated the responsibility for coaching the junior varsity team to an assistant coach and a parent of one of the players tells you that he does not think the assistant knows enough about the sport to coach the team. Explain how you would handle this situation.
5. Assume that you are an assistant coach and with a group of school patrons when one of them becomes critical of your head coach. Discuss the procedure you would follow.
6. Enumerate ways of establishing rapport with the coaches of opposing schools.

7. Give reasons why it is important for opposing coaches to exhibit mutual respect at athletic games.
8. You receive an eligibility roster from the opposing school containing the names of players certified eligible for your game with that school two weeks hence; you note that it contains the name of a player who you know competed in a nonschool game in the same sport the previous weekend in violation of your state association's independent or limited team competition rule. Outline the steps you would take in dealing with this case.
9. Discuss some of the values of belonging to a coaches' association.
10. List some worthwhile projects for a coaches' association. Describe any others you think would be questionable.
11. Your team is dressed and has gone on the field or floor to warm up for the game when you notice a college coach talking to one of your senior players. Explain the steps you would take in this situation.
12. Enumerate the factors you plan to consider in the approval of officials.
13. How do you plan to build and maintain proper relationships with officials?
14. Explain how you plan to instill good attitudes toward officials in your players.

BIBLIOGRAPHY

Donnelly, Richard J. "Relationship Between Athletic Officials and Coaches." *Athletic Journal*, 37 (May 1957), 30-32, 53-57.

Engle, R. Lynn. "Sports Officiating—An Aid to Coaching. *The Physical Educator*, 33, No. 3 (October 1976), 129–30.

Gallon, Arthur J. *Coaching Ideas and Ideals*, pp. 37–58. Boston: Houghton Mifflin, 1974.

A Guide for the College-Bound Student Athlete. Shawnee Mission, Kan.: National Collegiate Athletic Association, 1978.

Kenig, Robert B. "Seven Guidelines for the Assistant Coach." *Scholastic Coach*, 43 (December 1973), 129–30.

Veller, Don. "Head Coach and Assistant Rapport." *Athletic Journal*, 48 (April 1968), 66–69, 77.

CHAPTER 9

State High School Associations

State high school associations and the National Federation of State High School Associations have played prominent roles in the development of interscholastic athletics as one of the finest youth programs in the world. These organizations provide leadership and services with which every high school coach should be familiar.

History

Collective control of interscholastic athletics evolved through three phases.[1] The formation of area school conferences and leagues through which some common eligibility requirements and other regulations were established initiated some improvements among member schools. Only bona fide students were permitted to play on school teams, and more control was exercised over interschool competition. The fact that various conferences and leagues did not have the same regulations became a source of problems when schools from different conferences met in competition. Leading school administrators came to the conclusion that a broader type of organization was essential to further eliminate abuses.

High school principals in Illinois, Michigan, Indiana, and Wisconsin were among the earliest to give attention to the formation of statewide organizations to regulate athletic competition among the high schools of their states.

The Michigan association originated from action taken at the December 1895 meeting of the Michigan State Teachers' Association, when a

[1] Charles E. Forsythe and Irvin A. Keller, *Administration of High School Athletics*, 6th ed. (Englewood Cliffs, N.J.: Prentice-Hall, 1977), pp. 3-5.

committee was appointed by the high school section to formulate rules and regulations for athletic games. An Inter-School Athletic Association had been formed in the spring of 1895 to formulate rules for a track meet held at Jackson, Michigan. The records from that time until 1909 are somewhat obscure, but the organization started in 1895 became the Michigan Interscholastic Athletic Association in 1910 by action taken by the Michigan Schoolmasters' Club.[2]

The Wisconsin association had a similar history. A committee was appointed in 1896 to recommend rules to regulate athletic contests between schools following a state track meet sponsored by the University of Wisconsin in 1895. The committee's recommendations were made in December 1897 and provided the initial framework for the Wisconsin Interscholastic Association.[3]

The Illinois High School Association stemmed from a rump meeting of principals at the Illinois State Teachers' Association meeting in 1898. The records are not clear, but they show that it was in existence by or before 1903.[4]

The Indiana association was formed in 1903, and by 1925 statewide athletic or activities associations had been formed in virtually all states.[5] The work of these organizations played a leading role in improving interscholastic athletics, which led to their universal acceptance as part of the total secondary school program.

The National Federation

Cooperative action through a state high school association proved to be the solution to many problems faced by individual schools and conferences. However, because regulations among the state associations were not all uniform and other problems of mutual concern emerged, executive officers of the early associations wanted an organization through which state associations could work cooperatively.

ORIGIN AND GROWTH

The following excerpt from the national federation's *Official Handbook* provides the best summary available of its origin and growth:

[2] Lewis L. Forsythe, *Athletics in Michigan High Schools—The First Hundred Years* (Englewood Cliffs, N.J.: Prentice-Hall, 1950), pp. 72-73.

[3] Forsythe, *Athletics in Michigan High Schools*, p. 73.

[4] Charles W. Whitten, *Interscholastics—A Discussion of Interscholastic Contests* (Bloomington: Illinois High School Association, 1950), pp. 4-5.

[5] Forsythe and Keller, *Administration of High School Athletics*, pp. 48-49.

The national organization had its beginning in a meeting at Chicago on May 14, 1920. L. W. Smith, secretary of the Illinois High School Athletic Association, issued invitations to neighboring states and state association representatives came from Illinois, Indiana, Iowa, Michigan and Wisconsin. The primary purpose of the meeting was to discuss problems which had resulted from high school contests which were organized by colleges and universities or by other clubs or promoters. In many cases little attention was paid to the eligibility rules of the high school associations or to other high school group regulations and chaotic conditions had developed. At this first meeting it was decided that the welfare of the high schools required a more active part in the control of such athletic activities be exercised by the high school men through the state associations, and this control necessitated the formation of a national organization. A constitution and by-laws were adopted and the group decided on the name "Midwest Federation of State High School Athletic Associations." Principal George Edward Marshall, Davenport, Iowa, was elected President and Principal L. W. Smith of Joliet, Illinois, was elected Secretary-Treasurer.

In 1921, four states, Illinois, Iowa, Michigan and Wisconsin continued their interest and became charter members through formal ratification of the constitution. Largely due to their efforts, the national organization grew during the early years.

In 1922 the Chicago annual meeting was attended by representatives from 11 states, and the name of the National Federation of State High School Athletic Associations was adopted. A number of college and university representatives who attended the meeting expressed sympathy for and interest in the efforts to introduce a high degree of order in the regulation of interscholastic contests.

Since that time the National Federation has had a healthy growth to its present nationwide membership. By 1940 a national office with a full-time executive staff became necessary and such office was established in September of that year.[6]

In addition to the fifty state members, eight interscholastic associations from the Canadian provinces of Alberta, British Columbia, Manitoba, New Brunswick, Nova Scotia, Ontario, Prince Edward Island, and Saskatchewan hold affiliated memberships.

From 1920 to 1970 the national federation's functions were limited to interscholastic athletics, although by the last year the majority of its member state associations were *activities associations*, which were responsible for both athletic and nonathletic activities in their various states. The functions of the national federation were expanded by an amendment to its constitution, and its name changed from the National Federation of State High School Athletic Associations to the National Federation of State High School Associations. It now has responsibilities in both athletic and nonathletic interscholastic activities.

The office of the national federation was in Chicago, Illinois, for

[6]*Official Handbook* (Kansas City, Mo.: National Federation of State High School Associations, 1977-78), p. 6.

many years, but it was moved to Elgin, Illinois, in 1970-1971. A new office building was completed and the headquarters moved in 1979 to a location near the International Airport in Kansas City, Missouri.

Services of Associations

State high school associations provide many valuable services to their member schools. The earliest service, and still one of the most important, was the elimination of abuses and the establishment of standards in athletic competition.

The functions of high school associations can be understood by examining the objectives contained in their constitutions. Those of the Missouri association are a good example.

ARTICLE II—OBJECTIVES

Section 1. The Missouri State High School Activities Association is a voluntary, nonprofit, educational association of junior and senior high schools. Through it they work cooperatively in adopting standards for supervising and regulating those interscholastic activities and contests that may be delegated by the member schools to the jurisdiction of the Association.

Section 2. Stated more specifically, the general objectives of the Association include:

a. To ensure that interscholastic activities shall remain an integral part of the secondary educational program which will provide opportunities for youth to acquire worthwhile knowledge, skills, and proper emotional patterns.

b. To promote the educational values inherent in interscholastic activities which will contribute to the accepted aims of education.

c. To develop standards for the approval and direction of interscholastic activities and contests.

d. To formulate minimum uniform and equitable standards of eligibility that must be met by students to attain the privilege of representing their schools in interscholastic activities.

e. To develop standards to be met by schools participating in interscholastic activities under the sponsorship of the Association.

f. To avoid interference with the educational program of the school and to prevent exploitation of high school youth and the programs of member schools by special interest groups.

g. To foster a cooperative spirit and good sportsmanship on the part of school representatives, school patrons, and students.

h. To provide means of evaluating and controlling local, state, and national contests affecting secondary schools initiated by firms, organizations, and institutions outside organized educational agencies.

i. To develop standards of officiating and adjudicating to ensure greater statewide consistency and quality.[7]

[7]*Fiftieth Annual Handbook* (Columbia: Missouri State High School Activities Association, 1978), p. 11.

Among the many specific services state associations perform are the planning and administering of district and state contests, registering officials for interscholastic games, providing rules books for interscholastic sports, sponsoring meetings on interpretation of rules for coaches and officials, making films available for teaching and interpreting rules, printing forms necessary in the administration of the school's interscholastic program, providing group catastrophe accident insurance, and publishing official handbooks, journals, and special bulletins.

Each of us should study carefully the official handbook of our association. It is important to understand the standards of eligibility for players and the regulations schools must follow, which will help to prevent inadvertent violations that could embarrass us and our schools. These standards and regulations have been adopted cooperatively by the schools through the association and become the standards and regulations of each of our schools by virtue of their membership. The state high school association is not a separate entity that thrusts regulations on the schools. It is a voluntary association of schools which agree to uphold the same common minimum standards and regulations in their interscholastic programs.

Services of the National Federation

As its name implies, this is a *federation* of state high school associations, and each retains autonomy. Its authority is limited to making recommendations for each member association to consider. Its meetings provide a means of pooling the knowledge and judgment of leading high school athletic administrators, almost all of whom were formerly coaches, which supplies capable leadership in the development of recommendations for improving interscholastic athletics.

The role of the national federation is appreciated more when we understand the many services it offers. Its original functions of obtaining greater uniformity of standards among state associations and helping to prevent the exploitation of high school athletes and athletic programs are still important, but the numerous aids it provides to state associations, their member schools, athletic administrators, and coaches, which have increased tremendously over the years, have made it a real service organization. Its services and materials, which are made available through its member state associations, benefit the students in some 22,000 high schools in the United States. Among its services are the following:

1. *A program for writing rules.* Collegiate rules with some modifications were used for high school games for many years, but

representatives of the national federation and state high school associations concluded that rules could be better adapted to high school players and to the philosophy and objectives of interscholastic athletics. The program was initiated with the first *Official Interscholastic Football Rules Book* published in 1930.[8] From this beginning, the program has been expanded over the years until the national federation now publishes rules books for baseball, basketball, football, field hockey, gymnastics, soccer, softball, swimming and diving, track and field, volleyball, and wrestling. Supplementary materials are published in the form of case books, giving play situations and official rulings on them; officials' manuals; basketball and football handbooks for players, coaches, and officials; examinations of rules; and others.[9] Approximately two and one-half million copies of these publications are distributed annually.

The committees appointed to formulate and write the rules are comprised predominantly of some of the best high school coaches in the nation, which helps to assure that they are appropriate to the age and experience of high school athletes.[10]

2. *Keeping of national high school records.* A record book is published by the national federation which contains the winning teams of the various state high school tournaments, individual national marks set by high school athletes, and other records of interest to coaches. These records bring recognition to boys and girls whose performances are exceptional and help to stimulate interest in interscholastic competition.[11]

3. *Audio-Visual Aids.*[12] The films on teaching and rules are of great assistance in coaching. Coaches who wish to use any of the films should contact their state high school association.

4. *Legal Aid Pact.* A bibliography, including a synopsis of all known court cases in the United States related to interscholastic athletics, is compiled by the national federation and provided to state high school associations; this has proved to be an extremely valuable aid to their attorneys. Cases are grouped by alphabetically arranged topics and provide a ready reference in defenses against suits involving state associations and their member schools, which have increased significantly. This service also

[8] *National Federation Official Handbook*, p. 22.

[9] *Ibid.*, pp. 22-23.

[10] *Ibid.*, pp. 92-99.

[11] *Ibid.*, p. 18.

[12] *Ibid.*, p. 24.

helps state associations to reevaluate their standards and regulations and to amend them so that they will meet legal tests.

5. *Press Service.* Almost all state high school associations publish a monthly journal or bulletin. A National Federation Press Service supplies each state association with up-to-date information, announcements, data, current articles, and other material, which may be reprinted without special permission simply by using proper credit lines. This channel of communication makes it possible for coaches to keep abreast of developments at the national level.

Continual effort is exerted toward improving interscholastic sports through special projects and other activities. Various experiments are conducted through the National Federation office and rules committees, and these are evaluated by coaches, officials, and athletic administrators. Questionnaires are frequently used to obtain opinions regarding changes and improvements. Experiments in modifications of rules by state high school associations are also authorized. Reports are submitted to the national federation and referred to the proper committee for consideration. Some important changes have been made through these procedures.[13]

Careful attention is given to the health and safety of athletes through studies of the causes of injuries and ways to prevent them. Specifications for player equipment are included in the rules when considered necessary. For example, wearing the mouthpiece and facemask was made mandatory after experimentation and study showed they were essential in preventing dental injuries. Research by the national federation and state high school associations has been instrumental in establishing athletic accident insurance coverage, and catastrophe plans have been adopted by several state associations to cover the more serious injuries. The Wisconsin association was one of the leaders in this field.[14]

A *National Operating Committee on Standards for Athletic Equipment* was formed in 1970 through the cooperation of the National Federation, the Athletic Goods Manufacturers Association, the American College Health Association, the National Athletic Trainers Association, the National Collegiate Athletic Association, and the National Junior College Athletic Association. This committee sponsors research and experimentation and testing at Wayne University to improve the safety features of athletic equipment.[15]

[13] *Ibid.*, p. 25.

[14] *Ibid.*, pp. 25-26.

[15] *Ibid.*, pp. 26-28.

The *Official Handbook* is the best source of information regarding the National Federation's services and its current philiosophy and objectives.

Summary

The state high school association and the National Federation of State High School Associations were born out of necessity to protect and to improve the high school interscholastic programs. As a result of their collective efforts, interscholastic athletics evolved to become an important part of secondary education and the profession of high school coaching became significant.

QUESTIONS AND TOPICS FOR STUDY AND DISCUSSION

1. Describe the conditions that existed in interscholastic athletic competition before the formation of state high school associations.
2. Through what three phases did collective control of interscholastic athletics evolve?
3. Why was the National Federation of State High School Associations formed?
4. Discuss the functions of state high school associations.
5. Explain the services of state high school associations that help the coach.
6. Enumerate the services of the national federation that are important to interscholastic athletics and valuable aids to coaches.
7. Why are the playing rules developed by the national federation well adapted to the maturity of junior and senior high school athletes and to the philosophy and objectives of interscholastic athletics?
8. Explain benefits to high school athletes through the national federation and its member state associations that would otherwise be difficult to provide.
9. What is the significance of the National Operating Committee on Standards for Athletic Equipment?
10. Why do state high school associations and the national federation warrant the support of coaches?

BIBLIOGRAPHY

Forsythe, Charles E., and Irvin A. Keller. *Administration of High School Athletics*, 6th ed., pp. 3-5, 48-49. Englewood Cliffs, N.J.: Prentice-Hall, 1977.

Fiftieth Annual Handbook, p. 11. Columbia: Missouri State High School Activities Association, 1978.

Forsythe, Lewis L. *Athletics in Michigan High Schools—The First Hundred Years*, pp. 72-73. Englewood Cliffs, N.J.: Prentice-Hall, 1950.

Official Handbook, pp. 6, 22-28, 92-99. Kansas City, Mo.: National Federation of State High School Associations, 1977-78.

CHAPTER 10

The Health and Safety of Athletes

Successful high school coaches have an interest in the personal welfare of each athlete, which includes his or her health and safety. Such factors are involved as eating habits, conditioning, safety precautions, equipment, sanitation, and the prevention and care of injuries. It is the purpose of this chapter to examine practical ways of promoting the elements of health and safety essential to athletes' physical and mental welfare.

Proper Nutrition

All state high school associations require a player to have a physical examination showing that he or she is physically fit to participate in interscholastic athletics. Nutrition plays an important part in physical fitness and in its maintenance. Coaches cannot be expected to be expert nutritionists, but they should have sufficient knowledge to understand the nutritional needs of their students and to so advise them.

Coaches vary in the attention they give to the dietary habits of their players. Some will go so far as to attempt to prescribe diets; others take the position that athletes should eat what they are used to, because family meals will differ and too much insistence on changing diets can upset athletes emotionally and have adverse effects. A few coaches will pay no attention to nutritional needs, which can be seen as shirking their responsibilities to their players. Those coaches who try to control diets may have been influenced by their experience at athletic training tables in college, but this practice is not possible in high school athletics and is generally prohibited. A happy medium is the best procedure for high school coaches to follow. They should not attempt to dictate, nor to ignore, the dietary habits of their players, but the strategic position they occupy can enable them tactfully and effectively to influence them.

It is customary for high schools to provide meals for players away from home. Coaches follow two general procedures in furnishing such meals. A number will arrange a menu for all athletes, but others have found this to be unsatisfactory because of the probability that some players will not like some of the food. These coaches will tell their players the amount that can be spent on a meal and allow them to do their own ordering; they will also advise them on the type of food that should be included or not included. The disadvantage of this procedure is that it takes longer to order and prepare the meals. The best alternative if time is a problem is to find out foods that players do not like, or cannot eat, and arrange a menu in advance. All meals, either at home or away, should be eaten from three to four hours before game time. The wisest procedure is the one that appears to be the most appropriate for the players concerned.

INFLUENCING ATTITUDES TOWARD DIET

Children develop their eating habits by eating what is on the family table. Whether they receive proper nutrition depends on the education of their parents. Coaches can do little about the dietary knowledge of parents directly, but they can have some influence on the attitudes of athletes by providing relevant information. Students frequently snack between meals, which can be beneficial to teenage boys and girls engaging in strenuous physical activities, and they can be encouraged to choose snacks that will provide good supplements to their daily meals.

A positive approach should be used. Point out that one of the principal reasons children, in general, grow to be larger adults than their parents is a better diet during their childhood. If players note how they feel when they are hungry, after they overeat, and when they eat a good balanced meal, they will become conscious of the effects of good eating habits.

NUTRITION AND DIET

Each coach should have enough knowledge of basic nutritional needs to give athletes fundamental information. They should realize that proper nutrition will help them reach their maximum performance in sports.

The best source of necessary nutrients, vitamins, and minerals is natural foods. Common foods contain an ample supply of vitamins A, B, C, and D and the required minerals for good health. Supplementary vitamins and minerals commonly advertised are not needed and should be taken only upon the advice of a physician.

A balanced daily diet is important. There is a variety of foods available to meet good daily requirements. Students should eat three meals a day. They are prone to skip breakfast, which is an important meal and should contain approximately one-third of an individual's daily nutritional needs. Snacks between meals should be selected wisely. High school students, particularly athletes, should learn to eat fruits and other snacks which will supply better and more varied supplementary nutrition than sweets.

The United States Department of Agriculture suggests a simple and practical approach to a good daily diet in its Daily Food Guide for Fitness.[1] There are four basic food groups: meats, vegetables and fruits, breads and cereals, and milk. Proper selection of foods from these foods will supply a good daily diet.

It is recommended that two or more servings should be provided from the meat group, which includes beef, veal, pork, lamb, poultry, fish, eggs, dry beans, dry peas, and nuts.

Four or more servings are suggested from the vegetable and fruit group, including a citrus fruit or a vegetable such as tomatoes or raw cabbage which are good sources of vitamin C, a dark green or deep yellow vegetable, and other vegetables and fruits, including potatoes.

Four or more servings should be consumed from the bread and cereal group containing whole grain, enriched, or restored vitamins and minerals.

Other foods may be added as necessary to make up meals. It is not difficult to plan meals in accord with this daily food guide, nor for athletes to select servings that will meet their needs. The number of servings are based on average needs, and the amount consumed will vary with the age, size, and physical activities of individuals.

Caloric needs increase during periods of strenuous physical activity. The calorie is the unit of heat required by the body to produce energy. According to the United States Department of Agriculture the average caloric needs of teenagers are as follows:[2]

For boys 13 to 15 years of age......................... 3,100 calories
For girls 13 to 15 years of age .... 2,400 calories
For boys 16 to 19 years of age........................ 3,600 calories
For girls 16 to 19 years of age .... 3,100 calories

Athletes will require more calories than this because of the strenuous activity inherent in daily practice or competition. Most strenuous athletic activity will use an average of 390 calories per hour, and football

[1] *Food—The Yearbook of Agriculture* (Washington, D.C.: United States Department of Agriculture, 1959), p. 626.

[2] *Ibid.*, p. 102.

uses up to 400 per hour.[3] Thus athletes must eat more during the season to maintain their caloric needs. All good books on nutrition have charts showing the number of calories various foods contain. A chart posted in the gymnasium or dressing room will help athletes to know their needs and the number of calories they are consuming.

METHODS FOR TEACHING NUTRITION

It is impractical for coaches to devote all the time they would like to teaching nutrition and other matters related to athletics, which causes some to neglect important responsibilities. One or two short lectures at the beginning of the season supplemented by clippings and charts on a bulletin board can provide athletes with much information about nutrition. Weight charts showing weights at the beginning of the season and at selected intervals help indirectly to stimulate continued interest in diet, particularly if samples of good daily menus are posted. The bulletin board is a valuable visual aid and should be used for a variety of purposes.

MAKING WEIGHT IN WRESTLING

Many school administrators, physicians, and coaches consider the making of weight in wrestling to be a problem that can cause a lack of nutrition. The desire of wrestlers to compete in a lower weight class, because of what they consider an advantage in competition, causes many to go on diets, especially crash diets. Sweating off weight and not drinking for a period of time before weigh-ins are other practices that can cause serious problems resulting from dehydration. Coaches should be alert to any possible dangers to the health of high school wrestlers, although there is little or no scientific evidence concerning the harmful effects from properly making weight.[4] One of the best sources of information on wrestling is the booklet, *What Research Tells the Coach About Wrestling*, published by the American Association for Health, Physical Education, and Recreation.

Athletes can achieve some weight loss, which varies with the age, size, and build of the wrestler, without danger and even with some benefits when kept within reason. Studies show that there are no harmful effects on a wrestler's strength and ability when the loss is kept under approximately 10 percent.[5]

[3] Beulah Tannenbaum and Myra Stillman, *Understand Food—The Chemistry of Nutrition* (New York: McGraw-Hill, 1962), pp. 173-74.

[4] *What Research Tells the Coach About Wrestling* (Washington, D.C.: American Association for Health, Physical Education, and Recreation, 1964), p. 42.

[5] *Ibid.*

There is concern that weight loss from reduced food consumption can result in an insufficient supply of vitamins and minerals, which are extremely important to physical growth and development.[6] All crash diets accompanied by extra salt to secure dehydration are dangerous and should be condemned.

The time of the weigh-in can indirectly cause nutritional problems. It is often held late in the afternoon or early evening. To make weight, wrestlers may skip meals that day until they have weighed in, but the weigh-in may be too near the time of competition to allow a hearty meal. Some wrestlers have become sick during competition from eating too near the time of the match, when the food was not sufficiently digested. Athletes in all sports should eat their last meal at least three hours before competition starts. Whenever possible, the time of the weigh-in should be adjusted to allow some nutritional intake before the match.

The desire of some wrestlers to gain an advantage by reducing weight and qualifying for a lower weight class causes the nutritional concerns. If wrestling is to remain a respected high school sport, coaches must give careful attention to protecting the health of their athletes. Several state high school associations have adopted regulations to help in this matter. Having a physician certify the weight class in which a wrestler should wrestle is the best procedure, but this plan is difficult and expensive to administer. The wrestling coach is in the most strategic position to help resolve the problem satisfactorily.

Physical Conditioning

The fact that an athlete has had a physical examination and is certified fit by a physician does not mean that he or she is ready for strenuous athletic practice and competition. It simply means that the individual is healthy and devoid of any physiological weaknesses which might contribute to health hazards. To protect and improve health and to prepare for athletic activity require adequate conditioning for a minimum of three weeks prior to competition. State high school associations have regulations requiring a specified number of days of practice before competition in an effort to see that athletes are physically conditioned. Several require approximately a week of football practice without pads as a preventive measure against heat exhaustion.

Only a relatively small number of high school coaches will have the well-equipped training rooms found in college athletic departments. Frequently the only training room is the gymnasium, and many high schools cannot afford expensive training equipment. The coach must

[6]*Ibid.*, p. 43.

do the best he or she can with what is available and use initiative in improvising. Different sized food cans filled with concrete can simulate light weights and dumbbells. Homemade chinning bars and climbing ropes can be used for pull-ups. Calisthenics can be very effective in conditioning, and various isometric, isotonic, and isokinetic exercises can be devised that do not require expensive equipment.

PURPOSEFUL EXERCISE

The effectiveness of conditioning exercises will depend on the coach's knowledge of the muscles and joints used in particular skills. A fundamental knowledge of kinesiology can be very helpful in the selection of appropriate exercises for specific purposes.

The basic elements of conditioning include the improvement of strength, flexibility, agility, and endurance. The muscles, joints, and respiratory and cardiovascular systems (cardiorespiratory) must be appropriately exercised. The exercises should be adapted to the individual differences in the needs of athletes and to the sports in which they participate. The needs of tennis players are much different from those of football players, as are those of a tall, uncoordinated basketball player compared to a small, agile one.

Muscles work in groups, but some are stressed more than others in performing a skill. Strength can be built in the upper limbs (deltoid, triceps brachii, and biceps brachii), through push-ups, pull-ups, pulling, selected isometric exercises, and others.[7]

Leg presses, leg curls, leg pulls, and half squat (the full squat is not recommended) are helpful in building strength in the lower limbs.[8]

The back and abdominal muscles can be exercised by sit-ups, lateral flexions, and lying face down with one's hands behind the head and raising the head and shoulders.[9]

Flexibility can be increased by calisthenics, which stretch the muscles and flex the joints in the different parts of the body. A variety of exercises should be used including flexions, rotations, extensions, abductions (movement away from the midline of the body), and adductions (movement toward the midline). These movements are particularly important in exercising the joints in the hips, arms, legs, and cervix.[10] Developing flexibility is important in sports, particularly those involving numerous joint movements, such as swimming and basketball.

[7] Gene A. Logan and Wayne C. McKinney, *Kinesiology* (Wm. C. Brown Company, 1972), pp. 118-46.

[8] *Ibid.*, pp. 73-102.

[9] *Ibid.*, pp. 73-116.

[10] *Ibid.*, pp. 7-45.

Agility involves the ability to change directions, which requires both quickness and strength. No special equipment is needed for agility exercises. Crab drills (running on all four hands and feet); jumping forward and backward over dummies or similar objects; and directional drills in which players move right, left, forward, and backward on command are excellent agility drills for football. Directional drills in a crouched position with the weight on the balls of the feet is an example of a good exercise for basketball and many other sports. Quickness should be emphasized in most of these drills.

Endurance is developed through all types of exercises by extending the periods and increasing the physical requirements. Running is recognized as an excellent builder of endurance, especially cardiorespiratory endurance. Careful attention should be given to the gradual development of conditioning. Short rest periods will help to prevent injuries and overfatigue. Coaches must consider what is necessary, effective, and reasonable in developing endurance conditioning programs.

Many coaches utilize circuit training drills, which include exercises with a variety of purposes. Each of approximately eight stations provide an exercise with a specific purpose related to a particular sport. Players rotate individually through the exercises, spending a short time at each. An example of circuit training for conditioning in basketball could be (1) jumping rope; (2) practicing lay-ups, the shooter retrieving his or her own ball as quickly as possible to improve agility; (3) dribbling, involving quick starts, stops, and changes in direction; (4) tapping the ball against a wall and keeping it high by jumping as high as possible; (5) jump-shooting over the extended arms of a stationary player and "knifing" around the player to rebound or retrieve the shot (excellent drill to improve offensive rebounding); (6) defensive sliding: right, left, forward, and backward; (7) air sliding toward the basket, covering as much distance as possible; and (8) tapping the backboard as high as possible. Appropriate circuit training can be devised for any sport to exercise different parts of the body and improve skills.

The knee and the ankle are vulnerable joints in sports. Although the knee is considered one of the strongest joints in the body, it is also one of the most frequently injured.[11] It carries a lot of stress and is in numerous vulnerable positions. Special equipment such as knee pads and taping are used to help prevent injuries, and provisions in the football rules have been added to prevent piling on and blocking from the blind side, but knee injuries still occur in all sports.

Exercises to strengthen the muscles which support the knee—the calf, thigh, and hamstring muscles—can help it to withstand the stresses it receives. Knee flexions using weights can be very effective.

[11] *Tips on Athletic Training, VIII* (Chicago: American Medical Association, 1966), p. 16.

The ankle is a common point of injury in all sports. It is exercised in running and walking, but too many coaches fail to prescribe special exercises for the muscles which support it. Inverting, everting, and flexing the foot upward and downward several times each day will help strengthen these muscles.

Ankle sprains are one of the most common injuries in athletics and are more likely to happen in practices than in games (because more time is spent in practices). A doctor may be present at games but is seldom in attendance during practices. Preferably, an athletic trainer should be available to administer first aid, but very few high schools have qualified trainers to serve in this capacity, and seldom is one present or available immediately. Thus the coach must have sufficient knowledge of the steps to take when an ankle injury occurs. First, the shoe should be carefully removed and an ice pack placed over the injury, applying pressure by using an elastic wrap, to help keep down the swelling. The athlete should be referred to a physician for examination and x-rays to make certain there are no fractures. Ice or ice water baths are the best treatments during the first forty-eight hours, after which contrasting baths are advisable if swelling continues. The ankle must be acclimated gradually after a sprain. Other sprains can be treated in a similar manner.

Athletes must be acclimated to hot weather.[12] Sports such as football and baseball often involve practice and competition in hot and humid weather, which can result in heat fatigue, heat exhaustion, or heat stroke.

Heat fatigue is caused by the loss of salt and water from excessive sweating. It is the least serious of the three illnesses, but it does affect the physical alertness of the athlete and makes her or him more susceptible to injury. Advising athletes to use extra salt on their foods and supplying drinking water during practices and games can prevent heat fatigue and the other two heat illnesses. Salt tablets are not recommended because of the stomach irritation they can cause. It is far better to add salt to the drinking water at practices, using a ratio of one teaspoon of salt to six quarts of water.[13]

Heat exhaustion occurs from an excessive depletion of salt and water, and heat stroke results from a malfunctioning of the sweating processes.

Athletes should be acclimated to hot weather in graduated steps. The following are recommendations of the Committee on the Medical Aspects of Sports of the American Medical Association for preventing heat illnesses in athletes during hot weather:

[12]*Ibid.*, p. 6.

[13]*Ibid.*, p. 7.

1. Require a careful medical history and checkup prior to the beginning of practice.
2. Schedule workouts during cooler morning and early evening hours.
3. Acclimate athletes to hot-weather activity by carefully graduated practice schedules.
4. Provide rest periods of 15 to 30 minutes during workouts of an hour or more.
5. Supply clothing that is white to reflect heat, brief, loose, and comfortable to permit heat escape, and permeable to moisture to allow heat loss via sweat.
6. Furnish extra salt and water in recommended amounts.
7. Watch athletes carefully for signs of trouble, particularly the determined athlete who may not report discomfort.
8. Remember that temperature and humidity, not the sun, are the crucial factors. Measuring the relative humidity by use of a sling psychrometer on the field is advantageous in this regard. Heat exhaustion and heat stroke can occur in the shade.
9. Know what to do in case of emergency, including immediate first aid practices and pre-arranged procedures for obtaining medical care.[14]

PRESEASON CONDITIONING

The benefits of keeping physically fit should be impressed upon athletes and encouraged during off-seasons. Physical fitness cannot be stored and can be maintained only through exercise. As coaches, we are in a position to influence attitudes toward fitness and the importance of continuing exercise to maintain it in later life, which should be one of the ultimate objectives of interscholastic athletics.

Special attention should be given to what is commonly called preseason conditioning, which involves individual exercise and effort. Most state high school associations do not permit conditioning activities under the supervision of the coach before the first permissible practice date, but they will allow coaches to give suggestions to individual athletes to follow in conditioning themselves. The last week of the season is an appropriate time to provide an outline of recommended activities and exercises for the off-season, particularly during the two or three weeks before the beginning of the next practice season.

It is a good procedure to give an outline to each player and any others who plan to come out for the sport the following season. The outline should contain the reasons for the suggested activities, proposed exercises, and recommended time schedules. Athletes should be encouraged to participate in other sports during the off-season, which will provide exercise and help to avoid staleness that sometimes results

[14]*Ibid.*, pp. 7–8.

from year-round participation in a single sport. Coaches must be certain that the suggested exercises are safe and can be performed without their supervision. Strenuous exercises which might be dangerous without supervision should be delayed until practice starts. Running should be strongly recommended. Besides conditioning muscles, it provides one of the best means of conditioning the cardiorespiratory system. The best results will occur from preseason conditioning when the activities selected are adapted to the sport involved.

EARLY SEASON CONDITIONING

Although athletes may appear to be in good physical condition when they report for practice, additional conditioning should be provided before they engage in any strenuous activities. The amount and kind will vary with individual sports. They should be graduated until it is certain that the players are physically fit for the type of activity involved in the practice. Rest periods are a precaution against overexertion and possible injury.

Some coaches devise exercises adapted to the skills. Basketball coaches will have their squad members shuffle backward, forward, and sideways in a crouched position, the weight on the balls of the feet and the legs not crossed to strengthen leg muscles and to prepare them for movements on defense. Similarly adapted exercises can be used in other sports. Sufficient warm-up exercises are important before more strenuous ones are used. Running is commonly used, but light exercising of the arms, back, and abdominal muscles is also advisable.

Diagnostic and remedial teaching is important in supervising conditioning. Athletes who have any noted weaknesses should spend extra time on exercises that strengthen and improve the flexibility of the muscles and joints involved.

The Coach's Responsibilities

Proper attention to the safety of athletes is extremely important in the administration of the school's athletic program. Failure reasonably to provide for their safety can bring legal suits against coaches and school administrations. More important is protecting the physical welfare of the students. It is recommended that each school have an overall established school safety program, with the principal or someone designated by him or her as the coordinator. This program should include the following:

1. The adoption of safety policies to guide coaches and players.
2. Protective and safe athletic equipment.

3. Proper medical supervision.
4. The services of an athletic trainer.
5. Emergency policies and procedures.
6. Facilities devoid of any physical hazards.
7. Sanitation policies.
8. Athletic accident insurance for players.

The coach will be the person who makes certain that the safety policies and other phases of the safety program are implemented in his or her sport. There must be strict adherence by coaches and athletes to all policies and safety regulations adopted by the school, which must be clearly understood. If additional safety measures or policies are needed, they should be reported promptly to the athletic administrator together with any recommendations.

PRUDENT JUDGMENT

Some degree of judgment must be exercised in all phases of coaching, which include those pertaining to the safety of players. Some of these will be major decisions, such as the first step in the care of a player who appears to be seriously injured in practice. Others may appear to be minor; but some of them may be much more serious than they are thought to be and can have far-reaching complications. Health and safety are interrelated, and judgments and advice regarding nutrition and conditioning can involve safety.

For example, a player is absent from school in the forenoon, but reports for the afternoon session. He or she gives illness as the reason for absence, but contends that he or she is well enough to compete in the game scheduled that evening. Should that student be allowed to compete? What decision would you make if you were the coach? Suppose you took the player's word that he or she was well enough to play, and you allowed the player to compete. The next day he or she is ill again and develops a case of pneumonia. Could you be guilty of negligence? Such matters should be considered in making decisions that may at the time appear to be minor.

It is unwise to allow an athlete to practice or to play in a game when he or she was absent for any part of the day because of illness. *To be on the safe side*, the player who wants to play or practice on a date he or she was absent from school should be required to get a physician's permission to participate. A player should not be allowed to return to practice after any serious illness until certified to do so by a physician. It should always be remembered that regardless of the player's ability and the importance of the game, nothing is as important as the health of an athlete.

The element of safety must enter into the selection of exercises for conditioning. Hazardous or controversial exercises must be avoided. The duck waddle was once thought by a number of coaches to be a good exercise to strengthen the knee. Now it is considered one to be avoided. With the inclination of the public to seek court action for injuries, one's judgment must be exercised. The best general guideline to follow in making decisions related to athletic safety is to do what a reasonable and prudent person would do under the same circumstances.

SAFETY POLICIES

Policies regarding the safety of athletes should be established before any accidents occur. The establishment of the policies in itself helps to make coaches and players safety-conscious. One of the best procedures for formulating general safety policies is through cooperative action of the athletic administrator and coaches of the various sports. Because of the differences in the physical hazards inherent in different sports, coaches should be permitted to establish additional policies for their athletes as long as they are not in conflict with general policies. If the school does not have any official policies, it is advisable for the coach to develop policies considered essential and to have them approved by the school administration. Involving players in their formulation can help to create safety consciousness.

The establishment of clearly understood transportation policies is of vital importance because of the personal liability that could be incurred. The best arrangement is the use of school-owned buses or common carriers to transport the players. The coach should always be certain that all vehicles carrying athletes are fully insured and that he or she has a thorough knowledge of the insurance laws of the particular state. These differ from state to state, and in some states the insurance normally carried on automobiles does not always include coverage when the vehicle is used as a common carrier. Parental permission should be obtained for all out-of-town trips, and parents should be informed of the time the team is expected to return. Allowing athletes to drive automobiles should be avoided unless they are accompanied by parents. If buses are used, all athletes should be required to ride on them unless they have special permission to ride with their parents. Definite rules should be formulated to govern behavior while en route and at the site of the contest.

SAFETY GUIDELINES

Important in the safety of athletes are their own attitudes, actions, and judgments. Alertness to dangers and personal precautions help to prevent injuries. Safety policies for players can be established in the form of safety guidelines. The term *guidelines* often has a better effect than *policies*, which students frequently consider restrictive. The following is an example of the type of guideline that can be formulated for the athletes:

1. Engage in adequate preseason conditioning to be physically fit for the official opening of the practice season.
2. Have a physical examination and make certain the physician certifies you physically fit before the practice season and before you engage in any strenuous activity during preseason conditioning.
3. Make certain that any exercises you do have the approval of your coach.
4. Report immediately to your coach if you feel like you are becoming fatigued or ill or have any unusual feeling.
5. Report any injury, although minor, promptly to your coach.
6. Make certain that your equipment fits you properly and inform your coach if it does not.
7. Warm up adequately before engaging in any strenuous activity.
8. Be alert to any physical hazards which might exist or develop, such as unnecessary collisions with other players in practices or games.
9. Be alert to the actions of others that could accidentally injure you.
10. Follow proper sanitation practices.
11. If you are a swimmer, avoid hyperventilation.
12. Comply strictly with game rules related to safety to avoid injuring yourself and others.
13. Do not compete without athletic accident insurance.
14. Practice good eating habits and get plenty of rest.
15. Adhere to all school safety policies.

This safety precautions guideline can be adapted to various sports.

SAFETY EQUIPMENT

Athletic equipment can be classified into three categories: player equipment, playing equipment, and training equipment. Player equipment consists of that which is worn by the participant. Playing equipment comprises the materials essential to the game, such as bats, balls, hurdles, vaulting poles, and so on. Exercise bars, weights, and other things needed in conditioning make up the training equipment.

Adequate protective equipment must be provided in all contact sports and is particularly significant in football. Most of this type is furnished by the school. The equipment ordered should be of good quality and provide maximum protection to the player. Materials tested by the National Operating Committee on Standards for Athletic Equipment (NOCSAE) will meet the necessary requirements (see page 138) and relieve the coach and athletic administrator of much of the responsibility for meeting safety standards. Procedures for testing used football helmets have been established, and information can be obtained by writing NOCSAE at Wayne State University in Detroit, Michigan. Many reputable suppliers of athletic goods can also provide the needed information, and some will help make the necessary arrangements for retesting. All equipment bearing the NOCSAE seal can be considered to provide adequate protection, and football helmets carrying this seal are now required under the rules.

If the school purchases athletic equipment through a bidding process, the coach must specify the manufacturer's number of the desired article on the requisition form to make certain that the bid accepted will provide the desired quality and safety features. Coaches are asked to submit requisitions to the athletic administrator for the equipment needed, which makes it essential to keep an inventory showing the equipment on hand, its condition, and new equipment required. Figures 10-1 and 10-2 are examples of simple requisition and inventory of equipment forms.

Proper attention should be given to the fit of the equipment. This is of particular importance with football helmets and pads, but it is also important with shoes and other equipment in different sports. Shoes should be comfortable and good socks should be worn to avoid blisters, which are a source of infection.

Junior high athletics may present some problems in this matter. It is the custom in some schools to hand down used varsity equipment to the junior high school to save expenses. Junior high athletes are smaller and more difficult to fit. Coaches must conform to school athletic policies, but they have a right to insist that all players have adequate protective equipment because of the possible personal liability that could occur if they don't.

It is equally important to see that all wearing apparel is regularly laundered and sanitized. All equipment should be cleaned and sanitized before being stored for the next season.

Playing equipment should be inspected frequently to make certain that it meets safety standards. Damaged, badly worn, or weakened equipment should be replaced in any sport. An important responsibility of the coach is to see that all playing equipment, except that which is fixed or permanent, is promptly stored after practices or contests. If other or younger students have access to the gymnasium or field and their use of the equipment without supervision should result in serious injury, there might be grounds for negligence charges against the coach in some states. A discus, Javelin, and other similar playing equipment left out can be a physical hazard when used by nonathletes.

INSPECTION OF FACILITIES

We cannot assume that the school administration's inspection of facilities will be sufficient for adequate safety. Playing fields and gymnasiums need daily inspection to insure that no hazardous objects are left out and that no permanent hazards exist. I once coached a basketball team which used a tiled floor for practice. During the Christmas vacation it was cleaned and waxed by the maintenance department. Three players sprained ankles during the first practice following the vacation. Inspection showed that the wax used was not a nonskid type and that the floor did not provide proper footing for the players. Although there was no thought of any legal action on the part of the players or their parents and the wax was promptly removed and replaced with nonskid wax, the maintenance department was negligent in using an improper type of wax, and I as the coach was negligent in not carefully inspecting the floor before the start of practice.

Some older gymnasiums were both a gymnasium and an auditorium, with a stage on one end, and other, small gymnasiums had the walls too near the end boundary lines—both of which presented physical hazards. Unfortunately, a few of these are still used. Under such conditions, the stage, walls, and any similar part of the construction should be well padded to provide adequate protection.

Landing pits for the jumps in track and field should be properly constructed and regularly inspected before practice and competition. Playing fields should be examined to insure that they are free of holes and ruts. Coaches of all sports should regularly inspect their playing facilities for the safety of their athletes.

Synthetic turfs and fields have advantages in inclement weather, but whether they provide greater safety for athletes is debatable. Some people think that more serious knee and ankle injuries occur on artificial turfs than on natural ones, but the issue has not been sufficiently resolved for any conclusion, and manufacturers are constantly attempting to improve the safety features. Coaches are often asked whether synthetic turfs should be installed. Before making any recommendation, the coach should carefully investigate the latest data concerning the frequency of injuries and the newest safety features.

ATHLETIC EQUIPMENT
PURCHASE REQUISITION

Sport _____

Date _____

Note: If substitution cannot be made, indicate by writing *NO* in last column.

Item With Description	Supplier and Catalogue Number	Size	Quantity	Unit Price	Total	Substi- tution

Total Cost _____

Signed _____

Figure 10-1. Form for Requisition of Purchase of Athletic Equipment

INVENTORY OF EQUIPMENT

_____ High School

Close of _____ Season   Year: 19_____
                        (Sport)

Articles Used For This Sport	Previous Inventory Count	Number Purchased During Year	Total Number To Be Accounted For	Present Inventory (First Class Shape)	Present Inventory (Need Repairs)	Number Articles Not Accounted For	Estimated Number New Articles Needed Next Season

Date of inventory, _____ 19_____   Coach _____

Athletic Director _____

Student Manager _____

Figure 10-2. Sample Inventory of Equipment Form

No school should offer an interscholastic athletic program which has not made necessary arrangements for adequate medical supervision of the players. A satisfactory program must begin with the preseason physical examination by a doctor. Some schools are fortunate enough to have a school physician employed by the board of education whose duties include medical supervision of athletes. Others have a school nurse who can provide some help, but there are many schools in smaller communities where securing medical services is difficult. High schools usually are able to have a physician present at football games and many basketball games, but there are some communities which do not have a doctor at all. No school can have a physician present at all athletic contests, because the same school will be competing in two or more interscholastic sports on the same day, one or more of which may be away from home. Theoretically a doctor should be present at all football practices, but this has been found to be impractical, and it would be very expensive.

Each school must make the best arrangements possible under the conditions that prevail. Unfortunately in some of the smaller schools there is no athletic director, and because the principal and superintendent are overworked with routine administrative responsibilities and sometimes with teaching duties, they delegate to coaches the responsibility for medical services. The following are suggestions for making the necessary arrangements.

1. All coaches should have proper training in first aid and know what steps to take in emergencies, and a well-equipped first aid kit should be on hand for all practices and contests.

2. Schools that can afford it should have a physician paid by the board of education who will provide adequate medical supervision or help the school to arrange for such. He or she or another doctor should be present at all football games and as many basketball games and other contests as practical. For any games for which no physician can be in attendance and for practice sessions, prearrangements should be made for securing medical services as quickly as possible, including a communications plan which will enable the school to reach a doctor without delay. City and county health officials can frequently provide help in making arrangements.

3. Similarly, prearrangements should be made by schools that do not have a team physician or usually cannot have one present at games.

4. If there is no physician in the community, but there is a nurse, arrangements should be made to provide what assistance she or he can.

5. An athletic trainer can be helpful in providing for medical super-

vision. There are relatively few trained high school athletic trainers, but steps are being taken to provide training for faculty members and others to become certified athletic trainers through the efforts of such organizations as the National Athletic Trainers Association, Cramer Products, Inc., and others. Cramer sponsors summer athletic training workshops for coaches and student trainers. Faculty members other than coaches also can be chosen to serve as athletic trainers. (See Chapter 13 for information on the development of athletic trainers.)

6. Definite policies and procedures should be established for handling serious injuries, including the prearrangements referred to above. Parents should be contacted immediately and consulted about their choice of a physician or hospital when necessary.

7. A permission and authorization form should be signed by parents to relieve the coach and athletic administrators of liability. It is also vitally important that a copy of the athlete's physical examination record be on file in the school office. Figures 6-1 and 6-2 show the forms provided by the Missouri High School Activities Association to its member schools for these purposes. The use of the forms does not relieve school representatives of all liability, but it can help to reduce the possibility of legal suits.

SANITATION

The school may provide sanitary equipment and have sanitation policies, but they will not make significant contributions to the health and safety of athletes without proper attention from the coach. He or she is in the best position to influence the attitudes of athletes in the importance of forming desirable habits of sanitation and to supervise their practice. The policies established by the school administration will apply primarily to maintaining proper sanitation of the facilities. Those formulated by the coach are specifically for the purpose of improving and maintaining the personal sanitation habits of the players.

The first step should be creating a need for them by explaining the personal protection and benefits they afford. Among the policies and practices that might be considered are the following:

1. Sanitary drinking facilities must be used. Individual bottles or paper cups should be supplied at practices and contests.
2. Wearing apparel should not be exchanged among players without being sterilized.
3. Personal equipment must be aired and dried between practices.
4. Clean individual towels should be used.
5. All personal wearing apparel should be laundered regularly.

6. The footbath provided should be used daily.
7. All school-owned player equipment should be sterilized before being stored for the next season.
8. All wearing apparel should be returned to its proper place immediately after undressing.
9. The dressing room should be kept clean and neatly arranged.
10. Good sanitation habits should be practiced both in and out of school.

Many of the details of proper supervision, such as seeing that water and drinking cups are available and checking the dressing room, can be assigned to student managers. They can be of great assistance if wisely chosen and well instructed in their duties.

ACCIDENT INSURANCE

The school administration has the responsibility of either arranging for athletic insurance for athletes or adopting policies to ensure that they have adequate basic coverage. If the state high school association sponsors catastrophe coverage, the shool should participate in it. Many families will have their own health and accident coverage, which may include athletic accidents.

The coach should make sure that coverage is in force and suggest to the athletic administrator that a plan be considered if several athletes do not have protection. No athlete should be permitted to practice or compete without proper insurance.

Drug Abuse

The spread of drug abuse among students is one of the most serious problems facing our schools. Dr. Donald B. Louria notes in his book, *Overcoming Drugs*, that drug abuse in the United States is increasing at such magnitude that our society in the 1980s might appropriately be labeled as the *intoxicated society*.[15] Much research is going into efforts to determine the causes of the increase, but no general effective solutions have been found. These are not new problems, but as society has become more complex, so have the problems. The town drunk is no longer the major concern of even the smaller towns and communities; it is the spreading abuse of other drugs.

---

[15] Donald B. Louria, *Overcoming Drugs* (New York: McGraw-Hill, 1971), p. 5.

REASONS FOR ITS GROWTH

Attempts to analyze the contributing causes of the rise in drug use by high school and elementary school students provide varied explanations.[16] Among them are broken homes, personality and psychological problems, escapism, rebellious attitudes, affluency, availability, influence of the news media, curiosity, and the influence of peer groups. The influence of adults and the inclination of youth to imitate their elders has not received a great deal of public attention, perhaps because of the reluctance to admit it, but they are beyond a doubt contributing factors. For example, drinking alcoholic beverages became a social custom. Moreover, being on the cocktail circuit is a status symbol, and college and high school students started drinking at social functions held off-campus. The permissive parental attitudes which emerged certainly did not help to discourage its spread; neither did lowering the legal age for purchasing alcoholic beverages in some states. The *peer pressure* and the *desire to be accepted by the group* have been among the most potent causes of the extraordinary trend toward drug abuse among high school and college students.

The illicit use of drugs has been stimulated by the increase in drug traffic and the proselytizing of pushers and users. Proponents proclaimed benefits and made studies to support their contentions, but there is no scientific evidence to show that drugs taken for nonmedical purposes have any lasting beneficial effects. Studies pertaining to the use of marijuana are inconclusive, but there is abundant evidence of the harmful effects of LSD and hard drugs.

ATHLETES ARE NOT IMMUNE

Professional athletic practices have always had a profound influence on intercollegiate and interscholastic sports. Organizational plans for competition were imitated, many changes in rules were patterned after professional rules, and college and high school coaches are often influenced by the techniques of professional athletes and coaches. The use of drugs in professional sports for illicit purposes can affect the attitudes of high school and college players and coaches if the inherent dangers are not clearly understood. The pressures to win in professional sports are strong factors in drug abuse. Anabolic-androgenic steroids which are sympathetic male hormones, are used to increase weight and strength; pep pills (amphetamines), to get psyched up for the game; and pain-killing drugs, to enable athletes to compete with some injuries. Because playing is a means of livelihood for the professional athlete, he or she may be willing to risk the dangers of these drugs.

[16]*Ibid.*, pp. 14-20.

Similarly, the emphasis on winning in international athletics may be causing some amateur athletes to experiment with drugs. Steps are being taken to guard against improper use of drugs in Olympic competition.

The International Amateur Athletic Federation, National Collegiate Athletic Association, National Federation of State High School Associations, National Athletic Trainers' Association, and all other amateur athletic associations condemn the misuse of drugs in athletics. Moreover, there is no scientific proof that they improve performance.

The coach should obtain ample information about drugs and their effects to help athletes avoid their use and to help cope with any drug-related problems. This knowledge should include how to recognize drug users, the drugs that athletes are inclined to abuse, their dangers and harmful effects, how to deal with problems resulting from their abuse, and the street terminology used in reference to them. The NCAA has published a valuable pamphlet, *The Coach: Drugs, Ergogenic Aids and the Athlete*, with the cooperation of the United States Drug Enforcement Administration. Coaches may obtain copies from the NCAA at a small charge, and the National Federation also has provided copies to high schools through their state high school associations.

The drugs most frequently abused by student athletes are amphetimines, alcohol, marijuana, and anabolic-androgenic steroids. All can have serious health and psychological effects when used for nonmedical purposes.

RECOGNIZING DRUG USERS

The NCAA's publication outlines some of the symptoms to look for:

1. Decrease in motivation
2. Change in personality and facial expression
3. Changing patterns of behavior
4. Withdrawing from companionship
5. Decrease in performance both physical and academic
6. Poor personal hygiene and grooming
7. Isolation and/or association with only one group of persons
8. Inability to coordinate—standing or walking
9. Muddled speech
10. Impaired judgment (barbiturate user)
11. Restlessness

[17] *The Coach: Drugs, Ergogenic Aids and the Athlete* (Kansas City, Mo.: National Association of Intercollegiate Athletics, 1976), pp. 7-9.

12. Jittery
13. Muscular twitches, tremor of hands
14. Heavy sweating and bad breath (hallmarks of amphetamine abuse)
15. Nervous, highly talkative and overactive (amphetamine)
16. Marijuana abuse:
    —red eyes are fairly common symptoms
    —may begin to miss gym and then other classes
    —increases appetite with special craving for sweets
    —regular user is apathetic, listless, and careless
17. Needlemarks on arms and legs. Addicts often wear long-sleeved sweaters, even in summer, to keep warm and hide scars.
18. A person's language (his jargon) may indicate he uses drugs.
19. Episodes of stupor and incoherent speech may indicate acute intoxication from any number of substances.[18]

THE DANGERS

Coaches are respected by athletes and the bond that develops puts them in a position to be effective counselors. The first steps in dealing with a case of drug abuse are to determine the reasons for it and the drug involved to help the athlete know about its dangers.

Alcohol can have several chronic adverse effects upon the health of the individual.[19] One of the immediate effects is the inducing of vomiting when a sufficient amount is consumed before the body builds a tolerance for it. The person is then likely to drink more, and other effects of illnesses can result. Some of the more serious are these:

1. *There is danger of becoming an alcoholic.* There are two basic types of alcoholics: (1) those who get drunk frequently and (2) those who drink a large enough amount to obtain approximately one-half of their caloric needs from alcohol. As tolerance toward alcohol increases, the individual is apt to drink more and to become increasingly dependent on it.

2. *Excessive drinking causes cirrhosis of the liver.* It may occur in persons who regularly drink moderately.

3. *Judgment and reactions are lessened, which makes the individual more prone to accidents.* Drinking even moderate amounts of alcohol is one of the principal causes of accidents, particularly automobile accidents.

4. *Drinking results in temporary periods of elation followed by periods of depression.* In periods of elation the individuals overestimate

[18]*Ibid.*, p. 5.

[19]*Ibid.*, pp. 7-9.

themselves, and in depressions frequently feel inferior and lack ambition and will power.

5. *Continued alcoholic abuse often affects the blood vessels.* Those in the face appear red when the drinker is under the influence and purple when he or she is not.

6. *Extended use of alcohol causes permanent brain damage.*

7. *The use of alcohol interferes with the performance of physical skills.* This can occur from both extended and occasional use, and will reduce athletic abilities rather than improve them.

Alcohol abuse is recognized as the number one problem in the United States and coaches should do all in their power to discourage it. Television advertisements of alcoholic beverages sometimes show coaches and college students rushing to get a beer for relaxation after games and examinations. Setting an example by refraining from drinking is one of the best methods coaches can use to counteract the effects of such advertising.

Marijuana does have harmful effects. Coaches should understand that although some so-called "studies" of marijuana indicate that it is harmless, all the scientific data since 1850 show the opposite to be true.[20] It is the most popular drug among youth, and the dangers are widespread.

1. *The user tends to escalate to harder drugs.* Many addicts on hard drugs started with marijuana. Although the percentage who move on to LSD and more dangerous drugs is not definite, experts in the field consider the number to be sizable.

2. *Regular use can cause accumulative toxic retention, which can cause chromosome and sperm damage.* Even occasional use can cause these effects in some individuals.

3. *It can cause depression and panic.* A period of depression may follow occasional use; and the panic that may result when marijuana is smoked during a period of anxiety, may turn to despair. Some cases of suicide have been attributed to this cause.

4. *Temporary periods of persecution known as paranoia may result.*

5. *Excessive use can cause serious cases of psychosis.* This state occurs after the person has become so dependent on the drug that larger doses are taken. Both personality and psychiatric problems may arise and mental breakdowns occur.

6. *It interferes with motor performance and makes the individual more accident-prone.* Because of accumulative retention, this effect may still be present for a short period after use is discontinued.

[20] Louria, *Overcoming Drugs*, p. 39.

7. *The toxic influence can affect brain functioning.* A decline in memory is one of the most noticeable, but poorer judgment and other mental effects also occur.

Students can easily become confused by the fact that some individuals whose studies have been reported in the news media contend that occasional or moderate use of marijuana has no harmful effects, which ignores the data gathered over many years to the contrary. It is unfortunate that what are scientifically unfounded opinions are frequently given more publicity than those based on scientific research. The wise person makes his or her decisions on the basis of what a particular thing contributes to the welfare of that individual and to society. There is no solid evidence that marijuana has any lasting values for either.

Amphetamines are one of the most abused drugs in athletics. It is commonly acknowledged that they are used by some professional athletes as an artificial stimulant for competition. If they are used by college and high school players, it is probably without the knowledge of the coach; but the desire to be a star like the pros may prompt some individual athletes to experiment with pep pills without understanding their dangers. It is hard to believe that any knowledgeable coach would suggest their use. There is no scientific evidence to show that athletes perform better by using amphetamines because no comparison can be made with how they would have done without them in a specific game.

Some of the serious dangers their use involves are the following:

1. *They can seriously affect the cardiorespiratory system.* The nervous system can become stimulated to the point that blood vessels are restricted and the respiratory recovery time delayed, which can have serious effects.

2. *They can cause a loss of appetite.*

3. *If the usage becomes habitual, it may lead to dependency and overaggression.* Withdrawal after extended use may lead to depression.

4. *Increased use and dosage can lead to nervousness and insomnia.* There may be an inclination to use other drugs to offset these effects, that is, barbiturates to counter hypertension.

5. *Excessive use can become highly toxic and cause acute psychoses.* Personality and mental disturbances may be triggered in some cases.

6. *They may cause the individual to be unaware of the natural signs of fatigue and increase the chances of injury and heat exhaustion.*

Student athletes should be helped to understand that plenty of nourishing food, sufficient exercise, and ample rest will give them all the energy and stimulation they need. Artificial stimulation through the use of drugs has many times more dangers than advantages.

Some people believe that anabolic-androgenic steroids, which are synthetic male hormones, will increase the weight and strength of athletes, but this contention is contradicted by scientific studies.[21] The increase in weight is caused by the retention of fluid, and there is no scientific evidence that steroids increase strength.

Dangers in their use include these:

1. *They cause undesirable personality changes.*

2. *They cause adverse effects on growth and physical development.* The greatest danger to young athletes is in relation to the long bones of the body, and cases of stunted growth are known.

3. *They cause diseases of the liver.* The two most recognized are hepatitis and primary liver cancer.

4. *They cause the testicles and enlarged prostate gland to shrink.*

5. *They cause high blood pressure resulting from hypertension.*

6. *They encourage growth of any preexisting cancers or hormone-sensitive tumors.*

7. *They cause gastric ulcers.*

8. *Female athletes may become masculinized.*[22]

Anabolic-androgenic steroids should be taken only under the advice of a physician, and then not for athletic reasons.

LSD (lysergic acid diethylamide) is not a drug that athletes are prone to use, but it is one that presents serious dangers. It is a synthesized drug that has hallucinatory effects, and its abuse carries many of the same dangers as other drugs already discussed. In addition, it has been known to produce grave mental disorders and breakdowns from either regular or occasional use; it is considered a potential cause of genetic harm by inducing chromosomal breaks which can result in birth defects and abnormalities. It is a dangerous drug and should be avoided.

The references at the end of this chapter and other sources will provide more detailed and complete information to help coaches cope with individual cases of drug abuse.

TOBACCO

Smoking is a widespread practice among high school students. The United States Public Health Service Surgeon General's reports beginning in 1964 and the work done by such organizations as the National

---

[21] *The Coach: Drugs, Erogenic Aids, and the Athlete,* pp. 6-7.

[22] *Ibid.,* p. 7.

Center for Health Statistics, Cancer Society, Heart Association, Tuberculosis Society, and others have convinced many adults of the dangers of cigarette smoking; but students have not been influenced by the overwhelming evidence of the relationship between smoking and disease,[23] probably because they are still removed from immediate dangers by virtue of their age and because of peer influence. Peer pressure among high school students encourages many to smoke, even while there is increasing pressure from nonsmoking adults that smoking should be prohibited in public places.

Coaches are in a position to influence the attitudes of athletes and other students toward smoking. Some of the methods and techniques which can be effective are the following:

1. *To refrain from smoking ourselves.*

2. *To have students analyze their reasons for smoking and to evaluate their soundness.*

3. *To present the statistics that show the relationship between smoking and various diseases and premature deaths.*

4. *To adopt training rules that prohibit smoking.* The courts will uphold such standards when the reasons for them are first established and steps are taken to ensure that athletes understand the rules.

5. *To stimulate athletes to make their decisions on the basis of what something contributes to their welfare rather than on the possibility that it may not hurt them.* If it cannot be proved that benefits will accrue, they should avoid whatever the thing may be.

6. *To encourage them to dare to be different.* Youth strongly want to be *one of the group.* Any who do not conform to the mores and customs of the group are not likely to be accepted and may even face ostracism. This is a difficult situation for adolescents to face, and they need help. Efforts should be made to convince athletes that acceptance by some groups, usually social ones, may not be as important as they think and that the conditions are only temporary. Social sororities and fraternities are banned on school premises by several school boards and are prohibited by law in some states, yet they carry on outside the supervision of the school. They promote traditions, customs, and practices, such as smoking and drinking, to which many students object, but the students engage in them to be accepted into the organization. It is very helpful if athletes and other students can realize that leaders of these organizations may be among the most popular in the school but they are seldom real school leaders. Some schools have regulations providing that no member of a secret fraternity or sorority can participate

[23] W. K. Street, "Smoking in Schools," *The Physical Educator*, 29, No. 1, (March 1972), 25-26.

in extracurricular activities sponsored by the school. Organized student activities in almost all schools meet the interests and needs of the great majority of students, and these are the ones students should be encouraged to join.

It can be effective to have students understand that any benefits they may think peer groups have are short-lived. The groups that engage in illicit activities will provide no benefits once the students graduate. They will not help the students get their first job or qualify for college entrance. It is the evaluation of adults that then becomes significant. Teachers and school administrators will give the best recommendations to those who dare to be different and refrain from the use of tobacco and other drugs. They can be represented as individuals who will put first things first and exercise good judgment.

The School's Approach

The coach works closely with only a relatively small number of the school's total student population. If the school provides instruction about drugs that will reach all students, the coach may want to act primarily as a counselor to his athletes. If it does not, he or she should educate the players about drugs, their effects, and the dangers of their abuse.

No school can assume that it has no drug problem, which is no longer limited to the large metropolitan areas but has also spread to smaller communities across the country. Alert school administrators have established programs to cope with drug use by students, and laws to include drug education in the curriculum have been passed by some states. The coach must understand what instruction is offered, in what courses, to determine his or her own procedure.

TWO PHASES

An effective drug education program must instruct both the faculty and the students. A faculty committee can help determine the nature and scope of the problem in the school and what is needed in the program.

Very few teachers have had any instruction in the use and misuse of drugs. Workshops and seminars are frequently offered, but they must be carefully planned and administered to be effective. Teachers cannot be expected to be drug experts or even expert in drug detection, but they need to learn signs of drug abuse and the procedure to follow when they suspect it, particularly the legal regulations governing search and seizure.

The laws are not completely clear regarding the search of lockers and students' clothing. Most suits involving illegal searches and seizures have been brought under the Fourth Amendment, adopted in 1791 as part of the original Bill of Rights, which protects citizens from unreasonable searches and seizure. The key word is *reasonable*. A search warrant must be issued by a judge or magistrate to assure that a search is reasonable when it is made by a government official, although some exceptions are allowed under special circumstances.

School searches are almost in a class by themselves, but the matter of reasonableness is still extremely important to avoid court action. Because of the duties and responsibilities of school officials, however, lower standards are applied to the reasonable clause. According to the United States Supreme Court, they also have *good faith immunity* for personal liability for damages concerning their official duties and responsibilities if not conducted in ignorance or disregard of settled constitutional law (Wood v. Strickland, 1974).[24]

The reasonableness of searches balances the rights of an individual against the rights and protection of the majority of students. When a search is deemed essential to protect the welfare of other students, is specific to the student involved, and is not in disregard of the law, it will be considered reasonable. There may be instances when a proper search can be considered a duty of a school official in carrying out his or her responsibilities, and it could conceivably be considered negligent to fail to make a search when conditions warrant it. The following are guidelines for determining whether or not a search would be reasonable:

1. The duties and responsibilities of the school officials.
2. The purpose of the search.
3. The students' ages and conduct records.
4. The seriousness of the problem.
5. The necessity of conducting a warrantless search.[25]

DRUG EDUCATION FOR STUDENTS

Although it is widely recognized that education offers the most practical long-range solution to the drug problem, separate courses do not seem to be the best approach. A much better procedure is to include drug education in such regular courses as health where drugs can be discussed in relation to this subject. An extensive unit in such a required course will seem more purposeful to students than a special course that

---

[24]*Search and Seizure in the Schools* (Reston, Va.: National Association of Secondary School Principals, February 1979), p. 7.

[25]*Ibid.*, p. 7.

may adversely affect their attitudes and even glorify drug users. Also, those students who refrain might resent a special required course.

The teacher of any course must be carefully selected and well qualified. He or she must be the type of person who can communicate with students about their problems and one whom they trust and respect. The coach is often this person and is frequently assigned to courses in health in which drug education can be incorporated.

Both formalized and incidental teaching should be part of the school program. The work of school counselors, coaches, supervisors of student activities, and others in a position to counsel students should supplement the curriculum, and may be more effective with some students.

Regardless of the school's approach, truthfulness and honesty must be practiced. Students are too sophisticated to be influenced by slanted instruction or scare techniques. They should be taught the medical benefits of drugs prescribed by a physician as well as their effects and dangers when improperly used.

Basic to the success of any drug program are the attitudes instilled in the students. They should be taught to respect their bodies and minds. The attitude that the body and mind belongs to the individual to do with as he or she pleases is completely wrong. Who pays for the public health services many receive for illnesses stemming from drug abuse? Who pays for the injuries in accidents caused by the drug user? Everyone pays to some degree, and the use of illicit drugs is everybody's business. When the public accepts this attitude and does something about it, the drug problem may be alleviated considerably.

Summary

The health and safety of athletes must receive careful and continual attention from coaches and athletic administrators.

Good nutrition is essential to the health and safety of athletes. Coaches should help players understand what is needed in their diets to provide for their nutritional needs. The best source of the necessary nutrients, vitamins, and minerals is natural food from the family table. Making weight in wrestling may present special nutritional problems.

Physical conditioning is important in protecting the health of the athlete and in improving performances. Preseason conditioning under instruction provided in advance by the coach is recommended. The basic elements of conditioning include the improvement of strength, flexibility, agility, endurance, and the cardiorespiratory system. The coach should select appropriate exercises for conditioning to achieve the desired objectives. Care must be taken to acclimate athletes to hot weather. Warm-ups before conditioning exercises are begun and before practices and games are important in the prevention of injuries. Sufficient conditioning should be continued during the season to maintain a high level of physical fitness.

All coaches have responsibilities in the prevention and care of injuries, but these may vary with the size of the school and the athletic organization. The important thing is to understand thoroughly the responsibilities that exist and to take the necessary steps to assume them. If the administration does not have a plan to provide adequate medical supervision, the coach should assume that responsibility with the approval of the administration.

Safety policies should be developed and enforced. Adequate protective equipment must be provided and properly fitted. Facilities should be regularly inspected to avoid any physical hazards.

Attention must be given to sanitation and other measures to help protect the health of the players.

Players should have athletic accident insurance and should not be permitted to practice until verification is provided.

The drug problem in the United States has reached an epidemic stage in high schools, junior high schools, and even elementary schools. Athletes are not immune to drug abuse. Coaches and other teachers should know the types and effects of drugs commonly used and the signs of abuse. It may be necessary for the school to provide in-service training to teachers about drugs. Drug education should be given to students through health courses as well as through incidental counseling by teachers. Building desirable attitudes toward the use and abuse of drugs is most important. Most authorities agree that the best approach to a solution of the drug problem in our society is through education.

QUESTIONS AND TOPICS FOR STUDY AND DISCUSSION

1. Explain how you will attempt to impress on your players the importance of proper nutrition.
2. If you were a wrestling coach, explain the steps you would take to discourage wrestlers from excessive weight loss.
3. What are the basic elements of conditioning?
4. Give an example of an exercise with a specific purpose by stating the purpose and explaining the exercise you would prescribe.
5. Select a sport and describe a drill you would have your athletes perform to improve their agility.
6. Explain how the knees and ankles can be strengthened to help prevent injuries.
7. Discuss ways of acclimating athletes to hot weather.
8. Briefly outline your suggestions to players for preseason physical conditioning.

9. Prepare a set of safety guidelines for your players.
10. Briefly outline the policies you will want your athletes to adhere to on athletic trips.
11. Why is it personally important to the coach and athletic administrator to provide adequate protective equipment and to see that the athletic facilities are free of hazards?
12. Outline a plan for adequate medical supervision of athletes, including emergencies, in a school in which you plan to coach.
13. Prepare a brief outline of the sanitation policies you will have your players follow to build better personal habits.
14. What are some of the reasons for the increase in drug abuse among high school students?
15. List some of the signs which will help to identify drug users.
16. Prepare a chart showing the drugs students are most likely to abuse and the dangers they present.
17. Assume that some of your athletes smoke and one or two are suspected of experimenting with drugs. Discuss the procedures and techniques you would apply in coping with this problem.
18. What is the best approach for a school to take in providing drug education? Why?
19. Under what conditions would the courts be inclined to consider a search of a student's locker or clothing?
20. How would you try to convince a student that the abuse of drugs by one individual is the business of others?

BIBLIOGRAPHY

Answers to Health Questions in Physical Education, pp. 8-13. Washington, D.C.: American Association for Health, Physical Education, and Recreation, 1959.

Chilakos, Aristomen. "Cardiovascular Endurance Through Weight Training." The Physical Educator, 31, No. 4 (December 1974), 179-80.

The Coach: Drugs, Erogenic Aids, and the Athlete. Kansas City, Mo.: National Collegiate Athletic Association, 1976.

Food—The Yearbook of Agriculture, pp. 102, 266, 626. Washington, D.C.: U.S. Government Printing Office, 1959.

Forsythe, Charles E., and Irvin A. Keller, *Administration of High School Athletics*, 6th ed., pp. 266-95. Englewood Cliffs, N.J.: Prentice-Hall, 1977.

Gallon, Arthur J. *Coaching Ideas and Ideals*, pp. 61-114. Boston: Houghton Mifflin, 1974.

Hooks, Gene. *Application of Weight Training to Athletics.* Englewood Cliffs, N.J.: Prentice-Hall, 1962.

Johnson, Perry B., and Donald Stalberg. *Conditioning.* Englewood Cliffs, N.J.: Prentice-Hall, 1971.

Keelor, Richard O. "The Realities of Drug Abuse in High School Athletics." *Journal of Physical Education and Recreation*, 43, No. 5 (May 1978), 48-49.

Logan, Gene A., and Wayne C. McKinney. *Kinesiology*. Wm. C. Brown Company, 1972.

Louria, Donald B. *The Drug Scene*. New York: McGraw-Hill, 1968.

————. *Overcoming Drugs*. New York: McGraw-Hill, 1971.

Means, Richard K. "Drug Abuse: Implications for Instruction." *Journal for Health, Physical Education, and Recreation*, 41, No. 5, (May 1970), 22-24, 54-55.

Nutrition for Athletes: A Handbook for Coaches. Washington, D.C.: American Alliance for Health, Physical Education, and Recreation, 1971.

Resick, Matthew C., and Carl E. Erickson. *Intercollegiate and Interscholastic Athletics for Men and Women*, pp. 217-27. Reading, Mass.: Addison-Wesley, 1975.

Schiltz, Jack H. "Hyperventilation." *Journal of Health, Physical Education, and Recreation*, 43, No. 4 (April 1972), 67.

Schneider, Sue. "Care and Treatment of Ankle Injuries." *Woman Coach* (May-June 1975), pp. 24-25, 28-29.

Search and Seizure in the Schools. A Legal Memorandum. Reston, Va.: National Association of Secondary School Principals, February 1979.

Seaton, Don Cash. *Physical Education Handbook*, pp. 21-50. Englewood Cliffs, N.J.: Prentice-Hall, 1974.

Streit, W. K. "Smoking in Schools." *The Physical Educator*, 29, No. 1 (March 1972), 25-26.

Tannenbaum, Beulah, and Myra Stillman. *Understand Food—The Chemistry of Nutrition*, pp. 173-74. New York: McGraw-Hill, 1962.

Tips on Athletic Training, VIII. Chicago: American Medical Association, 1966.

What Research Tells the Coach About Wrestling, pp. 41-50. Washington, D.C.: American Association for Health, Physical Education, and Recreation, 1964.

Wilson, Holly. "Athletics Can Be Safe." *The Physical Educator*, 49, No. 5 (May 1978), 66-68.

CHAPTER 11

Legal Aspects of Coaching

Schools and state high school associations for many years could adopt and enforce regulations governing interscholastic athletics without any fear of interference from the courts. Few regulations were challenged by athletes or their parents. The first suit occurred in 1924 when the Ohio State High Athletic Association declared ineligible some players who were attending Scott High School in Toledo. It was not until 1938 that a second suit was filed, in the state of Oklahoma, after an athlete was declared ineligible for violating the award rule. This became a precedent-setting case. The Oklahoma Supreme Court dismissed the case, ruling that although the student had many rights as a citizen, he had *no vested right in eligibility*, and that vesting authority in the board of control was not unlawful. Thus the precedent was set that participation in interscholastic athletics is a privilege to be attained by meeting the standards established for it.

Changes in society and the assertion of individual rights and civil liberties through the courts eventually reached the interscholastic area, and numerous suits have been brought against high schools and their state associations since the late 1960s. It is now important that school administrators and coaches know the legal basis for establishing standards to help avoid liability and expensive legal fees.

The Tendency to Sue

The emphasis in our society on individual rights and freedoms without corresponding emphasis on individual responsibility has made it increasingly difficult to enforce rules and regulations. We have reached a state where the protection of the rights of one individual sometimes receives more attention than that of the rights of individuals who might be affected. A number of examples could be given to illustrate this statement, but the most glaring is the dismissal of charges by courts because of a violation of legal procedures. Whether the persons charged were guilty often appears to be of less significance than some minor violation of procedure. Because of the prevailing court philosophy, it is extremely important for coaches to know both how to protect the rights of athletes and the procedures to follow in enforcing established rules.

INDIVIDUAL RIGHTS

Although the courts have consistently held to the principle that participation in interscholatic sports is a privilege rather than a constitutional right, some high school association attorneys believe that the precedent set in the 1938 Oklahoma case may be challenged in the future. In that case, a boy who had accepted an illegal award and was declared ineligible sued the Oklahoma High School Athletic Association and was awarded judgment in a district court, which was appealed. The Supreme Court of the State of Oklahoma in dismissing the case stated:

> The Plaintiff has many rights as a citizen and as a high school student but he has no vested right in *eligibility* as dealt with at such great length in the rules of the Oklahoma High School Athletic Association. There is nothing unlawful or evil in either of those rules or in provision vesting final authority in the board of control.[1]

If students by court interpretation were extended a constitutional right to compete in interscholastic athletics, would schools have to give all students who wanted it this opportunity? Would the coach, the school, or the court have the final determination about who would play on the school team? Could the schools afford such an expansion of the interscholastic program? These are questions that would have to be answered. Changes in eligibility rules would be mandated, and all regulations would be more difficult to enforce. There is no doubt that more court cases would result. Fortunately for the welfare of interscholastic athletics, judgments of higher courts have not been awarded to plaintiffs whose complaints were based solely on the denial of a constitutional right. This does not mean that such suits will not be brought. Abridgement of the guarantees afforded by the constitution have been claimed in most of the cases involving interscholastic athletics, and they are difficult to substantiate; yet such claims persist.

---

[1] Oklahoma State High School Athletic Association v. Billy Roberts, 28653, Supreme Court of Oklahoma (1938).

The First Amendment of the Bill of Rights guarantees an individual the freedom of speech. Succeeding civil rights legislation and case law have added broader concepts to this provision than originally applied, and dress and grooming have become to be considered a means of individual expression. Restrictions on dress and grooming will be upheld in court only if there are valid and justifiable reasons for them in carrying out the educational functions of the school. For example, language that clearly disrupts classroom activities and interferes with the learning of others can be prohibited. Dress that would definitely have an adverse effect on the attitudes and behavior of others and make the wearer an object of antagonism can be prohibited if it can be well established that the standard of dress accepted is based on sound educational purposes. For a period of time, the length of hair was an issue, primarily because of the personal objections of coaches and school administrators, but this issue has subsided to a considerable degree. Football players can be required to wear their hair at an appropriate length to fit football helmets properly for their safety; or in wrestling the maximum length is governed by game rules based on valid reasons.

Most of the court cases relating to freedom of speech have involved the length of hair. The rulings handed down provide valuable guidelines for establishing and enforcing haircut rules. The court upheld the ruling of a high school in California in not allowing a student to participate in track events because of the length of his hair.[2]

The judge dismissed a case in New Jersey, stating that the dress code (re long hair) was an essential part of the sport of wrestling.[3]

The court ruled in Florida that wearing one's hair in a public high school in the length and style that suits the wearer is not a right protected by the U.S. Constitution.[4]

A grooming regulation applied only to athletes, except for the protection of the student, may not be upheld in court. Three athletes were suspended from a Vermont high school for violating grooming regulations that were applied only to athletes. The court held that the athletes must be reinstated, and school authorities were enjoined from enforcing the athletic grooming code.[5]

[2] Jay Neuhaus v. Tamalpais Union High School U.S. Dist. Court, Northern Dist. of California, No. C7030GBJ (1970).

[3] Craig S. Willet v. Freehold Regional High School, C-1210-71, New Jersey (1972).

[4] Chesley Karr v. Clifford Schmidt, Coronado High School, 31045, Florida (1973).

[5] Steven Dunham, Prentiss Smith, Paul B. Weber v. Vermont Superintendent of Schools, (1970).

Dress and grooming standards can be established and enforced when they are necessary for educational objectives and/or the safety of athletes. Regulations applying only to athletes may be deemed discriminatory unless it can be established that they are in the best interests of athletes only.

CIVIL RIGHTS

The equal protection clause of the Fourteenth Amendment has been the basis of several suits brought in federal courts claiming denial of the civil rights of athletes. There has been a notable difference in the views of state and federal courts pertaining to the relationship between eligibility and civil rights. State courts give much credence to the precedent that participation in athletics is a privilege, whereas federal courts are more concerned about any possible interference with the constitutional rights of the students. Since 1970, there has been a trend toward filing eligibility suits in federal courts. That federal judges view eligibility from a different perspective can be most clearly noted from state and federal cases involving the eligibility of married students.

The Supreme Court of Iowa upheld a rule prohibiting married students from participating in extracurricular activities[6] on the grounds that participation in athletics was a privilege and not an inherent constitutional right. The board of education was concerned that marriage would cause students to drop out, have an adverse effect on other students through conversations about intimate details of married life, and that without the married student rule more student marriages would result. The court held that there were sufficient reasons for the rule and it could not be considered unreasonable and arbitrary as claimed. The court did not find any violation of constitutional rights. There were five similar cases in other states before 1970 in which the decisions were essentially the same.

However, state court precedents were not considered by a federal judge to be sufficient, and a favorable ruling was given to a married student in 1972.[7] This and other federal cases have caused state courts to begin to view the constitutional rights of students under the Fourteenth Amendment in a different perspective.

The Texas Court of Civil Appeals held that the married student rule of that district violated the students' constitutional rights under the Fourteenth Amendment.[8] These federal court precedents are having

[6] School District of Waterloo v. Green, 147 N.W.2d 854, Iowa (1967).

[7] Holt v. Shelton, 341 F. Supp. 821. M.D. Tenn. (1972).

[8] Bell v. Loan Oak Independent School District, 507 S.S.2d 636, Texas (1974).

a significant impact on state court rulings, and have resulted in more eligibility cases being brought in federal courts.

Eligibility requirements must have a valid relation to educational purposes to be upheld by both state and federal courts. More attention must be given by athletic administrators to the protection of constitutional rights while still upholding the traditional values of interscholastic athletics in formulating and enforcing standards of eligibility. The same must be considered by coaches in establishing training rules and other regulations. Some people fear that the authority of schools to establish standards and regulations has been diminished by court rulings, but this is basically not the situation. The vital issue is the protection of civil rights, not the protection of the right to participate in interscholastic sports, which the Constitution does not guarantee. Essential rules and regulations can be established without abridging the civil rights of students. The view taken by the courts regarding the authority of boards of education and their representatives can be illustrated by an excerpt from the decision of the St. Louis District Court of Appeals.[9]

Along with entrusting the education of our children to teachers and administrators, we also entrust the control and supervision of the extracurricular activities incident to that education. Implicit in the responsibility for these activities is the power to make reasonable rules and regulations. We are dealing here with numerous schools who have voluntarily joined an association. As members of this association, they may, by majority vote, enact rules to govern their interaction. It is obvious that chaos would result without such rules. It is also obvious that the members are in the most advantageous position to appreciate the regulations under which they must act to achieve desired goals. The court should not interfere with the enactment of those regulations as long as they are reasonable and do not infringe on public policy or law.

DISCRIMINATION

The equal protection clause of the Fourteenth Amendment has been invoked in the courts when eligibility requirements were thought to be discriminatory. It was made clear in 1968 that no discrimination could be made because of race when the district court ruled that the Florida High School Activities Association must accept as members all former members of the Florida Interscholastic Athletic Association, an association of black schools, as made application and would permit examination of its membership records.[10]

---

[9] Art Gaines Baseball Camp, Inc. v. Clair Houston, et al., 4-314110, Missouri (1973).

[10] Walker and Harris vs. Florida High School Activities Association, U. S. District Court, Northern District of Florida, G. CIV. 406 (1968).

The issue of sex discrimination in interscholastic athletics arose in the 1960s when an increasing number of girls' physical educators began to show a greater interest in competitive athletic experiences. Before that time girls had fewer opportunities for competition than boys. Play days and sports festivals were emphasized, and there was considerable opposition to state championships in girls' sports. Many high schools offered interscholastic competition only for boys, and as many as nine state high school associations prohibited interscholastic games for girls as late as 1961.[11] There were varying degrees of interscholastic competition for girls in other states, and a few state associations (Iowa, Oklahoma, and Tennessee) sponsored district and state girls' tournaments.

Beginning in the middle 1960s, an increasing interest in interscholastic athletic opportunities for girls arose because of several factors. The issue of sex discrimination and the women's liberation movement had some influence. Publicity given to the Olympics and other international athletic competition, no doubt, played a part, particularly because of the public's desire for United States women to compete more favorably with foreign women. The Olympic Development Committee helped to stimulate an interest in more athletic opportunities for girls by initiating institutes to train women coaches and the developing plans to motivate interest in the Olympics, beginning in the elementary schools.[12] It was eventually recognized that the broad-based girls' athletic program consisting of physical education plus some interscholastic contests did not sufficiently challenge the athletically talented girl. By the late 1960s it was evident that the same type of interscholastic athletic program offered to boys was also needed for girls.

However, many boards of education and athletic administrators resisted the new trend and continued to offer a program only for boys. Girls whose schools had no interscholastic athletic programs for them then asked to compete on the boys' teams. When these requests were denied, they sought relief through the courts. The decisions in the first few cases were conflicting. A judge upheld the rule of the New Jersey State Interscholastic Athletic Association prohibiting girls from interscholastic athletic competition with boys,[13] and a Connecticut court ruled similarly in a case in which a girl was denied a request to run with

[11] National Federation of State High School Athletic Associations, *Official Handbook*, 1960-61, p. 59.

[12] Sara Staff Jernigan, *The Role of Women in Sports Development*, Proceedings of the National Conference on Olympic Development (Washington, D.C.: American Association for Health, Physical Education, and Recreation, 1966), pp. 14-21.

[13] Barbara Gregorio v. Board of Education of Asbury Park, C-1988-69, New Jersey (1970).

boys in cross country and indoor track.[14] The Nebraska School Activities Association was enjoined from prohibiting a girl from a boys' golf team because of her sex,[15] and the Michigan association was also an all boys' team solely because of their sex.[16] The inconsistencies in court decisions rendered in early cases involving sex discimination made the situation confusing for school administrators and coaches.
for school administrators and coaches.

Title IX

Title IX of the Education Amendments of 1972 (Public Law 92-318) has had a profound impact on the issue of sex discrimination in interscholastic and intercollegiate athletics, and will continue to have great influence over these programs in the future. It is intended to eliminate discrimination, not only in athletics, but also in other matters such as recruiting, employment, wages, and job classification. Some of these are no real concern to high school coaches, but there are some provisions with which all coaches should be thoroughly familiar.

The Guidelines for Federal Enforcement of Title IX issued by the United States Department of Health, Education, and Welfare in June 1975 were to become effective July 21, 1975, but there was provision for a three-year period for schools to comply fully with the requirements. Coaches should clearly understand those provisions contained under Subsection 86.41 Athletics, which are the following:

(a) *General.* No person shall, on the basis of sex, be excluded from participation in, be denied the benefits of, be treated differently from another person or otherwise be discriminated against in an interscholastic, intercollegiate, club or intramural athletics offered by a recipient, and no recipient shall provide any such athletics separately on such basis.

(b) *Separate teams.* Notwithstanding the requirements of paragraph (a) of this section, a recipient may operate or sponsor separate teams for members of each sex where selection for such teams is based upon competitive skill or the activity involved is a contact sport. However, where a recipient operates or sponsors a team in a particular sport for members of one sex but operates or sponsors no such team for members of the other sex, and athletic opportunities for members of that sex have previously

[14] Susan Hollander v. Connecticut Interscholastic Athletic Conference, Inc. Superior Court, New Haven County, Ct. 124927 (1971).

[15] Debbie Reed v. Nebraska School Activities Association, CV-72-L-145, Nebraska (1972).

[16] Cynthia Morris v. Michigan State Board of Education, 38169, Michigan (1972).

been limited, members of the excluded sex must be allowed to try out for the team offered unless the sport involved is a contact sport. For the purposes of this part, contact sports include boxing, wrestling, rugby, ice hockey, football, basketball, and other sports the purpose or major activity of which involves bodily contact.

(c) *Equal opportunity*. A recipient which operates or sponsors interscholastic, intercollegiate, club, or intramural athletics shall provide equal opportunity for members of both sexes. In determining whether equal opportunities are available the director will consider, among other factors:

(i) whether the selection of sports and levels of competition effectively accommodate the interests and abilities of members of both sexes;

(ii) the provision of equipment and supplies;

(iii) scheduling of games and practice time;

(iv) travel and per diem allowance;

(v) opportunity to receive coaching and academic tutoring;

(vi) assignment and compensation of coaches and tutors;

(vii) provision of locker rooms, practice and competitive facilities;

(viii) provision of medical and training facilities and services;

(ix) provision of housing and dining facilities and services;

(x) publicity.

Unequal aggregate expenditures for members of each sex or unequal expenditures for male and female teams will not constitute noncompliance with this section, but the director may consider the failure to provide necessary funds for teams for one sex in assessing equality of opportunities for members of each sex.

(d) *Adjustment period*. A recipient which operates or sponsors interscholastic, intercollegiate, club or intramural athletics at the elementary level shall comply fully with this section as expeditiously as possible but in no event later than one year from the effective date of this regulation.[17]

Coaches and school officials will recognize that not all of these provisions are actually applicable to secondary schools and that others are not completely clear. There are also other subsections applying primarily to the school administration which include some information of importance to coaches. It will take some time, and perhaps a few court cases, to clarify fully all the details of Title IX, but the following facts are understandable:

1. Both sexes must have comparable athletic opportunities.

2. There must be equality in scheduling, equipment, services, and facilities.

[17] United States Department of Health, Education, and Welfare/Office of Civil Rights, *Final Title IX Regulations Implementing Educational Amendments of 1972*, Federal Register, 40, No. 108, Pt. II, 24142-43.

3. Separate teams may be provided for boys and girls, and a student need not be permitted to compete on a team with the opposite sex if the same or a comparable sport is available and if the overall program for each sex is comparable to the other. An exact duplication of sports or an equal number is not required as long as the interests and needs are not the same.

4. The same amount of money is not required for the boys' and girls' programs if funds are reasonably allocated. It is recognized that some sports, such as football, are more expensive than others.

5. Girls do not have to be allowed competition in contact sports as defined in Subsection 86.41. (However, this provision does not mean that girls will not seek relief under the equal protection clause of the Fourteenth Amendment, or how a court will rule.) In a case[18] before the guidelines were issued a trial court upheld the Washington Interscholastic Activities Association's rule prohibiting girls from participating in tackle football as members of a boys' team; but the Supreme Court of the State of Washington reversed the decision, holding that the denial was a prohibited discrimination based on sex. The fact that Title IX only permits schools to *not allow* girls to compete with boys in contact sports and does not *prohibit* them from doing so may result in future court cases before the issue is finally settled.

6. Boys or girls must be allowed to try out for teams of the opposite sex when (a) the sport is not a contact sport, (2) there are not separate teams for boys and girls in that sport, and (3) opportunities for athletic participation for that sex have previously been limited. *Limited opportunity* is determined by comparing the total boys' program of a school with its total girls' program in relation to the interests and abilities of each sex.

7. Title IX does not prohibit married student rules, but it does provide that any rule dealing with marital status or pregnancy shall not be applied that treats students differently on the basis of sex. (Other legal difficulties may arise in married student cases, particularly as a result of previous court decisions applying the equal protection clause of the Fourteenth Amendment.)

8. A student cannot be discriminated against because of pregnancy. Pregnancies must be treated as any medical or health disability. Certification of physical ability to participate by a physician may be required provided it is also required of other students suffering from an injury or disease. For example, if the school requires a doctor's certifi-

---

[18] Delores Darrin and Carol Darrin v. H. D. Gould, Wishkah Valley School District (1973).

cation that a student is physically able to compete after suffering from a broken bone, or similar health difficulty, it may require a physician's certification in cases of pregnancies. The school must have a uniform policy covering all disabilities for the protection of its faculty as well as to avoid legal difficulties.

The additional guidelines, entitled *Title IX Intercollegiate Athletic Policy,*—issued in a *HEW Fact Sheet,* December 4, 1979, to colleges and universities receiving federal funds—have no particular significance for secondary schools other than some implications in the three areas: (1) financial assistance in the form of scholarships and grants-in-aid on the basis of athletic ability; (2) athletic benefits and opportunities, including equipment and supplies, travel, compensation of coaches, facilities, housing, publicity, and other aspects of an athletic program; and (3) accommodation of student interests and abilities.

High schools are not permitted by state association regulations to give athletic scholarships, which avoids any possible discrimination in the first area.

Policies promulgated for the second area make it clear that benefits and opportunities for men and women must be equitable, although they need not be identical. Comparable equipment must be provided, but it is recognized that equipment for some sports costs more than for others. Attention must be given to ensure fairness between the sexes in such matters as sharing facilities, travel, and scheduling.

The high schools have moved rapidly toward comparable opportunities for boys and girls, and the approximately 600 percent increase in girls' interscholastic sports in the 1970s is evidence that a concerted effort has been made. There is nothing new in the latest HEW guidelines that directly affects interscholastic programs.

Each coach must well understand those provisions related closely to his or her responsibilities, but it is advisable to become knowledgeable about all the requirements of Title IX. According to subsection 86.8 one employee in each school must serve as a coordinator of its efforts toward compliance and to establishing grievance procedures for the district. This person will be sufficiently informed to serve as a resource to coaches who are uncertain about specific policies.

Title IX concerns schools that receive federal aid to support educational programs and failure to comply can result in the denial of such funds. The guidelines to implement the Education Amendments of 1972, formulated by the U.S. Department of Health, Education, and Welfare, may in time help to resolve the issue of sex discrimination in interscholastic athletics, but it has created other problems in the administration of school athletic programs which will be discussed in Chapter 13.

Due Process

Because of the increasing attention given to due process by the courts, coaches and athletic administrators should be well informed about its requirements. These requirements relate to the clause in the Fourteenth Amendment which states, "nor shall any State deprive any person of life, liberty, or property, without due process of law." This provision has been expanded by court interpretations to apply to almost all regulatory organizations, including schools and state high school associations, and it is important that the right to due process is extended in all types of disciplinary cases.

Schools are not required to provide the same rigid procedures as are the arms of law, and the following fundamental elements will meet the requirements:

1. *Students have the right to be informed of the rules or regulations involved.* School regulations and eligibility standards should be carefully explained and well publicized. Copies should be posted in athletic dressing rooms.

2. *Students have the right to be informed of the charges if a violation occurs.* In serious cases, these should be given in writing. All charges should be well documented.

3. *Students have the right to a fair hearing.* The student must be allowed to tell his or her side. Some athletic administrators have established procedures for a hearing before the athletic director or school principal and the coach. If the athlete wants to have parents or other persons present, this wish should be granted. In some cases school officials themselves may want the parents present. It is always advisable for at least two school representatives to attend and for a record to be made of the hearing.

4. *Students have the right to appeal, including an appeal to the board of education.* The appeal procedure must be explained to the offender and a period set during which the appeal may be made, which is usually about seven to fourteen days.

5. *Students have the right to receive a copy of all rulings.* It is recommended that the statement contain the rule involved, the evidence substantiating the violation, and the penalty assessed or action taken. A copy of the ruling and summary of the hearing should be kept on file in the appropriate school office.

Each school should establish a formalized procedure of due process approved by the board of education, and it should be well understood by the faculty and students, although there may be few occasions when it is needed. Each case must be considered on its own merits. A more simple procedure may be followed in the great majority of cases involving school discipline, but it is always wise to afford the essentials of due process. A hearing before the principal or athletic director may be all that is necessary, provided there is an understanding that his or her decision can be appealed. This right is very significant in that judges are inclined to require all administrative remedies to be exhausted before the court will act. Several state high school associations have an official due process procedure which permits an athlete to request through his or her school an appeal of the school's ruling if the case involves a violation of an eligibility standard adopted cooperatively by the member schools of the association. This provides another step in administrative remedies. Athletic administrators and coaches should always be well acquainted with the procedures of their state association.

The coach, as much as or more than any person on the staff outside of the administrators, will face situations in which relief is sought through the courts. There are strong emotions attached to athletics, and particularly to athletic eligibility. The disciplinary procedures applied in coaching should comply with the simple elements of due process, which are not unreasonable and basically ensure fair treatment. This requirement does not involve routine, everyday problems, such as requiring an athlete to run ten laps around the gymnasium for reporting late for practice without good reason, but even in such instances, it is always best to learn why the tardiness occurred before taking any action. It is the more drastic cases, when an athlete may be suspended for a few days or expelled from the squad, that require careful attention to due process. If the school does not have a formalized procedure, the coach should establish his or her own, including the right of appeal.

Legal Status of Schools and Coaches

For many years public high schools, considered an arm of the state, enjoyed some degree of sovereign immunity. Sovereign immunity dates back to the period of the divine right of kings when it was accepted that the king could do no wrong and could not be sued. From this original concept the doctrine of governmental immunity evolved. The concept of governmental immunity was included in state constitutions and state governments were immune from suits. Public schools were considered agencies of the state, and therefore it is difficult to get legal judgment against school districts in several states. Thus legal action is more likely to be brought against school administrators and coaches personally than against the school district in those states where governmental immunity prevails. The laws of negligence adopted by some states have increased this danger, although changes in federal and state laws and court decisions have reduced federal and state immunity. It is now possible to sue the federal and some state governments under certain circumstances, but the danger of personal liability still exists. A convenient source of information about the laws of each state relating to athletics is a book by Andrew Grieve, *The Legal Aspects of Athletics.* [19]

BASIC LEGAL KNOWLEDGE

Coaches cannot be expected to be authorities in law, but they should have a sufficient knowledge of the law under which they could be held legally liable and which relates most commonly to the responsibilities of coaching.

Tort liability results when there is a breach of duty, except in the case of contracts, which causes damages to another person. Black's *Law Dictionary* defines a tort as a private or civil wrong. Liability ensues when there is failure to perform a duty, generally through negligence. Coaches must protect their athletes, and others, from unreasonable physical and mental dangers and harm.

Negligence may be an act or a failure to act. A failure to assume a duty owed to an athlete would be considered negligence, which is usually a primary issue in tort liability cases. Courts view it as failing to do what a reasonable and prudent person would have done, or doing what a reasonable and prudent individual would not have done, in the same or similar circumstances.

The proximate cause should be known in defending against charges of negligence. Persons are usually not negligent when their act or failure to act was not the proximate cause of the damage inflicted. For example, if a student unexpectedly threw a rock at football players engaged in practice and one of them was seriously injured, the coach would not be found negligent. No act or failure to act on the part of the coach was the proximate cause of the accident. On the other hand, if the coach saw students throwing rocks on the field and did nothing to stop it, and a player was struck and seriously injured, the coach could conceivably be found guilty of negligence because his or her failure to act might be considered the proximate cause.

Contributory negligence can relieve the coach of negligence. Courts in some of the states will relieve the person charged of all negligence, whereas in others it will only alleviate the charges. An example of contributory negligence might be the failure of a football player to wear a mouthpiece. If a football coach had discussed the protection provided by the mouthpiece and instructed his players to wear it during all prac-

[19] Andrew Grieve, *The Legal Aspects of Athletics* (New York: A. S. Barnes, 1969).

tices and games, but failed to check occasionally to see that they were worn, he could be considered negligent if an injury occurred. But a player who received a serious dental injury while practicing without the mouthpiece, after having previously been instructed to do so and warned of the dangers, would be guilty of contributory negligence. Then the negligence of the coach would be disregarded in some states and considered less serious in others.

Avoiding Legal Liability

A review of all the cases involving interscholastic athletics will show that it is difficult to obtain a judgment against a school or coach. The courts are inclined not to interfere unless there has been a violation of law or public policy; however, this does not protect the school district or its employees from expensive legal costs, and there have been a considerable number of negligence cases in the last decade. Proper steps and precautions should be taken to avoid situations from which legal action might arise and will help in defense should suit be brought.

Basically, there will be no liability unless there has been negligence on the part of a school employee or representative. Therefore, we will consider some of the duties coaches must perform and what precautions must be taken to avoid tort liability.

THE DUTY TO INFORM

Increasingly courts are giving attention to the *rights of students to know*, which makes it imperative that athletes be properly instructed in various aspects of athletics.

Legal action is initiated most often in cases involving violations of eligibility standards. Players and their parents often claim that the violation was caused by ignorance of the rule involved, frequently blaming the coach for not informing the students of the regulation. Most cases of this type can be avoided by carefully explaining the standards of eligibility and having the player sign a release form (see Fig. 6-4). Failure to inform players of the standards of eligibility may be considered negligence by a court.

Students must understand school policies. In addition to eligibility requirements, schools will have various policies concerning the conduct and administration of the interscholastic program. It is essential that students know these policies before they are disciplined for violating them. Official approval by the board of education gives school policies some legal status by virtue of the fact that the board of education in all states has the authority to adopt such rules and regulations necessary to govern the school, including extracurricular activities. Among some of the more important are those pertaining to student conduct and transportation to and from athletic contests.

It helps both to avoid legal action and to defend against it in court to make certain that school policies are understood and that there is ample dissemination of information about them. Publicizing the reasons for the policies also helps secure support and enforcement.

Athletes must be informed of all training regulations. The right of coaches to set reasonable training standards when they have an educational purpose has been well established through the courts. [20]

It is also clear that the courts will uphold reasonable standards of good conduct. A player lost his claim in court that he was deprived of a constitutional right when his eligibility was terminated following his misconduct in a football game.[21]

The procedures followed in establishing and enforcing training rules are extremely important in securing their support in court.

1. *Develop the reasons for the rule or regulation before it is adopted.* These reasons should be related to educational objectives, the performance of the individual, and/or the moral effect on others. It should be stressed that discipline is a part of education. No rule should be adopted that may be considered arbitrary or capricious. The reasons should be well publicized.

2. *Involve all appropriate individuals in the development of training rules, including the participants.* The level of involvement must be compatible with the level of the individuals' abilities and experiences. This procedure is consistent with the democratic principle of governing by consent of the governed, which is effective in legal action.

3. *Inform all individuals to whom the rules will apply of their adoption and make certain that they are understood.*

4. *Enforce all rules fairly and consistently.* Courts are not apt to uphold rules which are not applied consistently without good reason. Written policy statements pertaining to enforcement which are known by athletes and parents will help provide fair and consistent application of rules and regulations.

The great majority of parents who understand the standards adopted

---

[20] In Craig Thompson v. Winnebago High School, Minnesota State High School League, 43548 (1971), the court upheld the rule prohibiting the drinking of alcohol by athletes. Similar decisions were handed down in William H. Bunger v. Iowa High School Athletic Association (1971) and in Michael Winthers v. Jefferson County School District, Colorado, 42912 (1973).

[21] John C. Stock v. Texas Catholic Interscholastic League, *et al.* CA 3-7577-B (1973). The good conduct rule was also upheld in William B. Hurd, John W. Albohm, *et al.* v. William Pace, Virginia High School League (1975) when a restraining order was denied by the court.

and the reasons for them will support them, and many will make a special effort to see that their children conform to them. If a court case should arise, the testimony of parents who support a particular rule will be very valuable in defending that rule.

Interscholastic athletics are occasionally referred to as the last bastion of discipline in our schools because coaches and school administrators do enforce standards and regulations related to them. All rules and regulations should be periodically evaluated to determine whether they achieve any worthwhile educational purpose. If any do not, they should be changed or eliminated. Those that do should be staunchly supported and consistently enforced. It is evident that the courts will uphold those which are based on educational objectives and are not unreasonable, arbitrary, or capricious.

It is a duty of coaches to inform players of risks. When an athlete understands and appreciates the risk he or she is assuming in athletic competition through information provided by the coach, there is less likelihood that the coach will be charged with negligence in cases of serious injury. This is very important in such sports as football and wrestling, or in any others involving considerable physical contact. Players should be carefully informed of hazardous situations that might arise if proper care and precaution are not taken. The coach cannot guarantee absolute safety to athletes, or to their parents, in any sport, and they must be informed that personal risks are assumed when the athlete decides to play.

Athletes must be instructed in safety techniques. Many of the coach's responsibilities concerning the safety of athletes were discussed in Chapter 10. Proper assumption of these responsibilities will help to avoid liability for negligence in cases of injuries.

In a court case in New York it was established that a baseball player had been taught to slide feet first, but in a rundown play in a game, he voluntarily charged into an opposing player, head first, and received an injury resulting in paralysis. It was further substantiated that he had previously used the same technique of sliding head first in scoring a run, and that he had been congratulated by his coach, who said, "That 'a boy; nice play!" The jury awarded the plaintiff damages against the board of education but dismissed the charges against the City of New York that the athlete was given improper instruction on how to execute a squeeze play. The case was appealed. It is mentioned here to emphasize the need for care and thoroughness in instructing athletes in the techniques of safe play.

In football, butt blocking, spearing, and blocking with the head are prohibited by high school rules; although they might not be taught by the coach, he could be held negligent if he observed one of his players using any of these techniques and did not immediately stop it. The same principle applies to all other sports. For example, diving head first, after loose basketballs may provide excitement for spectators, but it is potentially very dangerous to the players.

Athletes must be trained in safety procedures and techniques. Moreover, they must be taught to use them in all occasions. Athletes are inclined to perform in a game as they perform daily in practice. Coaches can be liable for negligence in either, which makes it necessary to see that players habitually use precaution and proper safety techniques.

ADEQUATE SUPERVISION

The courts consider it a duty of coaches and teachers to provide proper and adequate supervision. A coach must never leave a playing or practice field for any reason without delegating the responsibility for supervision to a trained assistant or faculty member. A player would not be considered a qualified person. Damages were awarded in one case when a physical education teacher left the gymnasium to attend an injured student and a serious injury occurred to another student during his absence. Dressing rooms should also be supervised.

The number of supervisors considered adequate has not been tested in court, but schools should make certain that a sufficient number for safety are assigned to all activities and trips.

PHYSICAL EXAMINATIONS AND MEDICAL ATTENTION

State high school associations require physical examinations of athletes by a doctor for competition, but the requirement does not officially extend to practices. However, all athletes should be certified physically fit before being allowed to practice, and proper medical attention must be available.

SAFE EQUIPMENT AND FACILITIES

It is the duty of coaches and school officials to see that all player equipment and playing facilities are free of physical hazards and provide adequate protection to the athletes. Player equipment should be checked frequently and either properly repaired by an experienced repairman or discarded.

All new equipment must meet reasonable safety standards. Purchases should be made through reputable dealers who will guarantee the products sold and replace any which might be defective. If the particular equipment is tested by NOCSAE, such as football helmets, only that which is approved should be purchased. There has been a tremendous increase in the number of product liability court suits brought against manufacturers on charges of negligence in supplying defective equipment; they have run into well over two million dollars in claims.

Playing facilities must be kept free of hazards and frequently inspected by school officials. Inspection by the local fire department or other agencies will help protect school officials from liability. Steps for adequate protection against fire must be taken, including plans for emergencies.

Gymnasiums should be kept locked when not being used for school purposes. An unlocked and unsupervised gymnasium available to students for informal activities without supervision is risky and can subject school officials to claims of negligence should a serious injury occur. Coaches should not request an open gymnasium for basketball players to shoot baskets on their own, use weight-lifting equipment, or similar activities.

SAFETY RULES AND POLICIES

Each coach and each school should adopt such safety rules and policies considered advisable under existing conditions. Safety rules should be carefully explained and consistently enforced. Policies pertaining to safety in transportation, use of equipment and facilities, and other matters should always be posted in conspicious and appropriate places in the school.

ACCIDENT INSURANCE

The expenses incurred by parents in the medical treatment and care of injuries can prompt them to seek relief through the courts. The policy of some schools that athletes must show proof of accident insurance when the school does not provide it is a good one. Basic accident coverage supplemented by the catastrophe coverage provided through state high school associations are important aids in preventing a legal action.

PARENTAL WAIVERS

In many schools parents are required to sign waivers that the school and its representatives will not be held liable for any accidents. This policy is more effective in preventing suits than in freeing coaches and other officials from liability. It does not prohibit charges of negligence, and the courts follow the precedent that parents cannot sign away the rights of minors. However, the fact that it may help to prevent legal action makes it a good policy.

ACTING AS A PRUDENT PERSON

Exercising prudence in all areas of coaching is an important factor in avoiding personal liability. The coach is expected to act as a reasonable person whose good judgment, knowledge, anticipatory thinking, care, and emotional control directs his or her action in unusual situations or emergencies and in everyday duties. It is wise to anticipate what could happen and what should be done if it does and to prepare in advance for situations that commonly arise in interscholastic athletics. Some call it just using common sense, but it is more than that. For a coach it involves broad knowledge, an understanding of appropriate procedures, preplanning, prearrangements, the ability to anticipate the results of decisions, and basic legal knowledge.

LIABILITY INSURANCE

Because of the number of suits charging negligence, it is advisable to have the personal protection of liability insurance if at all possible. Many school districts provide this coverage for their employees, and several states have adopted legislation providing that public funds may be used to pay the premiums for it. Some people believe that the purchase of liability insurance admits that the party can be liable, but the advantages of having it far outweigh any legal advantages of not being covered. The insurance company will assume the cost of court cases, should any occur, which could be a financial burden to an individual or a school district. Each coach should investigate whether he or she can be held liable under the laws of his or her state, or whether the school district and its employees have governmental immunity, which is decreasing in almost all states. Any liability insurance carried by the school district should be checked to see whether it covers all employees, including coaches. If there is no protection from any of these sources, the coach may want to carry personal liability insurance.

Defense in Court Cases

Coaches will probably be called to testify in all types of cases related to interscholastic athletics. He or she should be well acquainted with the principal lines of defense and be prepared to give testimony in support. In cases claiming liability because of negligence, the following are the primary defenses attorneys will use, but not necessarily in the order presented:

1. *Establish that the person charged acted as any reasonable person would have acted.* This procedure may be used to deny negligence or to reduce the significance of the negligence that may have occurred.

2. *Prove that any negligence involved was not the proximate cause of the injury.* Witnesses should be prepared to testify that other factors were more direct and causative than the negligence charged.

3. *Show that there was an assumption of risk.* The witness should be able to testify about the steps taken to instruct players of risks, safety techniques taught to prevent accidents, proper use of playing equipment, and any other safety precautions called to the attention of the players. A waiver form signed by the player and parents that includes a statement absolving the coach and/or school from responsibility for any accidents—although it may not negate the charge of negligence—will help to substantiate the fact that the athlete and parents understood the risks and voluntarily accepted them.

4. *Prove contributory negligence.* If sufficient contributory negligence by the athlete can be established, the negligence of the coach usually will be disregarded. Testimony to show that the player committed an act he or she was warned against, the known and taught safety techniques or rules or policies were violated, and that other athletes knew the rules and abided by them will help to establish contributory negligence on the part of the injured.

5. *Show that the injury was the result of an act of God.* There are some causes of accidents beyond the control of the coach, the school officials, or the injured. In such cases it is important for witnesses to testify that there was no way of anticipating or controlling the cause.

In the case of any serious injury from which legal action may result, it is wise for the coach to gather information immediately and make notes that can be used in preparing testimony. The attorney will want the names of other persons, including players, who observed the accident or who possess information which will help the defendant.

Cases brought under the First and/or Fourteenth Amendment, claiming violations of the student's constitutional rights, are among the most common types against high schools and their associations. Defense attorneys may differ in their approach to these cases depending on the laws of a particular state or whether they are brought in a state or federal court. These suits usually concern standards of eligibility, training rules, and school policies and regulations. There are a few common facts that the attorney defending any such case will want to establish: that the rule or regulation involved is reasonable, that it is needed to further the cause of education, that it is not arbitrary, and that it is not capricious.

National Federation Legal Aid Pact

The National Federation of State High School Associations provides an excellent service to its members through its Legal Aid Pact, a bibliography of all known cases related to interscholastic athletics. The bibliography contains the court reference to each case, the year, and a synopsis of the court's decision. It is of great help to attorneys, and should a case arise, it is recommended that the state association be contacted immediately for a copy.

Summary

There has been a sharp increase in the number of legal suits brought against schools and their representatives during the past two decades, and a considerable number of these concern interscholastic athletics. The sharpest increase has been in cases that seek relief under the First and Fourteenth Amendments and the related issues of civil and individual rights.

The courts have held that participation in interscholastic activities is a privilege rather than a right guaranteed by the Constitution, but there are student rights which must be recognized.

Schools are allowed to place some limitations on freedom of speech, but only for sound educational purposes. Dress and grooming codes can be established when they are necessary to foster the cause of education, but they must be reasonable and consistently enforced.

The equal protection clause under the Fourteenth Amendment does guarantee students certain civil rights which cannot be denied by the schools. The courts recognize the need and right of schools to adopt rules and regulations to control interscholastic athletics, but any rule which is discriminatory can be overturned by legal action. Boys and girls must be given equal opportunities to participate in school athletics based on the expressed interests and needs of both sexes. Title IX was adopted by Congress in 1972 to eliminate discrimination between the sexes in public education. The guidelines formulated by HEW to implement Title IX allow separate teams for the sexes, provided equal opportunities to participate are offered.

The equal protection clause further provides that no person shall be denied rights or privileges without due process. Thus due process procedures must be established for students and the basic elements of due process must be followed in cases related to discipline or violations of eligibility. This process includes the right to be informed of the rule or regulation and the charges, the right to a fair hearing, the right to appeal, and the right to receive a copy of all rulings.

The governmental immunity of school districts and their employees has been diminished by legislation and court rulings, thus increasing the possibilities of legal action. Coaches and school administrators should understand the laws relating to liability, which include tort liability, duty, negligence, proximate cause, and contributory negligence.

A breach of a coach's duty can provide grounds for claims of liability because of negligence. Some of the important duties include informing players of risks of injury, teaching safety procedures and techniques, providing adequate supervision, requiring physical examinations, arranging for proper medical attention, and providing safe equipment and facilities.

The adoption and publicizing of safety rules and policies, accident athletic insurance, and player and parent waiver forms tend to help avoid court cases.

Because unpredictable damage suits can be brought, the school district should provide liability insurance for its employees, and a coach whose district does not do so should consider personal coverage.

Coaches should understand the principal primary defenses used by attorneys in defending against liability as an aid to being a good witness in a trial.

The National Federation of State High School Associations provides a bibliography of categorized court rulings on all cases concerning interscholastic athletics.

QUESTIONS AND TOPICS FOR STUDY AND DISCUSSION

1. Discuss some of the effects on interscholastic sports that could result if the courts established that participation in athletics was a right guaranteed by the United States Constitution rather than a privilege.

2. If you believe that there is need for a grooming rule for your athletes, list the reasons you would develop for the rule before adopting it.

3. Why has there been an increase in the tendency to bring civil rights cases in federal courts rather than in state courts? Explain.

4. Why are educational functions important in formulating rules and regulations for interscholastic athletics?

5. Has the authority of schools and coaches to establish rules and regulations been decreased? Explain.

6. Why is official approval of rules and regulations by the board of education significant in their enforcement?

7. Discuss the effects on interscholastic athletics of Title IX now and in the future.

8. Under what conditions can a school require boys and girls to participate on teams made up of students only of their respective sexes? When can it not?

9. What legal problems might result from the adoption of a married student rule prohibiting participation in interscholastic sports?

10. Why is it important to provide due process for athletes who commit rules violations?

11. You have established a no-smoking rule for your athletes and it is reported to you by some members of your squad that a team member has been smoking in the boys' toilet. Explain the due process procedures you would follow in this case.

12. Define the following legal terms: tort liability, negligence, proximate cause, and contributory negligence.

13. Discuss procedures and techniques that may be used to help avoid liability.

14. What assistance can the National Federation of State High School Associations provide to schools involved in a court case?

15. Discuss what you think will be some of the long-range effects of legal actions on interscholastic athletics.

BIBLIOGRAPHY

Arnold, Don E. "Sports Product Liability." *Journal of Physical Education and Recreation*, 49, No. 9 (November-December 1978), 25-28.

Chambless, Jim R., and Connie J. Mangin. "Legal Liability and the Physical Educator." *Journal of Health, Physical Education, and Recreation*, 44 No. 4 (April 1973), 42-43.

Clarke, Kenneth S., and Sayers J. Miller. "Sports Injury Data: Collection and Interpretation." *Interscholastic Athletic Administration*, 1, No. 3 (Summer 1975), 19-21.

Drowatzky, John N. "Liability: You Could be Sued!" *Journal of Physical Education and Recreation*, 49, No. 5 (May 1978), 17-18.

Flygare, Thomas J. "Schools and the Law: HEW's New Guidelines on Sex Discrimination in Collegiate Athletics." *Phi Delta Kappan*, March 1979, pp. 529-30.

Gallon, Arthur J. *Coaching Ideas and Ideals*, pp. 201-26. Boston: Houghton Mifflin, 1974.

Gradwohl, John M. "Reducing the Risk of Personal Liability." *Interscholastic Athletic Administration*, 4, No. 2 (Spring 1978), 9-12.

Grieve, Andrew. *The Legal Aspects of Athletics*. New York: A. S. Barnes, 1969.

———. "Physical Education, Athletics, and the Law: Safety of Facilities." *Journal of Health, Physical Education, and Recreation*, 45, No. 8 (October 1974), 24-25.

Groves, Richard. "Girls on Boys Teams." *Journal of Health, Physical Education, and Recreation*, 45 No. 8 (October 1974), 25-26.

Groves, Richard, and John T. Daly. "Athletic Eligibility." *Journal of Health, Physical Education, and Recreation*, 45, No. 8 (October 1974), 26-27.

Jernigan, Sara Staff. "The Role of Women in Sports Development." *Proceedings of the National Conference on Olympic Development*, pp. 14-21. Washington, D.C.: American Association for Health, Physical Education, and Recreation, 1966.

Johnson, T. Page. "Federal and State Courts Clash on Eligibility Rules." *Interscholatic Athletic Administration*, 2, No. 3 (Summer 1976), 20-21.

Leibowitz, Harold. "Good Samaritan Legislation." *Journal of Health, Physical Education, and Recreation*, 45, No. 8 (October 1974), 28.

Mallios, Harry C. "The Physical Educator and the Law." *The Physical Educator*, 32, No. 2 (May 1975), 61-63.

National Association of Secondary School Principals, *A Legal Memorandum*, September 1978.

National Federation of State High School Associations. "Final Title IX Regulations." *Interscholastic Athletic Administration*, 2, No. 1 (Winter 1975), 13-16.

————. "Additional H.E.W. Guidelines for Athletics." *Interscholastic Athletic Administration*, 2, No. 1 (Winter 1975), 16-17.

————. "Title IX: Sorting It Out." *Interscholastic Athletic Administration*, 2, No. 1 (Winter 1975), 18-20.

Obremsky, Peter L. "Courts Set Legal Guidelines for Coaches, P. E. Instructors." *The First Aider*, 46 No. 4 (December 1976), 1, 8-9, 15.

Thomas, Warren F. "Tort Liability of Teachers and Principals." *Bulletin of the National Association of Secondary School Principals*, 62, No. 415 (February 1978), 49-58.

U.S. Department of Health, Education, and Welfare/Office of Civil Rights, *Final Title IX Regulations Implementing Educational Amendments of 1972*, Federal Register, 40, No. 108, Pt. II, 24142-43.

CHAPTER 12

Self-Evaluation and Self-Improvement

All of us have an innate desire for greater recognition. If we want greater recognition, it follows that we must make attempts toward personal improvement. A college president once said in reviewing applications for a position on his faculty that the credentials a person had submitted indicated she actually did not have the twenty years of experience she claimed, but that she had one year of experience repeated twenty times. If one really wants to achieve self-improvement, one must make a conscientious effort to do a better job each year than the previous year.

Several factors are involved: First and foremost is a strong desire to improve. Second, we must be willing to see ourselves as others see us. It is vital that we understand both our most significant personal strengths and our weaknesses. Third, we must learn how to use our strengths most effectively and how to overcome our weaknesses.

Some coaches, and many others, believe that individuals advance by getting the breaks, but they fail to realize that the really important thing is to be prepared when the break comes.

Personal Qualities

Some very helpful thoughts and suggestions are offered by Brice Durbin in his booklet, *Personal Rewards: Self-Examination and Self-Realization—A Personal Counseling Aid*, from which the following excerpt is taken:

One of your most important goals should be the development of the neglected sides of your personality. The mind is a miraculous gift that is yours for the development. It is the greatest miracle of all creation. What we are and what we become depends on the ideas that gain admission to this miraculous chamber.

W. Gray Walter, British neurophysicist, states that one billion electronic cells would be needed to build a computer that would be a facsimile of man's brain.

The mind is a marvelous possession overlooked or little used by many. The humorist refers to it as *The greatest home of the unemployed.* Develop it and rise to the heights; neglect it and remain among the unknown or little recognized. Use it wisely and create a world of self that is a pleasant companion. Use the ever-increasing wisdom of the ages as guidelines.

> Lives of great men all remind us,
> We can make our lives sublime;
> and, departing leave behind us,
> Footprints in the sands of time.
>   . . . Longfellow

Study the Lives of the Masters. Create your own SELF-EXAMINATION and SELF-REALIZATION PLANS.

The Art of Living is the most distinguished and rarest of all the Arts. The nearer we approach excellency in this field, the greater our number of friends and the greater our earnings. The world is always searching for superior talent. Become an artist in your personal life by developing the factors and components of an Ideal Personality.

People of distinction are busily engaged in developing personal qualities to the highest degree and do it in a manner that leads and encourages others to do likewise. Admission to this group is not by invitation. You automatically become a member when you create and put into action self-examination and self-realization plans.

Creative people are happy people. One's greatest goal should be the creation of a noble life. You are the only one who can do this and, fortunately, others cannot prevent your doing it. You are being mean to yourself if self-improvement is not one of your goals. You are the greatest miracle of all creation—a human being. How great this miracle is depends on you. Self-neglect—indifference to personal interest and lack of purpose—heads the list of REASONS FOR FAILURE.

When do you begin to live? When we begin a self-discovery program, when we are willing to put the slide rule on ourselves, when we fully appreciate the great truth revealed in Robert Burns' lines:

> O wad some power the Giftie gie us,
> To see ourselves as others see us!
> It would from monie a blunder free us
>   An' foolish notion!

That person is most courageous who has the ability to look himself in the face and call himself by his real name. If you don't like his name, get busy and change it.

Each person determines, directs and acts out his own life. Our thoughts determine our destiny. If we are dissatisfied with the road we travel, we have the power to change directions by changing our thinking. Our ideas build or destroy. If we are really living, our world will improve FROM DAY TO DAY.

Life is not a broken record. It ever changes for better or worse—and we generate the ideas that determine a desirable or undesirable tomorrow. We build or wreck our tomorrows.

Why doesn't a person attract attention? Exert magnetism? Become better liked from day to day? He has ceased to grow mentally. If you would be desired by others, you must be desirable—and continue to add to your growing list of fine qualities. Quit growing and you become a broken record. A dull person is mentally starved. The mind demands activity—and mental activity, properly directed, prevents stupidity. Persistent mental growth in the Art of Noble Living is the key that unfolds a greater tomorrow.

Your plan of self-improvement should be your SECRET. Everybody's business is nobody's business. Plan secretly. Carry out your plans and you will be rewarded openly. Noble thoughts and deeds do not pass unnoticed. They are powerful invisible forces that are ever-creating a better world.

Don't overlook the Empire of the Mind. You have far more ability than you think. The mind is capable of becoming an amazing EMPIRE, but you and only you can develop this kingdom.

Knowledge of Self is all-important. Self-examination reveals strengths and weaknesses. Create a comprehensive Self-Inventory. Learn your strengths and weaknesses. Use the former to get rid of the latter.

Develop a Sense of Humor—but not at the expense of others. Laugh at your own foibles. We love the clown because he laughs at himself. The humorist blames his troubles on an incident that happened very early in his life—he was born!

Don't think you are short-changed on talents. You have more talents than you will develop. Activate your mind and discover your many talents. Put them to work for YOU. Your rewards will be many and add stature to your circle of friends.[1]

Our self-evaluation as a coach concerns two areas, examining our personal qualities and assessing our professional competencies. This section deals with determining our personal qualities and how to improve them.

HOW DO THE PLAYERS SEE US?

A Nebraska survey conducted in 1975 revealed that 47 of 104 principals listed difficulties in relationships with players as the most common reason for dismissing coaches.[2] The same study showed that in the opinion of the 232 principals surveyed, the failure to motivate players was the most common reason for coaches to leave the profession.

What kind of coach do our players see in us? What kind of coach do we want them to see? (If we have not yet coached but plan to in the future, what kind of coach will they see?) Do they see

[1] Brice Durbin, *Personal Rewards: Self-Examination and Self-Realization—A Personal Counselling Aid* (Columbus, Kan.: Portrait Publications, 1975) pp. 8–10.

[2] Donald Lackey, "Why Do High School Coaches Quit?" *Journal of Physical Education and Recreation*, 48, No. 4 (April 1977), 22.

a person who has a personal interest in and cares for each one of them?

one to whom they feel they can go when in trouble or to seek advice?

an individual whose example is worth imitating?

a coach who is fair and consistent?

one who is worthy of respect and appreciation?

a leader or a dictator?

a coach who is reasonable in his or her demands?

a person in whom one can have confidence and trust?

a coach who wants players to enjoy playing and who enjoys working with them?

HOW DOES THE STUDENT BODY SEE US?

How students other than athletes see the coach is a vital force in building school morale. Do they see

a person who has a genuine interest in all youth, or one who is interested only in the athletes?

a coach who is fair to all students, or one who is partial to athletes?

an individual whom they look up to, or a person they do not wish to emulate?

a person with whom it is easy to talk, or one who makes you feel ill at ease to be around?

a faculty member they would like to chaperone social events, or one who can't be bothered with them?

HOW DO PARENTS SEE US?

It has been said that the best public relations a school can have is through satisfied students and parents. Likewise a coach is best supported when students feel that he or she is worthy of emulation and parents see the kind of person with whom they would like to entrust their children.

Coaches must be aware of what parents want to see in them and realize that there will be different expectations. A few will be interested primarily in a coach who can make their son or daughter a star. Some may want a coach who will see their child as a great player. What they want to see must be carefully evaluated, and it must be recognized that not all parents will always be pleased by who starts the game, how much a particular substitute gets to play, or whether the team wins all its games. These are small matters. What we should really be concerned about and what we should ask ourselves are whether they see a person whose personal habits and attitudes will provide a good example for their children.

a coach who is as much interested in the physical, mental, and emotional welfare of their son or daughter as in the player helping to win the games.

an individual whose supervision can make them feel secure at home or away.

one who will exercise sympathetic but firm discipline.

a coach who will do what he or she thinks best for their child.

an individual they feel free to talk to about their child and who will be honest with them.

a person they will want to consult about any problem they may be having with their son or daughter.

the kind of coach we would want for our own child.

It is not easy for us to see what parents see in us, nor are there any established procedures for determining our image, but conversations with parents are one of the best techniques. Whether they appear friendly and at ease is an indication of their trust and appreciation. The types of questions they ask, more than the comments they make, often reveal whether they have confidence in us. Asking what we would do, or how we would do something indicates a respect for our opinion. If they are more prone to ask *why* questions, it may mean that they do not see in us a person with self-confidence, worthwhile convictions, and rational wisdom.

HOW DO SCHOOL ADMINISTRATORS SEE US?

How the coach feels toward the school administration is a strong indicator of what the administrators see in that coach. If he or she considers these school leaders as a source of advice and support, they are inclined to see in that coach one who will develop still greater competencies and who will be of increasing assistance.

The evaluations of athletic directors and principals are of vital importance to the coach. They are responsible to the superintendent and board of education for the interscholastic athletic program. They further understand that the quality of that program is determined largely by their coaches. Their estimates of the coach's personal qualities and abilities are most influential in awarding promotions, and sometimes in dismissals. What do our administrators see in us? Do they see

a coach whose personal habits and conduct are a positive influence on students?

one who is an asset to the morale and discipline in the school, or who is a liability?

an individual who is worthy of the respect and appreciation of students and parents?

a fellow faculty member who is interested in the total educational program, or one whose only concern is the interscholastic sport he or she coaches?

a cooperative staff member who can be trusted to adhere to established policies, or one who insists on setting policies of his or her own without interference from the administration?

a coach whose bench conduct and decorum contribute to good sportsmanship and crowd control, or one whose antics incite emotions which cause breaches of standards of sportsmanship and make crowd control more difficult?

one who exercises care and prudence, or one whose actions are sometimes based on impulses and emotional urges?

a coach who exhibits a philosophy of athletics compatible with the educational objectives of the school, or one who demonstrates a lack of understanding of the different philosophies of athletics?

It is also wise to try to see ourselves as others in the community see us. They want to see essentially the same things that students, parents, and the school administrators see. In addition, community leaders want to see a person who is willing to take an active part in community affairs, particularly in working with youth during off-seasons. Fellow teachers will want to see a coach who has as much interest in their responsibilities as he or she would like to have reciprocated.

Each of us should periodically find the time to be alone with ourselves to make our own personal assessment. As a part of this assessment, we should try to determine how others evaluate us. We should look for both our strengths and weaknesses, capitalize on our strengths, and try to correct or compensate for our weaknesses.

Our own attitudes are strong factors in the conduct of our lives. Recognizing whether we have a conservative or a liberal attitude can help us from going overboard in either direction. What is my attitude toward myself, my players, parents, colleagues, administrators, game officials, and interscholastic athletics? It must be remembered that we will be exhibiting and demonstrating these attitudes in our relationships with others, and that they will play a significant part in our success or failure.

GETTING OTHERS TO LOOK FOR OUR BETTER QUALITIES

One's personality attracts others. There are several definitions of *personality*, but for our purpose we shall consider it as those visible personal qualities others see in us. They may be either assets or liabilities, depending on the effect they have on those individuals with whom we come into contact. There are some who feel that we are born with a personality and can do little about it. These persons often confuse good looks with personality. Although handsomeness is an asset, it is not synonomous with personality, and there are many handsome persons with poor personalities. On the other hand, there are many homely persons with outstanding personalities. Our character is the sum total of all our traits. Our qualities of personality influence individuals to look for our stronger or weaker qualities of character and our strengths or weaknesses. Coaches must be of good character, and a good personality helps get others to look for our strengths of character and our professional competencies.

Personality can be cultivated. Because of the nature of their profession, in which many situations arise that can promote criticism, coaches should make every effort to improve their personality to help get and maintain support. However, in doing so, we do not try to be someone else. We must accept and be ourselves while also improving our personality.

The smile is a strong magnet. A young student teacher whose scholarship was superior had such difficulties in his first course in practice teaching that he had to be relieved of his assignment after just a few weeks in the classroom. He resented his supervisor and the students in his class and soon showed a belligerency that could not be tolerated. He was given the option of dropping from teacher education or being assigned to another class and a supervisor who had the reputation of being firm, but who was also appreciated for the significant help she had given many young teachers in developing their potential. She was noted for the little but important suggestions she offered to make teaching more effective. At the end of the first day the class had been turned over to the practice teacher to present a lesson, which she observed, and he was called to her office for a conference. It was sympathetically and kindly expressed that he appeared almost frightened before the class and that he was compensating by visibly displaying a tough attitude, which caused the students to appear tense and almost scared to respond. A crude drawing of a smiling and frowning face were shown to him. He was asked which of the two persons he would rather have as his teacher, and also which of the two he thought he appeared to be most like by his students. He stared at them for a few moments, showed great emotion, and then acknowledged that he was more like the one on the right. When his composure was sufficiently regained, it was pointed out that his knowledge of the subject matter was very good, that there was no reason why he could not become a successful teacher because his problem was one of personality—which the supervisor thought could be corrected without great difficulty. She requested him to practice smiling, force himself to if necessary, whenever giving instructions or asking questions. Also each time he saw one of his students, and other persons as well, he should meet them with a smile and be the first to say hello. He was an intelligent boy who, after recognizing what his problems were and following the suggestions, found that such a simple thing as a smile influences others positively and causes one to have a better feeling. It helped him adjust to the classroom and do a creditable job in his course in practice teaching, and a superior one in a second such course which followed.

Smiling is one of the most potent factors in cultivating a desirable personality. If we practice showing the proper expression, that emotion will be cultivated.

Attitudes affect personality. They are not as visible as smiles, being more sensed than seen. We show our attitudes through the feelings we express or exhibit toward players, their parents, fellow workers, and our responsibilities. We should try to seek more information about a matter before expressing our feelings. Our knowledge will then influence the attitudes we display and tend to improve them and our personality.

The attitude we have toward ourselves is highly significant. We must learn to accept ourselves as we are and realize that we have far more qualities and talents than we will use. We should try to develop those that can become strengths to compensate for any weaknesses.

Showing an interest in others creates an interest in us. We have a closer feeling toward those persons who demonstrate an interest in us and in our activities. Conversations with students, parents, school officials, and colleagues should not be dominated by athletic matters but should include inquiries about their likes and dislikes, occupational responsibilities, social activities, and accomplishments. Asking questions and listening is generally more helpful than talking about ourselves and our activities.

We are often judged by our appearance. Neat and appropriate dress and grooming, or the lack of them, indicate the personal attitudes and habits of an individual. Coaches are frequently on display, and their dress and grooming influence how people see them. A professor of educational psychology used to advise prospective teachers to look in the mirror each morning and feel satisified that they were neatly groomed and appropriately dressed, and then forget about themselves the rest of the day. His advice is worthy of our consideration. It is obvious that coaches must dress differently for games than they do for practice, but a carelessly dressed and groomed coach at games does not garner respect.

Good manners are still influential. Extending courtesies and amenities creates a favorable impression that enhances personal relationships.

Manners and conduct shown at games, where the coach is one of the most observed persons, have an effect on players and spectators and are strong influences on the sportsmanship prevailing at these events.

Poise and self-control contribute to personal credentials. Every coach will frequently face situations that can cause emotional stress: disappointment with players, criticisms from parents and others, controversial calls and even errors by game officials. Looking differently than we feel is not easy, but it must be practiced to maintain the kind of poise and emotional control that will win the respect of others. The loss of poise and self-control may catch the attention of athletic fans more than emotional control, but what does it gain? What personal impressions are created by bawling out players before others, stomping the floor or ground in disgust, throwing a towel, jumping from the bench in objection to an official's decision, and retorting to criticisms? Are those who observe such actions likely to evaluate the coach as being mature?

Self-control and poise can be developed by conscientiously practicing them regularly. They are too important to be neglected.

A sense of humor is an asset. It helps us relax, which is important in avoiding emotional strain, and tends to win the appreciation of others. We should be careful not to make others the object of jokes which might embarrass them. Coaches should not attempt to be comedians, but being able to laugh with others is a desirable personal trait.

Professional Competency

Success in coaching is determined by both our personal traits and our professional competency. A coach should not wait until things are not going well in competition to evaluate his or her coaching. The performance of players is influenced by what they practice daily, which makes it important that we start evaluating our coaching immediately following the first day of practice.

IN PRACTICES

Formulating a simple checklist to appraise our practices periodically can be of considerable help in making them more effective. The sample checklist given on page 103 provides a good example.[3]

These are simple but important criteria for evaluating practice sessions. Beginning and ending on time helps to develop habits of promptness and punctuality in players and enhance their respect for the coach. Extending practices beyond the time established can interfere with

[3] Brice Durbin, *How to Rate Your Coaching Qualities,* (Columbus, Kan.: Portrait Publications, 1977), p. 3.

transportation arrangements and with the family schedule. It is better to discontinue practice when players begin to show signs of physical or mental fatigue than it is to continue until these points are reached, which sometimes results in staleness.

Keeping the practice moving is essential to its effectiveness in developing concentration, stamina, and mental alertness. It is important to note whether players are continually exerting themselves, or whether they are just going through the motions. Lulls in efforts can be alleviated by providing sufficient rest periods, allowing athletes to relax and to regain their vitality. Strenuous physical activities can be interspersed with planned short rest periods, during which time attention can be devoted to oral remedial instruction or short lectures on the values of interscholastic athletics, attitudes, sportsmanship, and related matters.

Drills to develop fundamental skills should be evaluated frequently to note whether players are showing any signs of monotony, which can be avoided by providing a variety of drills involving the same skills. Learning and improvement will be minimized if the drills become boring.

Keeping all players busily engaged in drills and other practice activities is an important aid in maintaining good squad discipline. Also giving attention to only the starting players can result in neglect of younger athletes, who must be relied on in the future.

Charts and records of practice performances are valuable tools in appraising the abilities of athletes, and also help to motivate players to improve their fundamentals and playing skills. Free throw charts in basketball, time and distance charts in track, percentage records and others help evaluate progress made during the season and help coaches judge athletes more objectively. Statistics should show both accomplishments and errors. We must occasionally ask ourselves if adequate records are being kept and whether maximum use is being made of them. We should also ask ourselves if we are giving sufficient attention to seeing that fundamentals are executed correctly.

One criticism we will not want to hear is that we do not give all players a chance. We should frequently check to see that we are giving all athletes reasonable opportunities to prove themselves. Substitutes should never be neglected. Often there is a commanding lead, but the coach fails to send in substitutes until the last few seconds. No coach will want to risk losing a game by replacing his or her starters too soon, but after a safe margin is established, it should be remembered that in interscholastic athletics it is the victory that counts, not the margin of victory. The margin of victory should be used to provide opportunities for more players to participate in the game.

How often do we hold private personal conferences with our players? They are the best means of counseling players about their personal qualities and their athletic strengths and weaknesses. They should understand that this is a standard procedure to help them individually, which will help to create a better attitude toward the conferences and improve coach-player relationships. The quality of conferences is more important than their frequency. Athletes should be encouraged to express their likes and dislikes about the sports program and their athletic experiences. It is often better to listen to players than to talk to them. Athletes should be encouraged to evaluate their own strengths and weaknesses. We will want to examine whether we adequately compliment their accomplishments and contributions, and whether suggestions for remedying weaknesses are made sympathetically and tactfully.

This guide can be adjusted and supplemented to be appropriate for any sport, and similar ones can be formulated for other aspects of coaching.

IN COMPETITION

The real test of our coaching comes when what we have taught our players is compared in a game or contest with what is taught the opposing team. This does not mean that we should be measured by whether our team wins or loses. The important criterion is how well our team performed in relation to its potential as compared to that of the other team. If our players functioned well as a unit, we should analyze what and who contributed to a good performance and capitalize on them. To provide for improvement it is equally significant to examine weaknesses.

Teams tend to perform better when all players have mastered the fundamentals, but coaching for competition involves both the teaching of fundamentals and the teaching of plays or play patterns in which they are used. Each is interdependent, and the failure in either or success in both will be reflected in competition. If we are reasonably certain that our players have adequately mastered the fundamentals but the team does not perform to our satisfaction, we should then look for other causes. The following are taken from the *Causes of Coaching Failure*:

1. Offense too complicated
2. Too many plays
3. Wrong offense for the kind of material
4. Poor team spirit (morale)
5. Not enough defensive practice
6. Inadequate scouting.[4]

[4] *Ibid.*, p. 1.

Offenses planned for interscholastic competition must always be appropriate to the ability and experience of the players. It is best to start with simple basic offenses which they can understand and are capable of performing. There is sometimes a tendency for high school coaches to employ more complicated plays successfully used by college coaches without first evaluating whether their players have had sufficient background and the capabilities to execute them satisfactorily. After a mediocre season, coaches have been known to announce that they are going to install a new type of offense in the next season. Its success will be determined by whether it will be better adapted to the players. A total change in the style of offense alone can cause complications. It takes time for high school athletes to master play patterns sufficiently well for them to be used with maximum success, generally two or more years. Starting with the more simple plays athletes are capable of performing well, and building onto them as the athletes gain the necessary experience, is usually more successful.

Similar problems can result when high school players are asked to learn and to employ a large number of plays. It is often difficult for a high school student to remember specific responsibilities in a large number of plays in the excitement and tension encountered in competition. Before we criticize players for not remembering their assignments, we should ask ourselves if the number of plays are too numerous. Fewer plays may lead to better performance.

The best type of offense to use with the talent we have on the squad is a question we must contemplate carefully. Should we emphasize a running or a passing attack in football? The speed of backfield players must be compared with the abilities of the quarterback to throw and the capabilities of the receivers to make the proper determination. Will a basic fastbreak pattern be more effective than a deliberate style of play with the players on the basketball squad? Who should inbound the ball in the backcourt against a full court press? In the front court? It is easier to get better results by adjusting play patterns to the abilities of high school athletes than to try to attune players to offenses for which they lack the essential capabilities.

In team sports we must always reflect on whether the team performed better on offense or on defense. Each is equally important in competition. A 1 to 0 score in baseball indicates that the game might have been won more by the defensive play, including the pitching, than by the offense. A 75 to 70 loss in basketball may have resulted from weaknesses in defense rather than from offensive failure. Coaches sometimes spend much more time teaching offense than defense. Whether we spend enough time teaching and practicing defense must be considered.

Related to the proper selection of appropriate offensive and defensive patterns is the scouting of opposing teams. Are the basic offensive and defensive plays of the opponents well understood from the scouting report? Are their strengths and weaknesses shown? Does it reveal the capabilities and giveaway habits of individual opposing players? What type of offense and defense does it indicate we should use?

One of the most difficult problems coaches sometimes face is low team morale. Too often attention to morale is neglected until it becomes a factor in poor performance. It is wise to be alert to the morale of players at all times. The first step after a need for improvement is noted is to diagnose the causes. Second, we should examine what we have done that may have contributed to the situation and what we should do to try to correct it. Were our own attitudes a factor? Was there too much emphasis on winning? Have we put enough fun into our practices and games to provide enjoyment, which is one of the most significant means of maintaining good team morale and in improving it. Do we compliment our players frequently enough? Have we been conscious of the morale of individual players and what can be done for them?

PLAYER AND TEAM MANAGEMENT

Without proper player and team management our coaching will not be maximally productive. It must be realized that individual differences among athletes require a variety of techniques and methods which are psychologically sound and appropriate in relation to the players concerned, but there are some general procedures and factors worth considering.

Good discipline is crucial in player and team management. Adequate control over students facilitates learning in any situation, whereas the failure to maintain satisfactory discipline interferes with it. This is just as true on the athletic field or floor as it is in the classroom. It should be remembered that self-discipline is one of the significant educational goals in both curricular and extracurricular activities.

It is wise to evaluate periodically the type and quality of discipline we maintain. Some questions to help in our self-examination include the following:

1. Do the players understand the purpose and values of discipline?
2. Have standards of conduct and disciplinary policies been carefully explained and copies given to athletes or posted?
3. Do the athletes understand the reasons for the standards and policies?
4. Is discipline primarily based on mutual respect, or on the fear of punishment?

5. Are the standards and policies fairly and consistently enforced?

6. Is self-discipline continually emphasized?

The coach must evaluate whether due process is provided when disciplinary action such as suspension or expulsion from the squad is considered necessary. Do players understand the rules and regulations they must meet? Are there provisions guaranteeing a fair hearing? Are written records kept of player's misconduct? Are they available to players and parents for examination? Will the athlete and parents be given written copies of all findings and hearings in serious cases? Will the player be properly informed of his or her right of appeal?

Adequate supervision must be provided. To be assured that standards and policies are being followed and that other matters in management are receiving proper attention, coaches should observe daily whether adequate supervision is provided. Practical ways to maintain and to improve supervision should be studied.

The quality of our supervisory efforts can be measured by checking such matters as these:

1. Are our plans for supervision sufficiently complete?
2. Are all safety and sanitary precautions observed and good health habits regularly practiced?
3. Are checklists used by student managers to assure that all player and game equipment and first aid supplies are at hand?
4. Is the practice clothing regularly laundered?
5. Is any player and/or game equipment in need of repair or replacement?
6. Are the assistant coaches properly assuming their responsibilities?

A rating scale can be formulated by the coach to help evaluate various parts of his or her supervision, including such items as those listed above and in the previous section. The following example of a rating scale for supervision of the dressing room, which is important in management, is a simple one which can be used as a pattern.

Dressing Room

If the statement is not true, circle one; if partly true, circle two; if true, circle three.

1.	Do the custodians keep the dressing room clean and attractive?		1 2 3
2.	Do players help keep the dressing room clean by not leaving equipment around?		1 2 3
3.	Are players required to keep their equipment clean?		1 2 3

4. Are players required to keep their lockers orderly?	1 2 3
5. Is the dressing room free from any nauseating odors?	1 2 3
6. Is there a bulletin board?	1 2 3
7. Are notices posted attractively?	1 2 3
8. Are players responsible for noting all information on the bulletin board?	1 2 3
9. Do players keep practice equipment as neat as game equipment?	1 2 3
10. Do players take pride in keeping the dressing room, the lockers, and equipment looking nice?	1 2 3

Scoring: Add the numbers circled
Highest score: 30; lowest score: 10.[5]

Professional Knowledge

Although they may enjoy a noticeable degree of success, coaches should never become so self-satisfied that they fail to seek ways of improving their professional competency. We may convince ourselves that we are doing a satisfactory or superior job, but we often fail to ask whether we are doing as well as we are capable of doing, and how we could do better. To develop our maximum potential as a coach requires increasing our professional knowledge as well as improving our teaching and managing. Continual attention and effort are necessary to achieve this goal.

LATEST METHODS AND TECHNIQUES

A large number of coaches are inclined to coach as they were coached in high school and college. There is nothing wrong with this if it is used as a base on which to build, but it will not be sufficient to meet the competition encountered in high school coaching. Newer methods and techniques are often better in teaching fundamentals, and improved drills are continually being improvised by some coaches. A thorough knowledge of various offensive patterns must be gained as well as effective methods of defense.

BETTER CONDITIONING

Increasing attention is being given to physical conditioning to increase the strength, flexibility, and endurance of athletes as a means of improving performance, preventing injuries, and contributing to physical development. The coach must become familiar with the most

[5] *Ibid.*, p. 4.

appropriate exercises to achieve specific purposes as well as kinesological principles and their application. The benefits of preseason conditioning should be studied, and the methods and techniques employed to stimulate athletes to assume individual responsibility for a high degree of physical fitness during the off-season should be reviewed and evaluated.

RESEARCH

One cannot maintain an adequate professional knowledge in any field without keeping abreast of the research being done in it. The American Alliance for Health, Physical Education and Recreation has published a series of booklets on research in various sports, and coaches should become familiar with those studies.

MEDICAL SUPERVISION

The legal situation alone necessitates knowledge of the medical supervision which must be provided to avoid liability for negligence. The latest methods and proper administration of first aid must be well understood. The comments and suggestions of the Committee on the Medical Aspects of Sports of the American Medical Association will help coaches keep up to date, and its publications will help us attend to the health and safety of our athletes. Most of them are included in the National Federation Press Service and reprinted in state high school association journals and bulletins.

HISTORY, PHILOSOPHY, AND OBJECTIVES

All of us have some understanding of the history of interscholastic athletics and a philosophy to guide us. We also have certain objectives we try to achieve. But is our comprehension as good as it ought to be? Are we aware of influences and pressures which may affect interscholastic philosophy? Why has the number of three-letter athletes decreased? Why are there more attempts to sponsor national and international athletic competition for high school students? What is the position of educational organizations regarding postseason play? These are all pertinent questions. Coaches must understand the various athletic philosophies and the objectives stemming from them. They must also be alert to the possible effects of nonschool athletic philosophies on interscholastic philosophy.

How well do you understand the history of the sport you coach? Do you know it well enough to relate to your athletes in an interesting manner? An athlete's education through athletic experiences is not complete unless he or she has gained some knowledge of the history of the sport in which he or she participates. Were there any significant developments in techniques, styles, or patterns of play, or revisions in rules, which greatly changed the game? It is doubtful, for example, that many high school football players realize that at one time there was no such thing as a forward pass, and that its introduction resulted in a much more interesting and exciting game.

TRENDS

It is always difficult to predict trends, or to tell for certain when any change becomes a trend, but one's professional knowledge cannot be kept current without a realization of the changes taking place. We must study the trend toward more interscholastic athletics for girls. What will be the ultimate effects of Title IX, increasing specialization in high school sports, and financial conditions facing the schools?

IMPROVING PROFESSIONAL KNOWLEDGE

If we wish to continue to improve our professional competency, we must become familiar with some of the ways in which we can acquire this knowledge.

Coaching schools and clinics offer a practical source. A considerable number of clinics are offered each year, and the teachers are primarily either employed college or high school coaches. Most of the topics will consist of the teaching of fundamentals and patterns of offense and defense, but such matters as conditioning, motivation, athletic training, and first aid will be included. The coaching school or clinic should be selected with care. Many interscholastic coaches prefer those which have some high school coaches as speakers because they believe that such presentations will be more practical and appropriate for the high school level. Coaching schools and clinics are inclined to be up to date and abreast of the latest developments in coaching.

Wider professional knowledge can be gained through reading. There are a number of fine journals and magazines which publish reports of the most recent studies and research. *The Journal of Physical Education and Recreation, The Physical Educator, Athletic Journal, The Scholastic Coach, First Aider, Interscholastic Administration,* and others offer a wide range of articles on athletics.

Numerous books and booklets have been written on coaching particular sports, which can help the coach broaden his or her knowledge of methods and techniques for teaching fundamentals and different types of offensive and defensive play. Books on kinesiology will provide a better understanding of the principles and methods of conditioning and the types of exercises most productive in increasing strength, flexibility, and endurance. Booklets issued by the American Alliance for Health, Physical Education, and Recreation help coaches keep up with research and important developments. The publications of the state high school association should be read regularly for changes in regulations and standards. Official publications of such professional organizations as the National Association of Secondary School Principals periodically contain articles on interscholastic sports and the position taken by that organization toward them. A *Legal Memorandum* is regularly published which contains a synopsis of court cases, many of which are significant for athletic coaches. The high school principals who are members of the NASSP receive it and should make it available to their coaches and other staff members.

Current nutritional recommendations can help coaches suggest diets for athletes. Many coaches are classroom teachers of health and physiological sciences, and the knowledge gained from reading books and articles on nutrition will aid in their teaching of such subjects.

Reading should not be limited to just athletics. Coaches interested in professional advancement should try to become well-rounded persons, and keeping up with national and international events helps one converse more intelligently.

Schools should provide a professional library for the athletic department just as they do for other departments within the school. If it is not provided, the athletic administrator and coaches should request one and requisition the books and magazines they would like to have. If this is impossible because of financial or other reasons, it is advisable for all coaches within the department to subscribe to one or more good publications and to build their own library within the department.

Much professional knowledge can be gained through observation. Many ideas can be acquired by observing what other coaches do that contributes to their success. Their patterns of offensive and defensive plays should be studied, as well as pregame exercises and warm-up drills. The exchange of ideas and experiences between coaches can be mutually beneficial. Some coaches may be reluctant to discuss their offensive and defensive secrets, but most will not hesitate to reciprocate in discussing the many other aspects of coaching.

Athletic skills are widely exposed by the televising of athletic games, primarily intercollegiate and professional games. Watching how professionals execute skills can help us understand what skills should be taught and how to teach them. It must be remembered, however, that they play under a different set of game rules, which allow the use of some skills not permitted under high school rules. It is wise to indicate such skills to high school players who watch many games on television and want to perform like the professionals.

Additional professional knowledge can be developed through experimentation. Most of the research and studies in the various aspects of high school athletics are under the auspices of college physical education and athletic departments, which have provided some helpful information, but there are not enough studies and research being conducted and reported by high school coaches. To be sure there is considerable experimentation with different styles of play, but very little of a controlled nature or for which adequate statistics are kept. The coaching and teaching schedules of many interscholastic coaches cause them to feel that there is too little time left to engage in any extensive research, but more simple, and helpful studies should be conducted through experiments from which records can easily be kept.

For example, is it more effective in developing accuracy to have basketball players attempt twenty-five free throws per day, or to make twenty-five free throws regardless of the number of attempts required? Charts are often kept of the number made from the number of attempts required, which could be reversed by recording the number of attempts each player takes to make an established number. The squad could be divided into equal numbers of comparable abilities, with half using each procedure. Student assistants could keep the records. Percentages could be figured for each group and compared with the percentages of free throws made in competition by members from each group. The effectiveness of the procedures could then be evaluated to determine whether either one has any advantages over the other.

The use of student assistants to keep the records makes administration of experiments possible and allows coaches to conduct more of them. Keeping records of the types of injuries which occur can be helpful to football coaches. There are recommended exercises for strengthening knee and ankle joints. Collecting injury data from year to year after using selected exercises will help to reveal their degree of effectiveness.

An area which needs more careful experimentation and study is the most appropriate length of practice for high school players in various sports. Many experienced coaches have concluded that there is as much danger in practices which are too long as there is in practices which are too short, but there has been little reported on any experiments in this area.

Coaches should not hesitate to innovate and experiment with new ideas, but they should carefully evaluate them to determine their effectiveness more objectively.

There are benefits from participating actively in professional organizations. The principal function of any professional organization should be to improve the competency of its members. Meetings of local, state, and national associations brings one into contact with many other coaches from whom ideas can be gained. These meetings also keep coaches current on developments affecting interscholastic athletics and various high school sports. Also the associations sponsor coaching schools and clinics, valuable sources of information about the methods and techniques of coaching and of suggestions for professional and personal development. Active participation in an association offers opportunities to demonstrate and to develop leadership.

Coaching Excellence

All of us will strive for success in coaching, but how many of us will strive for excellence? It is only natural for young coaches first to seek success, but not all will be satisfied to be just another successful coach. Some will want to be the best coach the boys and girls will have. They are the type who are never completely complacent about their achievements and are continually in search of excellence. The following are some of the qualities and characteristics from Durbin's checklist for coaching excellence.

COACHING EXCELLENCE

A Quality Coach Check-List

1. Do you believe a coach never graduates from the school of coaching? That you are a student to the end?
2. Do you research the lives of successful coaches—successful people in all walks of life—looking for ideas that made them superior—and use them in your quest for quality?
3. Are you self-disciplined. A coach cannot control players if he or she cannot control himself or herself. Successful coaches, like all successful people, have self-discipline working for them.
4. Do you use silence and conversation in the right order? A *Quality Coach* thinks, then talks (sometimes). A failing coach talks, then thinks (maybe). Meditation, rightly used, saves irrelevant chatter—and prevents many headaches.
5. Do you accept defeat the morning after by saying. "Today is the first day of the rest of my coaching career. My defeats are guides for self-improvement!"
6. Are you creating an ever-evolving coaching plan? All players want to make the most of their lives by becoming mentally, physically, and philosophically tuned to athletic superiority. They want to be superior students of the game, physically at their best, and mentally tuned to meet every situation. A dedicated coach is always searching for better answers in these areas.
7. Are you constantly on the lookout for answers to three "Ever Important" Questions?
   (a) What's new in theory of the game?

(b) What are the latest physical fitness discoveries?

(c) What are the findings in the field of competitive thinking that strengthens player poise? Are your players mentally tuned to meet every situation?

8. Are you creating your own check-list of values that contribute to quality coaching? Do you check them from day to day to see that none are overlooked? It is not what we know, but what we remember to use that counts!

9. Are you wise to a practice that is loaded with *Coaching Power?* Successful coaching is based upon success in all areas of living—the classroom, home, other recreation, and the business of living—*Living* today is *Big Business!*

   You are taking advantage of this commonly over-looked practice if you are equally successful in the classroom, at home, and in all areas of living. "But," some may say, "I don't have time to do everything as well as I do my coaching." You don't have time not to do everything as well. They have to be done, and if done efficiently, they increase coaching stature.

10. Do you put life in your coaching? Your coaching plan requires many practices, but one is all-important—It Must Be Enlivening! It must put life in your players, kindle their enthusiasm. How do you do this?

    First, you must be fired up yourself. How do you generate this fire? Research the writings of successful coaches for inspirational quotes. Use them, giving recognition to their authors. Put people in your coaching and you put life in your coaching. Fortify yourself with quotes from the masters and you become a greater master in your own right. The accumulation and understanding of others create a spawning ground for inspirational quotes of your own making. All masters have traveled this road.

11. Do you know the coach is a leader in the educational program? If you are a quality coach, you are a central figure in the educational program simply because your players are learning values that register success in any area of life. Your program develops young people physically, mentally, and ethically. They are physically fit, mentally alert, and play the game according to the rules. They face reality—know they have a rough schedule and equip themselves professionally to meet the challenge.

12. Are your players mentally tuned? Many practices are required—and new ones are being discovered. One that rates high on the list is *Reality*—Giving players a clear understanding of things as they are—things they have to put up with whether they like them or not. What are some of these? The opponents to be faced, their coach, visiting field or court handicaps, imperfect officials, etc. When players accept unchangeable situations, they rid themselves of worry in these areas and can devote full-time to self-improvement. They equip themselves to play at their best regardless of circumstances. Only foolish people carry self-imposed handicaps into battle. False reasoning is spawning ground for disaster. Players who are coached to face reality transform handicaps into assets.

13. Do you coach players to *Run Their Best Race?* Do you remind your

player that his or her opponent may be running faster because he or she is performing second-class? Whether he or she runs slow, fast, or at their best is their own doing. His or her one great goal should be discovery of practices that enable him or her to *Run His or Her Own Best Race* and refuse to accept less than *Quality Performance.*

A quality athlete owes it to himself or herself, the coach and teammates to promote his or her best inerests in the proper manner and to the highest degree. It is the only way he or she can get the most out of life and enable others to do likewise. The athlete cheapens the team when he or she runs second-class, but, more important still, he or she *kicks himself or herself in the teeth.* Our greatest success comes when we become involved with others in the *Great Goal of Life—Everyone Living at His or Her Best. This is an Eternal Quest!*

14. Are players aware of the power within them? Are they made aware of the qualities possessed by players of quality—past and present? When players fortify themselves mentally with these qualities, they create an amazing inner power that produces miraculous performance.

15. Why is the Coach a Counselor? He or she is concerned with the development of the total athlete. Hence, because of this interest, students are advised to take subjects that develop personality.

   For example, speech and dramatics acquaint the athlete with his or her emotions—and athletic success is based upon carefully directed emotional buildups. These subjects, rightly taught, help players come alive— a *must* in any undertaking. The faculty members who intrigue coaches are those who are wide awake, alert, on the move, definitely going some place, and leave no doubt but that they expect to reach their destination.

   Music is important. If you don't believe this, then cut the band and quit teaching rhythm in plays. Music, rightly used, puts life in players.

   Business training is important. Players live in a business world. Those who know how to take care of their personal finances are better organized, happier, and understand business values in the field of coaching. An athletic program needs to be financially sound— so do players and coaches.

16. Is your work a sideline or do you consider it a valuable *School of Instruction?* To be eminently successful the coach must believe his or her work is based on principles that create success in all worthwhile fields of work. Sound coaching practices are used by proponents of quality and artists in all vocations and professions—and they are applauded by spectators.

17. Are you acquainted with the all-important value in coaching that stems from understanding the *know how* used by quality people, past and present? Sixth sense, hunch, intuition—call it what you choose—comes from an intense study of the successful techniques used by the masters— not only in sports but in all walks of life. This practice gives insight and adds to coaching stature. It is the ability to learn one thing in depth.

18. How do you justify your athletic program to your administrators, the faculty, and the public? If you are striving to become an artist in your

work, you are justifying your program. The qualities of a life of distinction and a championship coach are identical. A successful coach is not a gift but an achievement. Coaching success comes to the coach who year after year says, "Still I Learn." Stagnation sets in when one thinks he or she knows all the answers.

19. What are the guiding rules of coaching? A system of rules and regulations that enable each individual to work toward the development of his or her unlimited possibilities in such a manner that he or she doesn't interfere with the rights of others to do the same. For this reason, players should be allowed to ask questions. It is quite possible one could be using a practice that does not fit this cardinal rule. Everyone should be willing to put the slide rule on himself or herself. An unexamined life is not worth living.

19. Do players understand how highly correlated *Freedom* and *Restraint* are? Players conform to training rules because they work to the advantage of all concerned. Players resent freedom taken away unless they understand that they gain more freedom as a result. *Four-Way Stops* permit traffic to flow more freely and faster. In the *Race of Life* certain regulations are essential if all are to attain maximum performance. It makes sense to say there are situations where one speeds up when he or she slows down.

20. Does coaching success depend on who you are with or where you are? This is important, but the real key depends on what you do with those where you are.

21. Does your coaching plan have an automatic touch? Your coaching plan, ideally worked out, automatically makes a better person out of players the minute they become participants! Why?

   First, they are part of an orderly system, hence they assume orderly conduct. They proceed to take part in drills, practices, and mental attitudes that make them winners.

   Second, a coaching system rightly organized brings honor to those involved. All players are given the same opportunities day after day. They are diligently working toward a definite goal and becoming better individuals as a result.

   Finally, there are no player substitutes. All players are *First Class Citizens* in a *Coaching Plan of Distinction.*[6]

How Good a Coach Do I Want To Be?

This question was the center of our discussion in Chapter 2, but it is one that we should examine frequently. We all want to be successful coaches, but have we given sufficient thought to what constitutes success?

[6]Brice Durbin, *Coaching Excellence—A Quality Coach Checklist* (Columbus, Kan.: Portrait Publications).

Are we interested only in achieving that degree of accomplishment that will guarantee security in position, or are we striving to develop the personal and professional excellence that will make of us one of the greatest influences in the lives of our students? The latter become model coaches recognized as among the master teachers in our schools. It is not easy, but no accomplishment is easy that is really worthwhile. We must possess an insatiable desire to be the best, which compels us to evaluate continually our purposes in life and our personal and professional qualities and diligently search for means of self-improvement.

Summary

Coaching success is the product resulting from the blend of personal qualities and professional knowledge of the coach. Self-improvement is essential in the maximum development of achievement, and self-evaluation is fundamental to self-improvement. Coaches must see themselves as others see them and examine carefully their own strengths and weaknesses. They should capitalize on their strengths and make every effort to overcome their weaknesses in both personal and professional qualities. A checklist of qualities can be an important aid in self-evaluation and self improvement.

Personal qualities can be enhanced. These become important tools in stimulating others to look for our finer rather than our weaker traits, and help us to gain self-respect and self-confidence.

One cannot become a better coach without improving his or her professional competency. The methods and techniques employed must be appraised and better ones consistently sought in all aspects of coaching. Constant attention must be given to making practice sessions more effective for learning, and offensive and defensive patterns must be analyzed and those most appropriate for the players must be chosen for competition. Diagnostic and remedial teaching principles must be applied.

Effort should be made to improve player and team management. Maintaining good discipline is essential, and adequate supervision must be provided. Both should be assessed regularly for needed improvements.

Professional knowledge is one of the constitutents of coaching success, and the increase in professional knowledge is one of the principal determinants in augmenting competence. Continual study must be given to developments in methods and techniques of coaching, in conditioning, in research, in medical supervision, and in trends affecting interscholastic athletics. Some of the best sources for improving professional interscholastic coaching knowledge are coaching schools and clinics, extensive reading, observation of the best practices of other coaches, experimentation, and membership in professional organizations.

Many coaches achieve coaching success and some achieve excellence. To be individually most successful, each coach must try to become the best coach he or she is capable of becoming.

QUESTIONS AND TOPICS FOR STUDY AND DISCUSSION

1. Why is self-evaluation and self-improvement important to high school coaches?
2. Compose a chart consisting of two columns under which you list your strengths and weaknesses in coaching.
3. Make a list of the qualities and characteristics you believe players will want in a coach.
4. List the qualities you think parents will want to see in a coach.
5. If you were an athletic administrator, what qualities would you want in your coaches?
6. How can an individual influence others to look for his or her better qualities?
7. Formulate a list of guidelines for making practice sessions more productive.
8. What are some of the basic underlying reasons teams do not function well in competition?
9. Enumerate factors that will contribute to good discipline.
10. Discuss plans and procedures you will use to improve supervision over practices and dressing rooms.
11. Discuss possible ways of improving your professional knowledge.
12. What are some of the benefits of belonging to interscholastic professional coaches' associations?
13. Enumerate some of the qualities that distinguish coaching excellence.
14. Write a statement describing in some detail the kind of coach you wish to become.

BIBLIOGRAPHY

Allen, William. "A Working Experiment In Coaching Appraisal." *Interscholastic Administration*, 1, No. 2 (Spring 1975), 13–17.

Canfield, Verne. "Nine Ways to Improve Your Coaching." *Scholastic Coach*, 39 (December 1969), 48–49, 54.

Dodd, Robert L. *Bobby Dodd on Football*, Chapter 3. Englewood Cliffs, N. J.: Prentice-Hall, 1954.

Dougherty, John W. "Supervision and Evaluation of Teaching in Extracurricular Activities." *The Bulletin of the National Association of Secondary School Principals*, 62, No. 416 (March 1978), 31–34.

Durbin, Brice. *Personal Rewards: Self-Examination and Self-Realization.* Columbus, Kan.: Portrait Publications, 1975.

⸺. *Coaching Excellence.* Columbus, Kan.: Portrait Publications

⸺. *How to Rate Your Coaching Qualities.* Columbus, Kan.: Portrait Publications.

Emery, Don B. "Scoring the Factors in Successful High School Coaching." *Scholastic Coach*, 31 (March 1962), 62–65.

Frederich, John A. "Evaluating the Coach." *Athletic Journal*, 33 (January 1962), 42–45.

Grieve, Andrew. "The Coaches Handbook." *Scholastic Coach*, 38 (March 1969), 58–61.

Jones, Gary. "Do Coaches Make Better Administrators." *Journal of Physical Education and Recreation*, 49, No. 5 (May 1978), 32.

Karlgaard, Dick. "Discipline of Athletes." *Interscholastic Athletic Administration*, 5, No. 1 (Fall 1978), 14–15.

Lackey, Donald. "Why Do High School Coaches Quit?" *Journal of Physical Education and Recreation*, 48, No. 4 (April 1977), 22–23.

Resick, Matthew C., and Carl E. Erickson. *Intercollegiate and Interscholastic Athletics for Men and Women*, pp. 238–44. Reading, Mass.: Addison-Wesley, 1975.

Rice, Harry M. "Qualities of a Good Coach." *The Bulletin of the National Association of Secondary School Principals*, 43 (December 1959), 152–54.

Rice, Homer. "Self Management: The Attitude Technique." *Interscholastic Athletic Administration*, 1, No. 2 (Spring 1975), 9–10.

Roberts, John E. "Additional Training for Coaches." *Interscholastic Athletic Administration*, 1, No. 2 (Spring 1875), 11.

Veller, Don. "Get the Right Boy in the Right Job." *Athletic Journal*, 46 (March 1966), 45–54, 85–87.

Wilson, Gary. "Evaluating Yourself as a Coach." *The Physical Educator*, 34, No. 4 (December 1977), 192–93.

CHAPTER 13

Problematic Conditions and Developments

Predicting future results is often hazardous and frequently unreliable. However, coaches should be alert to any developments which may become trends affecting their future and which may have profound influence on the athletic programs offered by junior and senior high schools.

It is wiser to anticipate and prepare for major problems than to wait until the problem becomes critical. We shall look in this chapter at some of the conditions and developments that show signs of becoming trends.

Professional Athletics

The shorter workday and week have given the citizens of the United States more leisure time for recreation. Many people seek entertainment as a leisure-time activity, and professional athletics collectively provide one of the most popular programs for millions of our citizens. They are a legitimate big business, like many other enterprises, offering vicarious athletic experiences. It is not professional sports in themselves that cause concern among coaches and athletic administrators, but some of the practices in which they engage conflict with interscholastic philosophy and are negative influences. The primary objective in professional athletics is to win, which is essential in providing the type of entertainment the public will buy, and which is necessary to succeed as a business. In interscholastic athletics the primary purpose is to educate youth through athletic experiences; entertainment is secondary. The fact that many sports enthusiasts fail to understand this difference must be recognized by high school coaches.

INFLUENCES ON AMATEUR PROGRAMS

There are various types of amateur athletic programs in the United States, of which the interscholastic and intercollegiate programs are only two. The former differs from other amateur programs by its emphasis on education in addition to skills of performance. It is difficult to maintain a quality amateur athletic program in the United States for those over twenty-one because of the attraction of professional athletics to the outstanding college athletes. Why is it that the average age of foreign Olympic competitors is greater than that of U. S. athletes? One of the principal reasons is that the best college athletes usually become professionals. Many pro rookies receive contracts worth thousands of dollars, and they cannot afford to remain amateurs.[1] The loss of potential earnings plus personal expenses incurred in amateur competition motivate the most talented collegiate players to bypass national and international amateur athletic participation after graduation. The collegiate athletic program has become in essence the farm system for several professional sports teams. Its significance can be illustrated by the draft used in professional football to distribute the available talent and avoid the costs of competitive bidding.

This situation has had a profound effect on amateur programs in the United States: There are almost no organized high-quality programs available to older athletes except those sponsored by the national sports-governing bodies recognized by the international Olympic governing board. The result is that because of the influence of professional athletics, the United States must depend heavily on college and high school athletes for international amateur competition, which sometimes causes conflicts with interscholastic and intercollegiate sports seasons.

TELECASTS OF PROFESSIONAL GAMES

The sale of television rights is a source of significant income to professional athletics. The number of nationally televised games has increased, and night telecasts have been added. There has been encroachment on Friday nights, the time when many high school basketball and football games are played, which has adversely affected attendance and receipts. Federal law prohibits conflicting telecasts of National League football games on Friday nights, but the same protection is not provided to other high school sports. Telecasts of major league playoffs and World Series games on Friday nights have become a matter of much concern to athletic administrators because of the damaging effects on

[1] Stephen M. Bresset, "Is Amateurism Dying," *Journal of Health, Physical Education, and Recreation,* 44, No. 6 (June 1973), 21.

attendance. The National Federation of State High School Associations and the National Interscholastic Athletic Administrators Association have adopted resolutions requesting major league baseball to refrain voluntarily from telecasting games on Friday nights.

High school coaches should know that professional athletic organizations enjoy immunity from antitrust regulations under federal law. There is reason to believe that their representatives will not want to hazard the loss of this immunity. If they do not do so voluntarily, interscholastic coaches must cooperate fully with their athletic administrators, the National Interscholastic Athletic Administrators Association, and the National Federation of State High School Associations in a concerted effort to seek relief through federal legislation.

International Amateur Competition

Before 1950, and for some time after, international athletics seemed far removed from interscholastic athletics and had little, if any, influence; but this is no longer true. It became clear in the early 1950s that European nations were attaching great significance to international amateur athletic competition as noted in the 1952 Olympic Games, and this interest has continued to grow. European nations have established sports boarding schools to which athletically talented youth are sent for training for international competition, and particularly for the Olympics. Some of the most noted are found in the Soviet Union and East Germany, where many successful athletes are state subsidized all through their competitive lives.[2] Regular secondary schools lack the facilities and instructors for extensive athletic programs, and there is little interscholastic competition among them. The sports boarding schools, on the other hand, have highly specialized instructors. European nations depend primarily on these sports schools and amateur clubs to develop their national athletes, and not so much on the high school and college athletic programs as does the United States.[3]

Victory in international sports, such as the Olympic Games, is highly regarded as a national achievement which gains political prestige.[4]

[2] William Johnson, "Sports Development Programs in the USSR and Selected European Countries," *The Physical Educator*, 34, No. 3 (October 1977), 153-56.

[3] Raoul E. L. Mollet, "Current Trends in European Olympic Development," *Proceedings: National Conference on Olympic Development* (Washington, D.C.: American Association for Health, Physical Education, and Recreation, 1966), p. 130.

[4] *Ibid.*, p. 124.

U. S. OLYMPIC EFFORTS

International amateur athletic competition primarily involved adult athletes in the United States before the 1960s. By 1966 it had become clear that the Soviet Union and other European nations were making concerted efforts to support their ideological goals by developing the talents of athletes who could help to achieve international political prestige for their countries. There was some fear that this might result in lowering the image of the United States in the eyes of the world.[5] The interest of the federal government in the expansion of amateur sports for better performances of U. S. athletes in national and international athletic competition was expressed by Vice-President Hubert H. Humphrey in his remarks at the opening of the National Conference on Olympic Development held in 1966. He appealed for the identification of more talented athletes and for special training to prepare them for national and international competition.[6] It was clear that international amateur athletic competition had come to be considered by world political leaders as an important tool in the cold war.

The U. S. Olympic Committee in its efforts to upgrade the performance of U. S. athletes in the Olympics established the Olympic Development Committee in 1966, which sponsored the conference referred to above, and funds were allocated for its program. The primary thrust of the committee's responsibilities was the stimulation and encouragement of amateur athletic organizations to promote developmental programs, with the primary responsibility belonging to the schools, colleges, and sports-governing bodies.[7] It is clear that the school and college athletic programs in the United States are seen as important phases in the Olympic movement, and that they will play an ever-increasing part. High school coaches and physical education teachers will be involved in the broad basic programs reaching millions of boys and girls from which talented athletes will be discovered. Their talents will continue to be developed through intercollegiate athletics and special training under the auspices of the Olympic Development Committee.

The failure of U. S. athletes to win as many medals in the 1972

[5] Arthur Lentz, "Analysis of Olympic Development Needs," *Proceedings: National Conference on Olympic Development* (Washington, D.C.: American Association for Health, Physical Education, and Recreation, 1966), p. 1.

[6] Hubert H. Humphrey, "Foreword," *Proceedings: National Conference on Olympic Development* (Washington, D.C.: American Association for Health, Physical Education, and Recreation, 1966), pp. v-vi.

[7] Merritt Stiles, "Introductory Remarks," *Proceedings: National Conference on Olympic Development* (Washington, D.C.: American Association for Health, Physical Education, and Recreation, 1966), p. ix.

Olympics as anticipated resulted in renewed efforts of the U. S. Olympic Committee to upgrade its developmental programs, and additional funds were allocated. National training centers have been established in Colorado Springs and Squaw Valley, and hopes are for another to be set up on the East Coast. The center in Colorado Springs operates virtually all year in various sports. Talented athletes are chosen to receive specialized training under selected coaches recognized for their expertise. Some of the funds are used to pay expenses for travel, food, and lodging of athletes and coaches. The committee considers the establishment of training centers as one of its most important steps in the Olympic movement.

Events to attract outstanding performers are sponsored, including national sports festivals. The first of these was held in Colorado Springs in August 1978 and involved some two thousand selected athletes from across the nation, many of whom were in high school and college programs.

A new Olympic House, headquarters for the U. S. Olympic Committee, has been built on the grounds of the training center in Colorado Springs, and recognized national sports-governing bodies are being encouraged to move there. It could become the center of amateur sports in this country.

The training centers can provide continuing development of talented athletes after their collegiate competition. However, because many of the most outstanding will sign professional athletic contracts after graduation, several who would be capable of winning medals will be eliminated. Thus more undergraduate college stars and high school athletes will be selected for training at these centers, and perhaps younger students who show exceptional athletic talent. Many age-group programs in such sports as swimming are developing outstanding performers at an early age. Panel members attending the 1966 Olympic Development Conference recognized that one of the major difficulties inherent in age-group programs was maintaining interest in sports until the youth reached maturity.[8] How well the United States can fare in the Olympic Games under these conditions—in which out of necessity the average age of its competitors is younger than that of other countries— will be determined in the future.

Coaches may differ in their attitudes toward the Olympic Development Committee unless there is mutual understanding and cooperation. They will object if there are conflicts with high school sports seasons, but these can be avoided by cooperation in scheduling Olym-

[8]Panel Summaries, *Proceedings: National Conference on Olympic Development* Washington, D.C.: American Association for Health, Physical Education, and Recreation, 1966), p. 147.

pic training programs. Also, every effort should be made to avoid serious conflicts with the academic programs of students, for example, by holding events during the summer months, when the first National Sports Festival was held in 1978. The National Federation of State High School Associations recommends that its membership support the Olympic movement.

PAN-AMERICAN GAMES

The Pan-American Games are viewed in much the same light by high school representatives as are the Olympic Games. Next to the Olympics, they are considered important to the United States in developing goodwill and understanding, and warrant the support of coaches as long as serious conflicts with the high school academic and interscholastic programs are avoided.

NATIONAL SPORTS-GOVERNING BODIES AND FEDERATIONS

Two other types of organizations which sponsor international competition are the national sports-governing bodies recognized by the U.S. Olympic Committee and various sports federations.

The former receive some financial support from the U. S. Olympic Committee and contribute to the development of athletes for Olympic and Pan-American competitions. Some events have interfered with the academic and interscholastic responsibilities of high school athletes. The Competition Committee of the National Federation of State High School Association recommends that high school students be permitted to participate without loss of eligibility provided the high school principal's permission is received thirty days in advance of the event, prior arrangements are made for the athlete to complete academic responsibilities before the end of the semester, and the student misses no athletic contest sponsored by the School. The National Federation adopted a resolution at its 1978 annual meeting requesting national sports-governing bodies to work through the membership of the federation when selecting high school athletes.

The sports federations also contribute to the Olympic movement and provide for representation in interscholastic sports, intercollegiate sports, athletic competition in the various branches of the armed forces, and open competition from other forms of amateur sports. Many high school athletes are selected to participate in the events they sponsor.

It is suggested that high school coaches support the activities of both of these organizations provided proper channels are followed and steps are taken to protect the interscholastic program and the eligibility of high school athletes.

OTHER TYPES OF INTERNATIONAL COMPETITION

There are several other kinds of international competition promoted by various agencies which frequently conflict with interscholastic programs. Quite often the high school coach is the first to be contacted when high school athletes are selected. He or she should obtain complete information about the event, the sponsoring organization, and the promoter, and the athletic director and high school administrator should be consulted before the coach replies.

Tours by teams comprised of selected players are becoming increasingly common. So-called cultural exchange programs are one of them. Some do provide cultural benefits for the participants, whereas others have little value except to the promoter. Each should be examined carefully, including the credentials of the sponsor and specific prior arrangements for the cultural aspects of the tour. Unless it is clear that the cultural phase has been properly planned, the tour may be an attempt to exploit the athletes for the benefit of the sponsor. Tourist agencies are frequently among the principal promoters. The costs to the participants, arrangements for meals and lodging, types of teams to be played, provisions for supervision, medical care, and accident insurance are among the factors that should be determined. Athletes and their parents often need help in deciding whether to accept these invitations, and they are inclined to consult the coaches, who should have the necessary information before advising them. The costs may be more than the value of any benefits received. It is wise to contact the state high school association and the National Federation of State High School Associations for information about the tour and any competition involved. You must be sure that the competition will not jeopardize the interscholastic eligibility of the participants. Those events which would affect eligibility and/or conflict with the academic and interscholastic responsibilities of the athletes should be resisted.

An International School Sport Federation (the ISF) is centered in Europe. Full memberships are held by athletic organizations representing some twenty-five or more countries throughout the world, and there are provisions for associate memberships, including one for the California Schoolsport Federation, which is sponsored by an individual with no official connection with the schools in California.

World School Games are sponsored by the ISF. One of its stated purposes is to create and develop the sporting activity of boys and girls going to school.[9] The regular schools in Europe have not developed an interscholastic athletic program comparable to that in the United States, and athletic clubs and other types of amateur athletic organizations are prominent promoters of athletic activities for students. Participation in

[9]Federation Internationale Du Sport Scolaire et Association Du Sport Scolaire Et Universitaire, *Bulletin No. 2* (Paris) January 1976, p. 3.

the World School Games is limited to students not over seventeen years of age.[10] Two additional purposes of the games are to have the best athletes from the various countries meet each other in competition and have an opportunity to understand and appreciate each other.[11]

The number of U.S. teams which have participated in ISF world games and other projects is not certain, but there is an increasing number of organizations in this country attempting to send teams of high school age abroad each summer and some during the school year. Coaches and athletic administrators must keep abreast of these developments and any possible effects they may have on the interscholastic program.

National Competition

It is difficult to ascertain whether the significance attached to international athletics has stimulated more national competition for youth, but it is evident that both have increased. There are now regional and national tournaments for students not yet in high school, which were formerly limited to local and district levels. Most of them are held during the summer months and cause no direct conflict with school-sponsored programs. Because of the importance attached to the Olympic movement, some are identified with it by the word olympic or are referred to as an *olympic development program*, which leads to considerable misunderstanding. The Competition Committee of the National Federation of State High School Associations has defined an olympic development program as "one which is funded by the United States Olympic Committee and conducted or authorized by the National Governing Body of the sport involved."[12] This definition was made to help distinguish legitimate Olympic development programs, in which high school athletes should be allowed to compete without loss of eligibility, from those that are unacceptable.

The Amateur Athletic Union (AAU) was granted exclusive use of the term *Junior Olympics* after starting its Junior Olympic program in track and field in 1948. Its original immediate purpose was to provide a broad base of participation and competition for the youth of the nation.[13] It was the position of the AAU in the beginning that the competitions in the program should be limited to district association boun-

[10]*Ibid.*, p. 6.

[11]*Ibid.*, p. 3.

[12]National Federation of State High School Associations, *Official Handbook*, 1977-78, p. 45.

[13]John B. Kelly, Jr., "The AAU Junior Olympics," *Proceedings: National Conference on Olympic Development* (Washington, D.C.: American Association for Health, Physical Education, and Recreation, 1966), p. 97.

daries,[14] but they were later extended to a national level in some sports, and some teams representing the AAU have been sent abroad to compete.

The promotion of national meets and tournaments has increased, but it is not new. The interference with interscholastic programs was brought to the attention of the National Federation of State High School Athletic Associations (now the National Federation of State High School Associations) in the early 1930s, and the National Council, the legislative body of the National Federation, voted unanimously in 1934 to instruct the Exectuvie Committee not to sanction any meet or tournament held for the purpose of determining a national high school championship.[15] The principal sport at that time was basketball, in which a national tournament was being held. In more recent years the emphasis has been on promoting national championships in individual sports to which selected athletes are invited; and the impetus on Olympic development and the growing popularity of high school sports have stimulated an increasing number of amateur sports organizations, sports federations, and individual promoters to sponsor national meets. The athletes participating in these events compete unattached to their schools, but most of them received their training from high school coaching and interscholastic competition.

Problems of National and International Competition

High school coaches have always faced problems stemming from non-school-sponsored athletic activities, but although they are essentially the same problems, they are becoming more acute.

CONFLICTS WITH THE INTERSCHOLASTIC PROGRAM

Conflicts with the interscholastic program are more serious when national and international competition is held during the school year and the selected athletes miss some part of the interscholastic competition. Because outstanding high school athletes are selected, it affects the performance of the school team and other athletes participating on it. High school coaches naturally object to this type of interference and are inclined to feel that the time and effort devoted to coaching the selected individual are nonproductive in developing a school team.

However, participation in the Olympic Games should be considered differently than other types of international competition. Coaches can feel proud that one of their athletes was selected to represent the

[14] *Ibid.*, p. 99.

[15] *Official Handbook*, p. 31.

United States and their only concern will be to see that some kind of tutoring arrangement has been made.

CONFLICTS WITH THE ACADEMIC PROGRAM

Interscholastic coaches are trained in an educational philosophy that protects the academic interests of students. Previous arrangements must be made for athletes to continue their academic studies, particularly in such courses as mathematics and science.

CONFLICTS WITH COACHING THEORY

The coaching in Olympic participation and Olympic development programs will present no serious conflicts with high school coaching theory. Olympic coaches are specialists in their sports, and the instruction given high school athletes will help them to become better interscholastic performers. However, coaches of national teams and individual competitors may teach playing techniques and styles of play which are not as good as those taught by the high school coach; but because they are coaches of national teams, high school athletes may consider them authorities.

JEOPARDIZING ELIGIBILITY

All state high school associations have eligibility regulations pertaining to non-school competition which were adopted by their member schools. Most state associations have special provisions allowing students to participate in Olympic competition and development programs without loss of eligibility if specific conditions are met to protect the academic interests of the athlete. However, other types of national and international competition can affect the participant's high school eligibility. Because the regulations of state associations may differ, each coach should thoroughly understand his or her own and make every effort to properly advise any athlete involved.

STALENESS

No one has been able to adequately define staleness in athletics or to determine what causes it. Yet many people who are experienced in athletic activities recognize that it is a matter that warrants careful attention in athletic training.[16] The emphasis on year-round training is believed by some coaches to be a cause of mental and physical fatigue, which produces staleness. Also specializing in one sport over a long period of time, beginning in early childhood and continuing into high

[16] George Breen and Paula Welch, "Athletic Staleness—Fact or Fiction?" *Olympian*, July-August 1975, pp. 6-7.

school, is one of the reasons athletes sometimes drop out of high school sports before graduation.

There is a need for much more research and study of the short- and long-range effects of continuous, specialized, and strenuous training for highly competitive athletic activities on the physical, mental, and emotional education of students. Few high school coaches will have athletes participating in the Olympics. A few more will have players involved in Olympic development programs, but many will have athletes selected to compete in other types of national and international competition if the present trend continues.

Coping with the Problems

A coach is frequently the first person in the school to be contacted when an athlete is invited or selected to participate in national or international competition. Often he or she will first learn about it when a player inquires whether such participation will affect his or her eligibility. It is extremely important for the coach to thoroughly understand all standards of eligibility involved, and particularly those the school has adopted through its state high school association. As stated earlier, many associations permit athletes to participate in events sponsored by the U.S. Olympic Committee and national sports-governing bodies, and the National Federation of State High School Associations is taking steps to alleviate problems stemming from that participation. The problems presented by national and international athletic events sponsored by other organizations and individuals will cause coaches most concern.

THE ATHLETIC ADMINISTRATOR

The athletic administrator should be informed immediately when the coach learns of a national or international promotion involving one or more of his or her players. Questions should not be answered until complete information about the event and its sponsor has been obtained and carefully reviewed by both the coach and athletic administrator. The first determination that should be made is whether it is sponsored by the U.S. Olympic Committee or a recognized national sports-governing body. If not, the criteria recommended by the National Federation of State High School Associations for evaluating non-school competition can help determine if it is an acceptable event:

1. Is the primary purpose of the activity to benefit the participants?
   a. Will it benefit the participants more than the sponsor?
   b. Does it provide an activity not otherwise available to the students involved?

    c. Will the program develop needed abilities and skills rather than capitalizing on those students already highly skilled and served in other programs?

2. Will it contribute to the mental, physical, and emotional welfare of youth?

    a. Is the activity psychologically sound in regard to the physical, mental, and emotional maturity level of the participants?

    b. Is the individual participating because of a desire or because of outside pressure?

    c. Will it be conducted under standards appropriate for the age level of the youth concerned?

3. Will it interfere with the academic program of the school?

    a. Will it cause a loss of academic work?

    b. Will the time for competition, practice, etc., interfere with the home study of students?

4. Will it interfere with the interscholastic program of the school?

    a. Does it conflict with the philosophy and objectives of the interscholastic program?

    b. Will any standards of eligibility for interscholastic activities be violated?

    c. Does it involve students who are simultaneously participating in a similar school activity?

    d. Will it compete for the time the student devotes to other interscholastic activities?

    e. Will it exploit the interscholastic program?[17]

THE STATE HIGH SCHOOL ASSOCIATION

All state high school associations want to be kept informed about any national promotions, and they will have information about many of them. The state association office will be able to provide information as to whether participation in a national event will violate any association regulations. Many organizations sponsoring national meets and tournaments are highly organized, and schools frequently find that the best way to handle them is by the collective efforts of their state association.

THE NATIONAL ASSOCIATION OF SECONDARY SCHOOL PRINCIPALS

High school principals have been delegated authority for the supervision of interscholastic activities by boards of education and superintendents of schools. A resolution adopted at the 1979 Convention of the National Association of Secondary School Principals (NASSP) describes the stand of that organization and the great majority of secondary

[17]*Official Handbook*, p. 43.

school principals regarding certain types of athletic events and post-season play:

> Resolution No. 10. All-Star, Bowl, and Post-Season Athletic Contests
>
> RESOLVED, That the National Association of Secondary School Principals continues to support the establishment of a comprehensive physical education program in secondary schools, which includes regulated and supervised intramural and interscholastic competition where appropriate as part of a total educational program. However, the participation of students while still enrolled in high school in out-of-season, all-star, or bowl athletic contests, whether as part of a school team or on an individual basis should be prohibited. This overemphasis upon competition is detrimental not only on the total educational development of the individual, but is disruptive to the educational program of the school.
>
> NASSP believes that all-star, bowl, and out-of-season contests do not harmonize with the generally accepted educational philosophy of secondary school athletics which emphasizes varied seasonal activities with broad participation under school direction and supervision. There has been evidence of commercialism and exploitation of athletes through their participation in these contests. In too many instances where the contest has been conducted in the name of charity, pitfully small proportions of the receipts have been realized for that purpose. These contests have served more as a money-making scheme for the promoters and as a showcase where student athletes have been encouraged to display their talents in the marketplace with its recruiters for professional and collegiate athletics.
>
> NASSP suggests that administrators, coaches, and other instructional personnel refrain from participation, management, supervision, player selection, coching or officiating at any all-star, bowl, or out-of-season athletic contests in which secondary school students are participants.[18]

There are some important aspects of this resolution: First, it is clear that secondary school principals support interscholastic athletics as a part of the total educational program. Second, they are opposed to all-star, bowl, and postseason contests sponsored by non-school representatives who attempt to exploit high school athletes and the interscholastic program. Third, they do not approve of high school coaches participating in them in any way.

Pressures to Win

The fanatic desire to be the best has permeated many phases of our competitive society and has had a profound effect on athletics. The professionals understand that the public won't pay to see a team lose. The pressures to win in the Olympic games have caused political rami-

[18] National Association of Secondary School Principals, *Newsletter*, December 1978, p. 6.

fications, and governments are involved in training programs to develop top contestants. This tremendous urge to be the best has invaded the intercollegiate program and is why coaches who may have won more than their share of games but failed to win conference championships or postseason bowl bids were fired. Unfortunately, it is sometimes seen in the interscholastic program. Like supporters of intercollegiate athletics, high school patrons occasionally try to have coaches replaced if their teams fail to win the league championship or state high school regional and state tournament.

The pressure eventually reaches the individual high school athlete in different ways. First, there is the pressure to make the team by competing with fellow athletes. Second is the pressure to contribute to the team's efforts to be the best. Third, there is continuing pressure to become sufficiently outstanding to be offered a college athletic scholarship; pressure also comes from parents who want their children to receive special training to develop their athletic talents enough to become recipients of such scholarships.

COLLEGIATE ATHLETICS

The pressures in intercollegiate athletics most directly affect the high school athletic program, and secondary school coaches are sometimes critical of the practices found in intercollegiate athletics. However, they should understand that college coaches, in addition to the problems just discussed, face other problems of significance. The increasing costs and requirements of Title IX are causing growing financial problems. Winning under these conditions becomes even more financially important. Participation in bowl games has financial advantages to all schools in the collegiate conference, and sometimes as much or more to those that are not invited as to the one that competes.

The future success of college coaches is dependent on their ability to recruit top athletes from the interscholastic program. Although college recruiting can present problems to the high school coach, particularly when it involves an outstanding player, he or she must understand its importance to the college coach, while insisting that it be done legitimately in accordance with established regulations.

Regulations governing recruiting have been established by the National Collegiate Athletic Association and the Association for Intercollegiate Athletics for Women. Each group publishes a brochure available to high school coaches and solicits their cooperation in helping to enforce the rules. They are published annually and copies should be obtained from these organizations or the state high school association. If these guidelines are followed, there will be little interference with the interscholastic program and the problems coaches face concerning recruiting will be minimized. If a violation of the regulation does occur, each of the above associations urges the high school coach to report it.

The interscholastic coach must be perfectly honest in providing the requested information about athletes: the type of academic program the player is carrying, academic average, SAT scores, and class rank in addition to athletic accomplishments. Some high school coaches prefer to refer the recruiter to a school counselor for this information.

The most serious problems will be encountered when the coach has an athlete sufficiently talented to be sought by several college coaches. The number of contacts received and time taken by several recruiters can interfere excessively with the player's academic and interscholastic programs. Sometimes the high school coach must cooperate with the parents to protect the athlete's academic and interscholastic interests. A few coaches and parents have made arrangements to collect and hold all letters and other materials sent to the athlete until the end of the school season.

TEACHING STUDENTS TO COPE

All coaches realize that extreme pressure to win can have adverse psychological effects on athletes' performances. Although perfect win-loss records are cherished, some coaches feel that their teams are better prepared psychologically for district and state high school meets and tournaments if they have experienced defeat, which the coaches believe reduces some of the pressure.

If winning is kept in proper perspective and students are taught that it is also noble to learn how to accept defeat and profit from it, athletes will still strive to win without being as greatly affected by pressure.

ANTICIPATION AND PREPARATION

Pressures are not always harmful. All individuals will feel tensions and pressures at times throughout their lives, which are a direct cause of their accomplishments. It is when the person becomes unable to cope with pressures that they can become damaging. Feeling pressures and tensions and learning how to deal with them can be valuable in preparing for later life. Facing pressures in interscholastic sports can be educational in learning to live in a competitive society.

OVERSPECIALIZATION

The increasing emphasis on year-round competition in a single sport, which many think is necessary to excel in athletic competition, is leading to what may be considered overspecialization in interscholastic athletics. The number of three-letter athletes in high school is decreasing proportionately.

There are arguments for and against specialization.[19] There is some degree of specialization in all interscholastic athletic programs. Because of concurrent seasons, athletes must decide in which sport to participate during a particular season. Our society is becoming increasingly specialized and some people think that specialization is essential to success, even in interscholastic sports. But when decisions are made at an early age to participate in a single sport all year round instead of a variety of sports, before it can be determined in which sport the individual may have the most potential, it may then be considered over-specialization.

There are increasing pressures on youth to specialize in sports before they reach high school, beginning as young as ages seven and eight. The age-group Olympic development programs encourage it, and parents frequently make decisions for their children to specialize and participate in these or other types of specialized programs. Most of these parents believe that it is necessary to specialize at an early age to excel in a sport, make the high school team, and eventually receive a college athletic scholarship. Children differ, and a few become vitually interested in a particular sport before they reach junior high school; but the majority *just want to play*, and there is no accurate way to indicate in what sport they will excel.

Non-school-sponsored athletic programs are encouraging overspecialization. At the close of a particular high school season athletes used to begin participating in another sport, and many still do, but an increasing number are being solicited by non-school organizations to compete in their programs in the same sport. Some of these programs are in progress during the academic year outside the high school sport season, and others continue into or are operated during the summer months. Many sports which used to be seasonal are now year-round activities. Some of the programs are highly organized as leagues, which include league and interleague championships, and interfere with the interscholastic athletic program by siphoning off many athletes who would otherwise participate in different sports in the school program. The result is an increase in specialization.

Specialized sports camps and clinics also encourage high school athletes to specialize. There has been a considerable increase in the number of camps sponsored during the summer months by professional or former professional players and college coaches, and they have become a lucrative enterprise. Camps conducted by college coaches also provide recruiting advantages by putting them in a position to identify future athletic talent. The NCAA considers it a recruiting violation for a col-

---

[19] Donald Staffo, "Will Sport Specialization Reduce the Number of All-Around Athletes? *The Physical Educator*, 34, No. 4 (December 1977), 194-95.

lege coach to participate in any coaching school which is attended by a graduated high school athlete who is eligible for admission to college, but there is no restriction applied when the athletes still have junior or senior high school eligibility. Thus the college coach can identify potential collegiate athletic talent and follow the athlete's progress through the individual's interscholastic competition.

High school coaches differ in their attitudes toward specialized camps and coaching schools. Some encourage attendance, which they think will aid their high school program. Others look on them with disfavor because of possible conflict with their own coaching theories and what they consider exploitation of the athletes. Some do not believe that the advantages gained from attending a specialized camp or coaching school for one or two weeks, the most common term for most of them, are worth the costs to the athletes and their parents. Athletic administrators and high school principals sometimes feel that specialized camps are discriminating because only those whose families can afford to pay the costs can attend; it would be a violation of most state high school regulations if others would pay their camp fees.

Specialized athletic camps have presented problems for state high school associations. Because of the opposition of many school administrators to the camps, some state associations adopted regulations that athletes who attended specialized camps in some sports would make themselves ineligible in those particular sports; but these restrictions have been removed because of the fear of legal action, which indirectly has further encouraged specialization. A few state associations have adopted regulations governing the amount of time a student may attend a specialized athletic camp without jeopardizing his or her eligibility. The Missouri State High School Activities Association, for example, has a standard providing that an athlete can attend a specialized camp for a period of no more than two weeks in any one calendar year. It was challenged in court,[20] claiming restraint of trade, but was upheld by both the Circuit Court of St. Louis County and the St. Louis District Court of Appeals. The appeals court ruled that there was sufficient evidence to show justification for the enactment of the rule, which was summarized as follows:

1. the rule helped to prevent inequalities and unfair advantages between students with different economic means, as well as between schools located in areas of differing economic wealth;
2. the rule helped prevent conflicts between campers and their coaches over theory;
3. the rule was necessary to prevent young athletes from being "burned out" in a sport;

[20]Art Gaines Baseball Camp, Inc. v. Clair Houston et al., No. 34693, Missouri (1973).

4. the rule promoted development of the whole child by preventing premature specialization and by exposing students to sports in which they could participate throughout life;

5. the rule helped to prevent overprofessionalism, exploitation, and undue pressure on students from parents, coaches, and booster clubs;

6. the two week period represented a balance between no camp at all and the alleged abuses of prolonged camps;

7. the recommendation of the National Federation and adoption by the Missouri member schools indicated reasonableness of the rule.

The complaint in this case, based on restraint of trade, is evidence that some camps are operated as a business enterprise. It is also important to know that the courts will uphold standards adopted by schools when they are based on educational reasons which can be substantiated. A statement of a court relevant to the authority of schools to adopt reasonable rules was referred to in a previous chapter (see p. 178).

What position should a high school coach take when asked about specialization? Many coaches are asked by athletes and parents what sport to participate in, whether to compete in any other sport, whether to attend a specialized summer camp, and other questions about specialization. The decision should be made by the athlete. The coach's responsibility is to provide information which will help the player to make a reasonable and realistic decision. The advantages and disadvantages of specialization should be carefully explained to the athlete, and to parents if the occasion arises. The decision to specialize is often made while or before the student is in junior high school.

Some of the advantages and reasons for specialization that might be given include these:

1. One can better prepare for a particular sport in high school.

2. One can develop sufficient talent to be offered a college athletic scholarship. The coach must be honest in discussing the possibilities of receiving a college athletic scholarship. Only a very small percentage of high school athletes will be offered scholarships. A study made by the Missouri State High School Activities Association in 1971-1972 showed that only 1.1 percent of high school athletes were awarded athletic scholarships that school year; 37.2 percent of the scholarships were in football, 22.4 percent in basketball, and 15.6 percent in baseball.[21] Although this study cannot be considered conclusive, it does indicate the small number of high school athletes who will be offered a scholarship. One can surmise from this type of study that high school students still participate in interscholastic

[21]Missouri State High School Activities Association, *Missouri High Activities Journal*, September 1972, p. 18.

sports primarily for the fun and enjoyment of competition. It is important that both athletes and parents, particularly those of junior high school age and below, understand the limited possibilities of receiving college athletic scholarships.
3. Exceptionally talented youth may specialize for the purpose of participating in the Olympics and other types of international competition or in national competition in individual sports.
4. Some will begin specializing at an early age with the hope of becoming professional players.

These reasons may be acceptable for some youth who have the ability and desire for excellence, but they may lead to frustrations for others.

The disadvantages of specialization should also be made known:

1. It will interfere with the enjoyment of participation in other sports.
2. Competing in organized leagues and attending specialized athletic camps and coaching schools during the summer months conflicts with summer jobs and vacations.
3. Specializing in a single sport over an extended period of time may result in adverse psychological effects or in staleness.
4. Specialized camps and coaching schools can be costly.
5. There may be a loss of opportunity to gain experience in lifetime sports.
6. There is danger of specializing in a particular sport before it is certain in which sport the individual has the most potential, and greater opportunities would thereby be by-passed.

Coaches should encourage athletes to make decisions concerning specialization which are realistic, rational, and in keeping with their life goals.[22]

Qualifications of Coaches

After physical education became a requirement in the curriculum, schools began to employ qualified physical education teachers who were assigned to coaching duties. This provided considerable improvement in the qualification of coaches as long as the interscholastic program was limited to just a few sports. School administrators began to

[22] Staffo, "Will Sport Specialization Reduce the Number of All-Around Athletes?" pp. 194-96.

look upon physical education teachers as being better qualified, and when a vacancy in a coaching position existed, more and more of them looked for physical education teachers to fill it. The fact that many college students who aspired to be coaches considered physical education as a logical major or minor field also helped to alleviate the problem of finding more fully qualified coaches.

AN EXPANDING INTERSCHOLASTIC PROGRAM

The tremendous expansion in interscholastic sports has had an immense indirect effect in lowering the qualifications required of coaches. The increase in the size of schools resulting from school district consolidation and reorganization and population growth stimulated many schools to broaden their interscholastic athletic programs to accommodate the interests of more students, thereby creating the demand for more coaches per school. Many schools added the so-called minor sports, which resulted in a considerable expansion in the sports offered to boys. Further increase was stimulated by the surge of public interest in athletics following World War II. The participation records compiled by the National Federation of State High School Associations and published in its annual handbooks show a steady growth in both the number of interscholastic sports offered and the number of schools offering them.

The greatest impact on the expansion of the interscholastic program began in the 1960s when more girls began to demand opportunities to compete, a force which gained momentum and was climaxed by the advent of Title IX to enforce the Education Amendments adopted in 1972.

During the 1960s, high school administrators began to have difficulty finding enough fully qualified coaches for all the coaching positions in their schools. No longer could these positions be filled by physical education teachers because the school could not accommodate enough physical educators to fill all the coaching positions in a much increased interscholastic program. Teachers who had a proficiency in a sport but lacked the professional training for coaching began to be assigned to coaching positions in emergencies in greater numbers, particularly in individualized sports. Concern began to be expressed by professional physical educators and athletic administrators about the possible increase in danger to the safety and well-being of athletes under the supervision of coaches who were not fully trained, particularly in first aid and the prevention and care of injuries.

A move to formulate programs to certify coaches began in teacher-training institutions, and recommendations were made to require coaches to be certified physical education majors or minors or to hold special coaching certificates. These programs are designed to assure that those holding coaching certificates would have some degree of understanding and competency in the following:

1. The history, philosophy, and objectives of interscholastic athletics.
2. Medical aspects of sports.
3. Theories, methods, and techniques of coaching.
4. Administration of interscholastic sports.
5. Principles and problems of coaching.
6. Kinesiology of movement.
7. Physiological foundations of athletics.

Separate courses are not always required for each area, and some subjects may require more time than others. Efforts were made by college physical education administrators to have state departments of education and state high school associations to adopt minimum coaching certification requirements. By 1970 nine states had some form of coaching certification requirements beyond the traditional requirement that all coaches must be certified teachers.[23]

These efforts to assure that high school players are under the direction and supervision of coaches who meet minimum standards for coaching are commendable, but not enough individuals could be found by all school administrators to meet the demand of the expanding interscholastic program in the 1970s, and some high schools began to engage some nonfaculty persons to coach high school sports such as gymnastics, tennis, and golf. It was reported at the July 1978 meeting of the National Federation that of the forty-two states responding to a survey made of state high school associations, thirty-three state associatioons permitted nonfaculty coaches in one way or another.[24]

There has been a growing tendency for a number of teachers to resign from their coaching duties because they are no longer inclined to devote the time required for successful coaching. There are some nonfaculty persons who are sufficiently experienced in a sport and have some knowledge in related aspects to coach in various communities, but their employment can result in a loss of administrative control, greater emphasis on winning and less on educational values, lack of

[23]Matthew G. Maetozo, ed., "A Survey of Special Certification Requirements for Athletic Coaches of High School Teams," *Journal of Health, Physical Education, and Recreation*, 41, No. 7 (September 1970), 14.

[24] David Harty, *Non-Faculty Coaches*, Report made at July 1978 meeting of National Federation of State High School Associations, National Federation Press Service, July 1978.

loyalty to the school, poorer sportsmanship, internal staff dissension, and other problems.[25]

In some states there is a question whether a nonfaculty person can legally be allowed to coach. Some state laws prohibit allowing any individual to teach or supervise students who is not certified as a teacher. Under interscholastic athletic philosophy, coaches are considered teachers, and it is not certain how courts would rule on this matter. The number of court cases charging negligence against teachers and administrators has increased. If there were a serious injury because of the negligence of a nonfaculty coach, could the principal, superintendent, and members of the board of education be held liable for negligence for permitting a noncertified person to coach? These are questions which warrant careful consideration.

THE PREPARATION OF COACHES

During World War II, when there was a great shortage of teachers, standards for certification were lowered to help meet the emergency. A number of individuals who would have lacked the ability and academic background to become certified teachers under normal conditions obtained temporary teaching certificates, and eventually became tenured teachers. They condoned lower standards of performance by students, which was instrumental in bringing criticism on the teaching profession. Coaches, as well as athletic administrators, might well be concerned about the possible effects lower standards might have on their profession and on the interscholastic athletic program.

One of the primary functions of any professional organization should be to help its members improve their competency. Incompetency on the part of some coaches can cast a reflection on others and their profession. The coaching certification movement will help to improve competency, and practical training in medical aspects of sports can help many coaches to assume better their responsibilities. Study should be given to in-service programs for coaches who are certified teachers but who do not have a major or minor in physical education or a special coaching certificate. Cooperating with athletic administrators in developing these kinds of programs can help cope with a shortage of qualified coaches.

Interscholastic Athletics for Girls

The greatest development in interscholastic athletics since the beginning of the 1970s has been the increased participation of girls in interschol-

[25] *Ibid.*

astic competition. According to data compiled by the National Federation of State High School Associations, the number of interscholastic sports offered to girls approximately doubled from 1970 to 1975,[26] and the number of girls participating, although still approximately half that of boys,[27] increased some 600 percent from 1970 to 1978. Some 2 million girls and 4.4 million boys participated in interscholastic athletic activities in 1978-1979, which is a total of over 6.4 million. Title IX (see Chapter 11) has had a tremendous impact on the increase in girls' participation, but boys' competition has also grown steadily although at a much lower rate.

OTHER EFFECTS OF TITLE IX

In addition to being a strong factor in the increase in girls' athletic competition, Title IX has had other notable effects on the interscholastic program.

The issue of equal opportunity required under the Title IX guidelines is much debated and interpreted. Does prohibiting girls from competing in contact sports provide equal opportunity? Can equal opportunities be provided without spending the same amount of money per capita on each of the programs regardless of the number participating respectively or the cost involved in different sports? Do separate but equal opportunities meet the requirements?

If a girl were to inquire about the possibility of playing on the boys' football team, how would you reply? Title IX guidelines allow a school to prohibit girls from competing in contact sports, but it is not certain how courts might rule under the Fourteenth Amendment. The Washington State Supreme Court ruled that this prohibition was discrimination, and other court decisions are divided on this issue.

Most coaches believe that equal opportunities can be best provided through separate but equal programs for both sexes. However, there is some difference of opinion on the part of those particularly interested in opportunities for the exceptionally talented girl athlete.[28] There are some people who believe that separate programs cannot provide equal opportunities because girls are not permitted to compete in the best competition essential for maximum achievement. Others fear that

---

[26]National Federation of State High School Associations, "Expanding Opportunities for Girls in Athletics," *Interscholastic Athletic Administration*, 2, No. 1 (Winter 1975), 4-5.

[27]National Federation of State High School Associations, *News Release*, September 15, 1978.

[28]Patricia L. Geadelmann, "Equality in Athletics—Can They Be Equal?" *Journal of Physical Education and Recreation*, 49, No. 9 (November-December 1978), 32-33, 72.

siphoning off the best female athletes to compete with boys will impair the quality of girls' sports, and that if it is permitted, boys will have to be allowed to compete on girls' teams, which would also reduce the opportunities for many girls.[29]

A number of women physical education educators are concerned about the possible effects Title IX may have on intramural sports, which have provided broad athletic opportunities for great numbers of girls. Will concentration on interscholastic competition by the talented result in lessening the importance of intramural activities for which the girls' physical education program has always been noted?[30]

These examples illustrate some of the issues and problems stemming from Title IX and the need for keeping informed of current developments. Closely related are problems resulting from various interpretations of the Fourteenth Amendment. The emphasis has been on the protection of civil rights, which has been interpreted by several students to mean the right to participate but thus far has not been recognized by the courts. An issue that needs to be further clarified is whether the amendment is intended to avoid individual sex discrimination or collective sex discrimination, which could have additional effects on interscholastic athletics.[31]

A number of internal school problems have resulted from the impact of a greatly expanded interscholastic program, and accommodating both sexes requires many compromises.

SHARING FACILITIES

Relatively few schools have sufficient athletic facilities to meet the needs of the interscholastic program and it is difficult to vote levies to construct more. The accommodation of both sexes strains existing facilities and requires greater sharing. Coaches must cooperate in developing plans which will provide for fair and equitable use of buildings and fields.

CONFLICTS IN SCHEDULING

Avoiding conflicts in scheduling contests and practice sessions has become increasingly difficult, complicated further by avoiding conflicts with nonathletic student activities. It is becoming more and more necessary for master scheduling plans to be developed to provide the

[29] Florence Grebner, "Sex as a Parameter of Athletic Eligibility," *The Physical Educator,* 31, No. 4 (December 1974), 205.

[30] Danae Clark, "Intramurals: A Casualty of Title IX," *Journal of Physical Education and Recreation,* 48, No. 5 (May 1977), 66–67.

[31] Grebner, "Sex as a Parameter of Athletic Eligibility," p. 207.

best equity possible. With boys' and girls' varsity contests and practices, finding time for junior games and practices becomes more difficult. Coaches must try to protect their own program, but they must be aware of the needs of each other's programs and cooperate in working out arrangements. In some cases it may mean reducing the length of practice sessions to provide additional practice spaces in the schedule, which would require the maximum use of the time allowed.

BUDGET ALLOCATIONS

It is typical in school administration that additional offerings are squeezed into existing budgets before additional sources of funding are secured, which means that often there must be a greater sharing of the athletic dollar. Taking from one sport to finance others can cause friction among coaches, but decisions have to be made by athletic directors and boards of education. Each coach has a right to insist that his or her sport receives its fair share, but he or she must also cooperate by taking better care of equipment and saving expenses whenever possible without damaging his or her part of the athletic program.

School Finances

Boards of education traditionally have subsidized interscholastic athletic programs, providing facilities and utilities and paying salaries of coaches from school funds without charge to the athletic department. Receipts from admissions seldom, if ever, would supply sufficient funds to cover all these costs. In addition, because interscholastic athletics are considered an important part of the total educational program, boards of education allocate monies from its funds, much of which is derived from local school taxes on personal property, to support the athletic program.

The growth in interscholastic offerings for boys and the tremendous expansion in girls' athletic programs have increased the costs of the interscholastic athletic program.

THE TAXPAYERS' REVOLT

Problems in school financing began to occur when the public started to resist the rising costs of government, stimulated further by the exposure of tremendous waste and considerable corruption in the use of state and federal funds. The fact that local taxes, including school taxes, were the only ones on which citizens had an opportunity to vote prompted them to reject proposed school tax increases to meet rising costs due to inflation. This created financial crises for a number of boards of education, which found it necessary to reduce its curricular and extracurricular programs. In such circumstances, the interscholastic athletic program is often the first to be affected, and in some instances, eliminated.

The tax revolt was climaxed by the much publicized passing of Proposition 13 by the voters in California in 1978.[32] The limit set on property taxes of 1 percent and the requirement that local tax increases must be approved by two-thirds of all eligible voters had a two-pronged effect on the school programs in California. It reduced considerably the amount of state funds available to schools and made it much more difficult to pass local school tax levies. Both curricular and extracurricular programs were drastically affected. Most schools managed to maintain their interscholastic athletic programs, but many found it necessary to decrease allocations considerably, reduce the number of coaches, eliminate some sports, and limit junior varsity and freshmen programs. The wide attention given by the news media greatly expanded the influence of Proposition 13, and it would be difficult to determine its ultimate and far-reaching effects on interscholastic programs throughout the nation.

NEED TO BE INFORMED

Coaches have always been concerned about athletic budgets, but they should also be well informed about the school's total education budget and the financial conditions of the district. Because of the strategic position they occupy, they have many occasions to discuss athletic costs with school patrons and community groups. It is important that the citizens in the community be better informed of the cost of the interscholastic program in relation to the school's total budget. Few realize that interscholastic athletics utilize less than 1 percent of the total school budget, exclusive of the use of facilities and utilities.[33]

COPING WITH FINANCIAL PROBLEMS

Financial problems facing the school district are not just the concern of the board of education, but they affect the future of interscholastic athletics and of coaches themselves.

Practicing economy helps to avoid and alleviate financial problems. Care must be taken not to reduce the quality of the program unnecessarily or to sacrifice safety and the well-being of athletes, but some measures can be taken without undesirable effects.

Coaches must take excellent care of equipment and see that any

[32] Richard G. Fawcett, "Proposition 13: The Shot Heard Around the World," *Interscholastic Athletic Administration*, 5, No. 2 (Winter 1978), 4-16.

[33] "Interscholastic Athletics: Their Cost and Value," *Interscholastic Athletic Administration*, 3, No. 2 (Spring 1977), 17-18.

necessary repairs are promptly made to lengthen its use. Players also must be required to take excellent care of the equipment.

Only equipment that is actually needed should be requested. Purchasing through bids can save money and, this procedure should be suggested if the school does not use it already. To assure receiving equipment of the quality desired, coaches should list the brand and catalog numbers on each item let to bid.

Money can be saved in providing meals and transportation. The practice of some coaches of wanting to supply players with better meals on athletic trips than they enjoy at home and providing meals after home games is unnecessary. Having athletes eat as many meals at home as possible helps to economize, and they are inclined to perform better when they eat meals they are used to. Scheduling games as near to home as feasible can help reduce transportation expenses and provide for better attendance.

Avoid lengthy practice sessions requiring use of facilities which add to the cost of utilities. There will be increasing pressure to conserve energy. Coaches can cooperate by limiting practice sessions to what is necessary. Practice requiring the use of gymnasiums during vacation periods should be avoided as much as possible. Athletes sometimes perform better when they have rest periods during the season, and there is less interference with family activities when practices are not held.

The use of private funds in financial crises should be accepted with qualifications. Private organizations and individuals occasionally offer to provide financial assistance, particularly during periods of financial difficulties when discontinuing the interscholastic program is considered. Money should be accepted only when it will not influence school policies. If it is designated for a particular use or for a specific sport, policy is then being determined by the donor. If it is offered for the athletic program without any strings attached, it can then be accepted without interfering with the policy-making responsibilities of the school administration and board of education.

Another problem that can develop from the use of private funds is that it is a temporary aid, which may not be continued for an extended period, and causes the interscholastic program to remain in a precarious position without a permanent solution. It may also influence citizens in the community to think that athletics can be supported without the use of school funds, which can further complicate the problem.

Special projects to raise finances are used by some coaches. A few coaches have always employed special techniques to help finance their sports, for example, soap games between teams chosen from the squad for which the admission may be a bar of soap (or some other commodity). Others hold an intrasquad game before starting the competition season to raise funds for season expenses and for which a reduced admission is charged. They have found that fans are willing to help support the team in this manner. Other projects may be used, but care should always be taken to avoid excessive use of the students' time or to interfere with their other responsibilities.

Athletic Trainers

The emphasis on better medical supervision warrants serious consideration by coaches and athletic administrators. The number of court cases involving athletic injuries has increased, which makes it important that more attention be given to avoiding legal liability for negligence in the medical aspects of athletics.

It was reported in 1971 that only about one hundred schools in the United States had a full-time teacher-athletic trainer on their faculties, and that approximately one-fourth of the head coaches of junior and senior schools had sufficient professional training to qualify as an athletic trainer.[34] The need for trainers has been recognized, but additional expenses are involved when professional trainers are available.[35]

Fortunately, steps have been taken to help remedy one of those conditions. The National Athletic Trainers Association formed in 1950 has devoted continual effort to developmental programs for trainers and has formulated standards for approving programs already offered. Courses also are now given in workshops and seminars to train student athletic trainers. It can be expected that more professionally prepared trainers will be available in the future.

What should the coach do if there is no athletic trainer? Because of the possibility of liability for negligence coaches should discuss the matter with the athletic administrator and high school principal. They could offer to acquire the necessary professional training, which would help greatly in providing personal protection, but because of conflicts in duties this may not be the best solution.

The school administrator could be encouraged to employ a teacher-trainer, or to have a faculty member trained as a trainer and given a reduced teaching assignment to allow time for the new responsibilities. This person could serve both the athletic and physical education programs.

The possibility of establishing a student-trainer program could be suggested. A few schools have held summer programs offering a course

[34] Walter C. Schwank and Sayers J. Miller, "New Dimensions for the Athletic Training Profession," *Journal of Health, Physical Education, and Recreation* (September 1971), p. 41.

[35] *Ibid.*, pp. 41-42.

in athletic training to high school students.[36] It is best that students trained in this type of program assist a head trainer, but they can serve also when the school finds it impossible to employ a full-time teacher-trainer.

A number of colleges and universities have summer programs for teacher-trainers and student-trainers. No school should designate a person as an athletic trainer unless he or she has had the proper professional training. Medical societies are recommending that schools have a qualified trainer on their staffs, and some state legislatures are considering requiring it.

Summary

Interscholastic athletic coaches must keep abreast of existing conditions and developments and anticipate their effects on interscholastic athletics and coaching.

Professional athletics continue to influence interscholastic athletics directly or indirectly. They also influence other amateur athletic programs. The fact that they siphon off the great majority of the most talented athletes in the United States results in more dependence on high school and college athletes in the Olympic Games and Pan-American Games and other international competition. Televising professional games adversely affects attendance at high school games, and encroachment on the traditional time for interscholastic games must be resisted.

The fact that the Soviet Union and other European countries view victory in the Olympic Games and other international competition as a national achievement which gains international political prestige and supports their ideologies is affecting amateur athletics in our country. The U. S. Olympic Committee is developing programs to identify talented athletes at an early age and prepare them for the Olympics. High school coaches and administrators should support the Olympic movement but must insist that it not damage the interscholastic athletic program, which is an important part of the total U. S. Olympic development program.

Schools must cope with proliferations of the Olympic movement. International athletic tours are sponsored by non-school organizations and individuals and tend to exploit high school athletes and the interscholastic program. International meets and tournaments are promoted by foreign sports federations, which solicit the participation of U. S. high school teams and individual athletes. These events may interefere with the academic and interscholastic responsibilities of students.

[36] Bill Beckman, "Organization of a Student Trainer Program," *Interscholastic Administration*, 1, No. 2 (Summer 1975), 9–10.

The attention given to the importance of Olympic competition and other international events has stimulated an increase in national competition for high school students, which sometimes intereferes with the interscholastic programs. Coaches should always work with their athletic administrators in coping with any such difficulties. The state high school association and the National Federation of State High School Associations can provide advice and aid in these matters.

There is increasing pressure to win stemming from the desire of high school athletes, and their parents, for college athletic scholarships and the stress on international competition. This pressure is causing some youths to begin overspecializing in athletics at an early age. Winning and specialization must be kept in proper perspective, and athletes must be taught how to cope with pressures, which can be an educational experience.

The expansion in interscholastic athletics, caused in large part by the increase in interscholastic sports for girls, has created a shortage of high school coaches. Nonfaculty coaches have been employed to fill positions in some states to avoid eliminating some sports from the program. Coaching certification programs have been developed by teacher-training institutions to certify coaches who are not physical education teachers and who already have the qualifications. There is a recognized need for more well-trained coaches.

The impact of more interscholastic athletics for girls has presented problems for schools and coaches. The requirements of Title IX for equal opportunities for girls has broad implications. Facilities must be shared equitably, budget allocations must be equitable, and practice and playing time must not favor either sex.

The taxpayers' revolt has had some drastic effects on the interscholastic offerings of a number of schools and is a matter of concern for all coaches. The coach must be informed about the school's finances and should have factual evidence when discussing athletic financial matters. Every effort should be made to help the district cope with financial problems by practicing economical prudence and seeking other solutions.

Consideration should be given to securing the services of a professionally prepared athletic trainer for better medical supervision of athletes to prevent legal action for negligence.

QUESTIONS AND TOPICS FOR STUDY AND DISCUSSION

1. Why is it wise to anticipate and prepare for major problems in interscholastic sports?

2. Discuss ways that professional athletics affect interscholastic athletics. How do they affect U. S. Olympic competition?

3. What is the major difference in the way that the Soviet Union, West Germany, and some other European countries develop athletes for Olympic competition compared to the United States?

4. What part do interscholastic and intercollegiate athletics play in the U. S. Olympic efforts? In what ways does this affect the interscholastic athletic program?

5. How do the activities sponsored by national sports-governing bodies and sports federations sometimes conflict with interscholastic athletics?

6. Under what conditions does the National Federation of State High School Associations recommend that high school athletes be permitted to participate in events sponsored by these bodies without loss of eligibility?

7. Discuss some ways the interscholastic program and high school athletes are exploited through international athletic competition.

8. Give what you think are some of the major causes of the increase in national competition for junior and senior high school students. Discuss some of its possible effects on the interscholastic athletic program and on high school coaching.

9. Assume one of your players has been invited to join a team selected to participate in an international athletic meet or tournament to be held in Europe; outline the procedure and steps you would take, including the factors to which you would give consideration.

10. Enumerate four major guidelines for evaluating nonschool competition to determine whether it is acceptable.

11. Discuss some of the factors that are increasing the pressure to win and show how each affects interscholastic athletics.

12. When and how can facing up to pressures be educational for high school athletes? How can the coach help?

13. What are the causes of the increasing tendency of high school athletes to specialize in one sport?

14. What is your position in regard to specialized sports camps? Why do you take this position?

15. The parents of a twelve-year-old boy asks you whether you would suggest that he choose one sport in which to participate in junior high school or whether he should compete in more than one. Explain how you would try to help these parents.

16. Why has there been an increasing tendency for schools to employ a non-faculty coach? Give reasons why you think this is a good or bad step.

17. Give examples of situations with which you are familiar illustrating the effect of the financial crisis on interscholastic athletics. Why is the interscholastic program one of the first to be affected when a school faces financial difficulties?
18. Why is it important for a coach to be well informed about the school's financial status? What information should he or she have when discussing athletic financial matters with school patrons?
19. Discuss possible ways a school can provide for the services of an athletic trainer.

BIBLIOGRAPHY

Adams, Samuel H. "Certification in Coaching: A Sorely Needed Aspect of Education." *Athletic Purchasing and Facilities*, 2, No. 6 (November 1978), 20-22.

Breen, George, and Welch, Paula. "Athletic Staleness—Fact or Fiction?" *Olympian*, July-August 1975, pp. 6-7, 15.

Bressett, Stephen M. "Is Amateurism Dying?" *Journal of Health, Physical Education, and Recreation*, 44, No. 6 (June 1973), 21.

Clark, Danae. "Intramurals: A Casualty of Title IX." *Journal of Physical Education and Recreation*, 48, No. 5 (May 1977), 66-67.

Crase, Darrell. "Athletics in Trouble." *The Physical Educator*, April 1972, pp. 39-41.

Fawcett, Richard G. "Proposition 13: The Shot Heard Around the World." *Interscholastic Athletic Administration*, 5, No. 2 (Winter 1978), 4-16.

Federation Internationale Du Sport Scolaire et Association Du Sport Scolarie Et Universitaire. *Bulletin No. 2* (Paris), January 1976.

Geadelmann, Patricia L. "Equality in Athletics: Can Separate Be Equal?" *Journal of Physical Education and Recreation*, 49, No. 9 (November-December 1978), 32-33, 72.

Grebner, Florence. "Sex as a Parameter of Athletic Eligibility." *The Physical Educator*, 31, No. 4 (December 1974), 205-207.

Harty, David. "Nonfaculty Coaches." Survey report given at the 1978 annual meeting of the National Federation of State High School Associations. *National Federation Press Service*, July 1978.

Hibler, Richard W. "Ideals and Realities of the Olympic Games." *The Physical Educator*, 33, No. 3 (October 1976), 119-21.

Johnson, William. "Sports Development Programs in the USSR and Selected European Countries." *The Physical Educator*, 34, No. 3 (October 1977), 153-56.

Keith, Forbes. "Practice Coaching." *Journal of Physical Education and Recreation*, 47, No. 9 (December 1976), 18.

Kelly, John B., Jr. "The AAU Junior Olympics." *Proceedings of National Conference on Olympic Development*, pp. 97-101. Washington, D. C. : American Association for Health, Physical Education, and Recreation, 1966.

Long, Ruth, Robert Buser, and Michael Jackson. "Student Activities in the Seventies." *National Association of Secondary School Principals*, 1977.

McKinney, Wayne C., and Robert Taylor. "Certification of Coaches: The Missouri Approach." *Journal of Health, Physical Education, and Recreation*, 41, No. 8 (October 1979), 50-51, 56.

Maetozo, Matthew G. "Required Specialized Preparation for Coaching." *Journal of Health, Physical Education, and Recreation*, April 1971, pp. 12-13.

Maetozo, Matthew G., ed. "A Survey of Special Certification Requirements for Athletic Coaches of High School Interscholastic Teams." *Journal of Health, Physical Education, and Recreation*, 41, No. 7 (September 1970), 14, 16.

——. *Certification of High School Coaches*. Washington, D.C.: American Association for Health, Physical Education, and Recreation, 1971.

Mollet, Raous E. L. "Current Trends in European Olympic Development." *Proceedings of National Conference on Olympic Development*, pp. 123-32. Washington, D.C.: American Association for Health, Physical Education, and Recreation, 1966.

Moyer, Lou Jean. "Women's Athletics—What Is Our Future?" Article adapted from a speech presented at the Northwest District Convention in April 1976. *Journal of Physical Education and Recreation*, 48, No. 1 (January 1977), 52, 54.

National Association of Secondary School Principals. *Newsletter*, December 1978, p. 6

National Federation of State High School Associations. "Athletics: Their Cost and Value." *Interscholastic Athletic Administration*, 3, No. 2 (Spring 1977), 17-19.

——. Expanding Opportunities for Girls in Athletics." *Interscholastic Athletic Administration*, 2, No. 1 (Winter 1975), 4-5.

——. "Making a Place for Interscholastic Athletics." *Interscholastic Athletic Administration*, 3, No. 2 (Spring 1977), 23-25, 31-32.

——. *Official Handbook*, 1977-78, p. 31.

——. "The Role of Private Funding." *Interscholastic Athletic Administration*, 3, No. 2 (Spring 1977), 20-22.

National School Boards Association. "All About the Real Cost of School Sports and How Not to Get Your Signals Crossed." *The American School Board Journal*, 162, No. 6 (June 1975), 19-34.

Proceedings: National Conference on Olympic Development. Washington, D.C.: American Association for Health, Physical Education, and Recreation, 1966.

Schwank, Walter C., and Sayers J. Miller. "New Dimensions for the Athletic Training Profession. *Journal of Health, Physical Education, and Recreation*, September 1971, pp. 41-43.

Staffo, Donald. "Will Sport Specialization Reduce the Number of All-Around Athletes?" *The Physical Educator*, 34, No. 4 (December 1977), 194-96.

Stiles, Merritt. "Introductory Remarks." *Proceedings: National Conference on Olympic Development*, p. ix. Washington, D.C.: American Association for Health, Physical Education, and Recreation, 1966.

CHAPTER 14

In Perspective

Financial problems, criticism of public education, abuses in intercollegiate athletics, and other outside forces cause some people to question the future of interscholastic sports.

All coaches should look at interscholastic athletics in proper perspective, which becomes a little more clear when athletics are viewed retrospectively, introspectively, and prospectively.

In Retrospect

We have noted in early chapters how interscholastic athletics evolved from a stage in which there was considerable opposition to them to one in which they are considered an indispensable part of secondary education.[1] Most secondary school administrators view underparticipation as one of the biggest problems in student activities.[2]

Coaches have played an important part in this development. We have seen how the position of the coach emerged from that of an outsider in the earliest days to that of a qualified faculty member.

Organizations were formed to foster the values of athletic activities for students. State high school associations and the National Federation of High School Associations have and are performing notable functions in improving the benefits of interscholastic sports. Coaches should be familiar with the standards of these organizations and the services they offer.

[1]Ruth Long, Robert Buser, and Michael Jackson, *Student Activities in the Seventies*, National Association of Secondary School Principals, 1977, p. 1.

[2]*Ibid.*, p. 19.

In Introspect

Legal challenges are being confronted, and coaches should be aware of the liability the courts are placing on them and how to avoid any possible negligence (see Chapter 11). Outside influences stemming from the differences in the philosophies and objectives of professional athletics, national and international amateur competition, and pressures to win can conceiveably adversely affect school athletics. As coaches, we must be prepared to cope with these influences to maintain the significant role of interscholastic athletic competition.

An expanding program and financial problems in school districts are matters that warrant serious attention. Boys' interscholastic sports increased some 6.3 percent and girls' about 26 percent from 1976 to 1978, despite the beginning of financial problems in the schools during this same period.[3] Increasing financial difficulties and declining enrollments resulted in a decline of around 5 percent in boys' and 12 percent in girls' interscholastic competition in 1980.[4]

Taxpayer revolts and economic conditions are matters of concern to coaches and school administrators. It is typical in financial crises that much publicity is directed toward the possibility of eliminating the interscholastic program. Threats to delete this program, a popular one in all communities, is often used by boards of education to dramatize the need to pass school levies, and interscholastic athletics sometimes become the whipping boy. Yet they comprise only a very small percentage of the total school budget. Despite threats, it is probable that they will not be reduced any more than other parts of the school program, including the academic program from which some elective courses are frequently dropped. The attention given by the news media to possible effects on interscholastic sports tends to create some misconceptions. There have been no comprehensive studies published to show that the interscholastic program is reduced any more during periods of financial difficulties than are academic courses. The number of elective academic offerings discontinued during such times remains relatively unknown because of the lack of publicity.

It is only logical that schools will have to make adjustments during financial crises. Athletic budgets may be reduced, and it will become necessary to economize. Some nonrevenue producing sports may have to be eliminated, but most schools will make every effort to continue an interscholastic program. Even the California schools, hard hit financially by Proposition 13, maintained interscholastic athletics.

In financial crises, boards of education tend to insist that student activities become more self-supporting. Schools may need to look for

[3] *National Federation Press Service*, 39, No. 2 (September 1978).

[4] *National Federation Press*, 1, No. 2, (September-October 1980), 1.

additional sources of financing, but the use of private funds should be considered with caution. Patrons will support intrasquad games before the start of the season, for which an admission can be charged, if they understand the need for them. Various fund-raising projects may be employed, but principals will insist that they not interfere with the academic responsibilities of the students. A participation fee has been tried in some school districts, but state laws should be carefully checked to determine whether it is legal. The involvement of students in fund-raising plans can be educational when properly handled and can enhance the teaching of responsibility.

There are differing opinions among school administrators regarding the position of student activities in the educational program, ranging from that of a few who think they are being overemphasized to that of others who believe interscholastic athletics should be part of the academic curriculum. The position of the majority lies somewhere between these two extremes. The National Federation refers to student activities in its publications as *the other half of education*. Some prolems could arise if interscholastic athletics were made a part of the academic curriculum and academic credit given for them. There is a strong probability that the courts would then no longer consider participation in them as a privilege and that students would have a legal right to compete. It could then become more difficult to enforce eligibility standards.

Interscholastic athletics are well established today as an important part of the modern secondary educational program. Attitudes, ideals, respect, self-discipline, and other emotional controls are often taught better in a well-planned and well-administered athletic program than in the classroom. Some six million high school boys and girls receive educational benefits each year from their athletic experiences, and many times that number participate as spectators. Interscholastic sports is one of the most wholesome and most respected youth programs in our nation.

In Prospective

Any coach or school administrator who is concerned about the future of interscholastic sports should be conscious of the students' attitudes toward them. After all, it is primarily to meet the interests and needs of the students that schools provide opportunities for athletic participation. A survey sponsored by the National Association of Secondary School Principals shows that 70 percent of the students responding participated in interscholastic athletics.[5] Thirty percent felt that extracurricular activities (including all student activities) were more im-

[5] Long *et al., Student Activities in the Seventies*, p. 8.

portant than their courses.[6] A large number, 79 percent, thought that more opportunities should be given to girls to compete in interscholastic competition.[7] The failure of some students with athletic ability to participate should not be interpreted as a general lack of interest. The survey shows that 68 percent of the students surveyed believed that employment outside of school was the greatest factor causing nonparticipation in extracurricular activities.[8]

These data, plus the growth in interscholastic sports reported by the National Federation and the recognition by administrations of their value, are evidence enough that interscholastic athletics will continue to be an important part of the total educational program. However, there are some apparent developments which will influence coaching in the future.

The public will demand better teaching. Better teaching will be expected not only in the classrooms but in the gymnasiums and on the playing fields as well. It will become increasingly important to convince the public and school administrators that students are being taught important lessons through athletic experiences, as well as sports skills, both of which will have to be of higher quality.

School boards will be concerned that the school district gets its educational dollar's worth from interscholastic athletics. When members cope with financial problems, they will look more and more at which courses and offerings are essential. Some will question what is being taught through interscholastic athletics that could not be taught as well and cheaper through physical education and intramurals.[9] Thus it is even more important for coaches to increase the educational values of the sports they teach.

Coaches will be held more accountable. Many claims have been made for interscholastic sports in the past without sufficient evidence to support them. More supervision will be extended to see that the values claimed for athletics are actually being achieved.[10] Good sportsmanship and conduct will be increasingly emphasized.

Better qualified and more competent coaches will be desired. Although there may be some relaxation of standards in the qualifications of coaches during periods of shortage, principals realize that the quality of coaching will depend on the qualifications established for coaching.

[6]*Ibid.*, p. 7.

[7]*Ibid.*, p. 7.

[8]*Ibid.*, p. 11.

[9]National School Boards Association, "All About the Real Cost of School Sports and How Not to Get Your Signals Crossed," *The American School Board Journal*, 162, No. 6 (June 1975), 21.

[10]John W. Dougherty, "Supervision and Evaluation of Teaching in Extracurricular Activities," *National Association of Secondary School Principals Bulletin*, 62, No. 416 (March 1978), 32-34.

Athletic administrators will look for better trained coaches,[11] as seen by the movement for coaching certification.

Keeping up with developments will be important. Anyone interested in anticipating the future if interscholastic athletics and of high school coaching must keep abreast of developments which may affect both areas. Court decisions, long-range effects of Title IX, nonschool competition, and national interest in the Olympics and international competition are all matters which must be continually studied.

In The Final Analysis

All coaches realize that you score on the offense, not on the defense. Too often, when criticisms and problems are faced, defensive techniques are employed to disprove them, when offensive tactics would be much more effective. Striving to make interscholastic athletics a still more important and indispensable part of education will influence their future much more than proclaiming values for them as they are. Gathering facts to show how the costs of providing interscholastic athletic competition compare with the costs of other parts of the school program before financial problems arise will be much more influential than arguing against reduced budgets. Studying better ways of teaching youth through athletic experiences will be much wiser than merely acclaiming the educational benefits they offer now.

In the final analysis, we must realize that the place that interscholastic athletics occupy in the secondary program in the future will be just as good and as secure as each of us, as coaches, help to make them.

QUESTIONS AND TOPICS FOR STUDY AND DISCUSSION

1. List ways you think coaches helped to establish the importance of interscholastic athletics.
2. What are some of the reasons the interscholastic program is one of the first to be affected in time of financial crisis?
3. Would you favor making interscholastic athletics a part of the academic program? Why or why not?
4. Do you believe that student interest in interscholastic athletics is decreasing? Give reasons for your position.
5. Can you give reasons why a smaller percentage of students in large high schools participate in interscholastic activities than in small high schools?

[11] Phil Ball, "State Leaders View Coaching," *Interscholastic Athletic Administration*, National Federation of State High School Associations (Fall 1980), pp. 14-15, 28.

6. Why is a knowledge of student interest important in trying to anticipate the future of interscholastic athletics?
7. Why is the collective position of high school principals significant to the future of interscholastic athletics?
8. What changes do you think will take place in the interscholastic program within the next ten years? Explain.
9. In what ways do you believe coaches can influence the future of the interscholastic program?

BIBLIOGRAPHY

Allison, Bradford. "Student Activities as the Ultimate Academic Department." *National Association of Secondary School Principals Bulletin*, 63, No. 426 (April 1979), 95-98.

Ball, Phil. "State Leaders View Coaching." *Interscholastic Athletic Administration*, National Federation of State High School Associations (Fall 1980), 14-15, 28.

Dougherty, John W. "Supervision and Evaluation of Teaching in Extracurricular Activities." *National Association of Secondary School Principals Bulletin*, 62, No. 416 (March 1978), 32-34.

Long, Ruth, Robert Buser, and Michael Jackson. *Student Activities in the Seventies*, National Association of Secondary School Principals, 1977.

National Federation Press, 1, No. 2 (September-October 1980), 1.

National Federation Press Service, 39, No. 2 (September 1978).

National School Boards Association. "All About the Real Cost of School Sports and How Not to Get Your Signals Crossed." *The American School Board Journal*, 162, No. 6 (June 1975), 19-34.

Thawley, George. "My Crystal Ball Is Clouded." *The 80s: Where Will the Schools Be?* National Association of Secondary School Principals, 1974, pp. 47-50.

Index